GIFT FROM

**AMERICAN
INTERFAITH INSTITUTE**

Education for Shalom

Education
for
Shalom

Religion Textbooks
and the Enhancement of the
Catholic and Jewish Relationship

Philip A. Cunningham

THE AMERICAN INTERFAITH INSTITUTE
Philadelphia, Pennsylvania

Cover design by David Manahan, O.S.B.

This edition published for The American Interfaith Institute, Philadelphia, Pennsylvania.

1	2	3	4	5	6	7	8	9

Library of Congress Cataloging-in-Publication Data

Cunningham, Philip A.
    Education for shalom : religion textbooks and the enhancement of the Catholic and Jewish relationship / Philip A. Cunningham.
      p.   cm.
    Includes bibliographical references.
    ISBN 0-8146-2248-8
    1. Christian education—Textbooks—Catholic. 2. Judaism (Christian theology)—Study and teaching. 3. Christianity and antisemitism—History. 4. Judaism—Relations—Catholic Church. 5. Catholic Church— Relations—Judaism. I. Title.
BX930.5.C86 1995
261.2'6'071—dc20   94-10630
                                                CIP

To my mother,
Helen Burke Cunningham,
for trying to instill in her sons
an awareness of anti-Semitism and racism.

Contents

Tables

Graphs

Acknowledgments

This study owes much to the advice and support of my dissertation committee at Boston College: the committee chair, Mary C. Boys of the Institute for Religious Education and Pastoral Ministry, Kilburn E. Culley of the School of Education, and Anthony J. Saldarini of the Department of Theology. Special thanks are due to Eugene J. Fisher, director of the Secretariat for Catholic-Jewish Relations of the National Conference of Catholic Bishops. All of you were immensely helpful.

My thanks, also, to two friends who assisted in gauging the reliability of the study's analytic instrument: Leon E. Abbott, Jr., pastoral associate at St. Mark's Parish in Londonderry, N.H., and Michael J. Corso, a doctoral fellow at Boston College.

Aid in acquiring certain textbook series was provided by Msgr. Charles Crosby, director of the Office of Faith Development of the Diocese of Manchester, N.H., and Sr. Phyllis M. Heble, N.D., director of the Salem Christian Life Center. Thank you.

I am also indebted to the following publishers who provided samples of some or all of their textbook series. My thanks to: Brown Publishing/ROA Media, The Center for Learning, Hi-Time Publishing Corp., Loyola University Press, William H. Sadlier, Inc., Silver Burdett and Ginn, and Winston Press.

Finally, my deepest gratitude must be given to my wife, Julia Anne Walsh. She not only provided precious proof-reading assistance, but, more importantly, constantly supported me with her patience, understanding, and love throughout the research process. I love you very much.

Abbreviations
and Bibliographic References for Ecclesial Documents

Vatican Council II

Vatican Council Documents are found in Abbott, Walter M., ed. *The Documents of Vatican II.* New York: Guild Press, 1966; and Flannery, Austin, ed. *Vatican Council II: The Conciliar and Post-Conciliar Documents.* Northport, N.Y.: Costello Publishing, 1975.

Vatican II, *Dei Verbum* (1965)

Dei Verbum, The Dogmatic Constitution on Divine Revelation, November 18, 1965. Abbott: 111–128; Flannery: 750–764.

Vatican II, *Lumen Gentium* (1964)

Lumen Gentium, The Dogmatic Constitution on the Church, November 21, 1964. Abbott: 14–101; Flannery: 350–426.

Vatican II, *Nostra Aetate* (1965)

Nostra Aetate, The Declaration on the Relation of the Church to Non-Christian Religions, October 28, 1965. Abbott: 660–668; Flannery: 738–742.

Papal Statements

A collection of the present pope's relevant statements is found in Fisher, Eugene J., and Leon Klenicki, eds. *Pope John Paul II on Jews and Judaism: 1979-1986.* Washington: U.S.C.C., 1987.

John Paul II, "To American Jewish Leaders" (September 11, 1987).

Origins 17/15 (September 24, 1987) 241–243.

John Paul II, "Apostolic Letter on the 50th Anniversary of the Beginning of World War II" (August 27, 1989).

Origins 19/15 (September 14, 1989) 253–256.

John Paul II, "Apostolic Letter on Jerusalem" (April 20, 1984).

Redemptionis Anno in Fisher and Klenicki, 53–57.

John Paul II, "To a Delegation of the American Jewish Committee" (March 16, 1990).

Origins 19/43 (March 29, 1990) 714–716.

John Paul II, "To Archbishop John May" (August 8, 1987).

Origins 17/12 (September 3, 1987) 181–183.

John Paul II, "To Christian Experts in Jewish-Christian Relations" (March 6, 1982).

Fisher and Klenicki, 37–40.

John Paul II, "To European Bishops preparing for the 1991 European Synod of Bishops" (June 5, 1990).

Origins 20/6 (June 21, 1990) 90–93.

John Paul II, "To the Jewish Community in Australia" (November 26, 1986.

Fisher and Klenicki, 95–97.

John Paul II, "To the Jewish Community in Rome" (April 13, 1986).

Fisher and Klenicki, 79–85.

John Paul II, "To the Jews in Warsaw" (June 14, 1987).

Origins 17/13 (September 10, 1987) 200.

John Paul II, "To Representatives of the Anti-Defamation League of B'nai B'rith" (March 22, 1984).

Fisher and Klenicki, 51–52.

John Paul II, "To Representatives of Jewish Organizations" (March 12, 1979).

Fisher and Klenicki, 23–26.

John Paul II, "To the West German Jewish Community" (November 17, 1980).

Fisher and Klenicki, 33–36.

Vatican Commissions

Congregation for Catholic Education, "Study of the Fathers of the Church" (1990).

Idem, "Instruction on the Study of the Fathers of the Church in the Formation of Priests." *Origins* 19/34 (January 25, 1990) 549–561.

Int. Cath.-Jew Liaison Com., "Uprooting Anti-Semitism" (1990).

International Catholic-Jewish Liaison Committee, "Uprooting Anti-Semitism." *Origins* 20/15 (September 20, 1990) 233–236.

Pontifical Biblical Commission, "The Bible and Christology" (1984).

Idem, "Instruction on the Bible and Christology," in Fitzmyer, *Scripture and Christology,* 3–53.

Pontifical Biblical Commission, "Instruction on the Historical Truth of the Gospels" (1964).

In Fitzmyer, *A Christological Catechism,* 131-142.

Pontifical Justice and Peace Commission, "The Church and Racism" (1988).

Idem, "The Church and Racism: Toward a More Fraternal Society" *Origins* 18/37 (February 23, 1989) 613–626.

Vatican "Guidelines" (1974).

Vatican Commission for Religious Relations with the Jews, "Guidelines and Suggestions on Implementing the Conciliar Declaration *Nostra Aetate, 4,"* in Croner, *Stepping Stones,* 11-16.

Vatican, "Notes" (1985).

Vatican Commission for Religious Relations with the Jews, "Notes on the Correct Way to Present Jews and Judaism in Preaching and Catechesis in the Roman Catholic Church." *Origins* 15/7 (July 4, 1985) 102–107.

National Conference of Catholic Bishops and Sub-committees

NCCB, *Dramatizations of the Passion* (1988).

Bishops' Committee for Ecumenical and Interreligious Affairs, National Conference of Catholic Bishops. *Criteria for the Evaluation of Dramatizations of the Passion.* Washington: U.S.C.C., 1988.

NCCB, *God's Mercy Endures Forever* (1988).

Bishops' Committee on the Liturgy, National Conference of Catholic Bishops. *God's Mercy Endures Forever: Guidelines on the Presentation of Jews and Judaism in Catholic Preaching.* Washington, U.S.C.C., 1988.

NCCB, "Guidelines" (1967).

Idem, "Guidelines for Catholic-Jewish Relations," March 1967, in Croner, *Stepping Stones,* 16-20.

NCCB, "Guidelines" (1985).

Secretariat for Catholic-Jewish Relations, Bishops' Committee on Ecumenical and Interreligious Affairs, National Conference of Catholic Bishops. *Guidelines for Catholic-Jewish Relations.* 1985 Revision. Washington: U.S.C.C., 1985.

NCCB, "Guidelines on Doctrine" (1990).

National Conference of Catholic Bishops. "Guidelines on Doctrine for Catechetical Materials." *Origins* 20/27 (December 13, 1990) 429–436.

NCCB, "Statement" (1975).

National Conference of Catholic Bishops, "Statement on Catholic-Jewish Relations," November 1975, in Croner, *Stepping Stones,* 29–34.

NCCB, "Toward Peace in the Middle East" (1989).

Idem, "Toward Peace in the Middle East: Perspectives, Principles, and Hopes." *Origins* 19/25 (November 23, 1989) 401–413.

NCCB-ADL, *Within Context* (1987).

Secretariat for Catholic-Jewish Relations, National Conference of Catholic Bishops; Adult Education Section, U.S. Catholic Conference; and the Interfaith Affairs Dept., Anti-Defamation League of B'nai B'rith. *Within Context: Guidelines for the Catechetical Presentation of Jews and Judaism in the New Testament.* Morristown, N.J.: Silver Burdett & Ginn, 1987.

Other Episcopal Conferences

Bishops of West Germany, Austria, and Berlin, "Accepting the Burden of History" (1988).

Bishops' Conferences of the German Federal Republic, of Austria, and of Berlin. "Accepting the Burden of History." *SIDIC* 22/1–2 (1989) 36–42.

French Bishops, "Pastoral Orientations" (1973).

French Bishops' Committee for Relations with Jews, "Pastoral Orientations on the Attitude of Christians to Judaism," April 1973, in Croner, *Stepping Stones,* 60-65.

Polish Bishops, "Jewish-Catholic Relations" (1990).

Idem, "Pastoral Letter on Jewish-Catholic Relations." *Origins* 20/36 (February 14, 1991) 593–595.

West German Bishops, "The Church and the Jews" (1980).

In Croner, *More Stepping Stones,* 124–145.

Local Diocesan Statements

Dioceses of New York, Rockville Center, and Brooklyn, "Catholic-Jewish Relations" (1969).

"Guidelines for the Advancement of Catholic-Jewish Relations in the Archdiocese of New York, the Diocese of Rockville Center, and the Diocese of Brooklyn" (1969) in Croner, *Stepping Stones,* 20-27.

Archdiocese of Galveston-Houston, "Guidelines" (1975).

Croner, *More Stepping Stones,* 65–73.

Joint Catholic-Jewish Statements

Archdiocese of Los Angeles-AJC, "The Holocaust: At the Edge of Comprehension" (1990).

Catholic-Jewish Respect Life Committee, Los Angeles Archdiocese and the American Jewish Committee. "The Holocaust: At the Edge of Comprehension." *Origins* 19/37 (February 15, 1990) 601–604.

See above NCCB-ADL, "Within Context" (1987).

Introduction

In the last three decades numerous instructions concerning Jews and Judaism have been issued by Catholic ecclesial authorities. Inspired by the groundbreaking 1965 Vatican II declaration *Nostra Aetate,* they have insisted upon a totally accurate presentation of Jews and Judaism in Catholic teaching and preaching. They have promoted "not only objectivity, justice, [and] tolerance, but also understanding and dialogue."[1] Some have urged that Catholic religion textbooks be examined to ensure their conformity with the outlook of *Nostra Aetate.*[2]

This book is based upon such a textbook study. It was conducted as a doctoral dissertation at the Institute of Religious Education and Pastoral Ministry at Boston College in 1992. Technically described as a "content analysis," it reviewed current Roman Catholic religion textbook series, on both primary and secondary levels, in order to assess their presentation of Jews and Judaism. The study had three purposes: (1) to evaluate how well textbooks dealt with topics shown to be problematic in earlier research; (2) to assess the effects of Church statements and theological reflection in the 1976–1991 period on American religion textbooks; and (3) to offer recommendations for future textbook treatments of Jews and Judaism.

Presented here under the title of *Education for Shalom,* this volume has some further aims. Agreeing with previous research, the study showed that certain anti-Jewish themes have pervaded Christian teaching and have endured through the years only to reappear in modern religion textbooks. Some of these themes have lasted so long because they can be found in the New Testament. Therefore, the first part of this book will explore the origins and history of Christian anti-Jewish speech and its modern renunciation in the post-*Nostra Aetate* Church.

The second part, besides describing the present educational situation, should also serve as a guide for undertaking similar evaluations in the future. Religious educators, liturgists, and others can easily adapt the criteria and procedures presented herein in order to assess a wide variety of materials in terms of their treatment of Jews and Judaism. Such materials could include lectionary-based programs, homily services, catechesis in R.C.I.A. programs, passion plays, Bible study texts, etc.

The book concludes with recommendations for compensating for the weaknesses in current textbooks, which, hopefully, will add to the volume's usefulness in religious education programs.

There has been considerable progress in Catholic textbooks and their presentation of Jews and Judaism. But there remains much to be done. The title of this book includes the Hebrew word *shalom* which refers to the wholesome peace brought about by right-relationship. By seeking to provide *Education for Shalom,* the Church confirms its indebtedness to Judaism, promotes friendship with the contemporary Jewish people and tradition, and thereby becomes more "whole," more authentically Christian.

Notes

[1] Vatican, "Notes" (1985) 27. All ecclesial documents are cited in accord with the abbreviations on xii–xvi.

[2] E.g., Vatican, "Guidelines" (1974) III; NCCB, "Guidelines" (1967) III, 5.

PART ONE

THE ONSET AND DEMISE
OF THE
CHRISTIAN ANTI-JEWISH TRADITION

1

The New Testament Origins
of Anti-Judaic Themes

The Christian community began to say negative things about certain Jews and particular aspects of the Jewish tradition fairly early in its two-thousand-year history. However, two crucial facts must be kept in mind: (1) the earliest Churches were entirely Jewish in their composition, and (2) first-century Judaism was extremely dynamic and diverse.[1]

Emerging as one Jewish movement in competition with other Jewish groups, the Church soon began using polemical language as part of the normal sociological processes of self-definition, membership and boundary delineation, and the delegitimization of rival authority figures.[2] This originating setting amid competing Jewish viewpoints explains the early appearance of unfavorable assessments of (other) Jews and Judaisms, sentiments which were expressed according to the conventions of first-century polemic.[3]

This picture of competing claims among Jews is complicated by the fact that the earliest Christians were debating among *themselves* on a wide range of issues involving self-definition and group boundaries.[4] Opinions on Torah fidelity and Gentile admissions standards, for example, ranged from those demanding total observance of the Torah by both Jewish and Gentile believers to those who claimed that the Mosaic Law was terminated and should no longer be observed by anyone.[5] Such debates rebounding among the various types of Jews and Gentiles in the first-century Church were another factor which helped shape early Christian attitudes toward Judaism.

Thus, the setting within which the Christian Scriptures were composed was very complex. This chapter will examine the New Testament's negative assertions about Jews and Judaism in order to discern the origins of long-lasting anti-Judaic themes. It will be seen that this negativity is primarily the consequence of the social forces which accompany the formation of a new group identity and is not the product of divine revelation.

A. The Letters of Paul

These earliest New Testament books contain a significant amount of polemical language, much of it concerned with the Law of Moses. However, there presently exists considerable scholarly disagreement over Paul's exact views on the subject.[6]

The Letter to the Galatians contains particularly forceful language: "all who rely on the works of the law are under a curse" (3:10),[7] "Christ redeemed us from the curse of the law by becoming a curse for us" (3:13); "Stand firm, therefore, and do not submit again to a yoke of slavery" (5:1).

It is obvious that Paul was immersed in a great controversy over the requirements for the admission of Gentiles into the Church. Sociological concerns over membership delineation, on the boundaries between Jews and Gentiles in Christ, and the resultant effects on the boundary between the Church and other Jewish groups provide the immediate context for Paul's words.

All agree that Paul sees himself as the divinely commissioned Apostle to the Gentiles, that he argues for their full inclusion in the Church without becoming Jews, and that he is consumed with the desire to save as many Gentiles as possible before Christ's return in glory and judgment. It has become less clear in recent years what Paul felt about continued Torah observance both by Jews "in Christ" and other Jews.

Until recently it was generally held that Paul had come to realize that Judaism was fundamentally flawed because it sought to earn salvation by performing the Law. Paul, therefore, opposed continued compliance with the Law of Moses.[8] However, it has been convincingly demonstrated that there is no evidence of such a "works righteousness" theology in any of the varieties of first-century Judaism for which there are records available.[9] Instead, it seems that the term "covenantal nomism" would better describe the pervasive essence of all the diverse strands of first-century Judaism, including, presumably, the Pharisaic tradition with which Paul was familiar. Covenantal nomism denotes the view that a person's place in God's salvific plan is the result of the free and unmerited gift of the covenant by God to Israel, and that this covenant requires conformity to God's Teaching, together with atonement for any transgressions, as the proper responses to divine graciousness.[10]

Since it seems that in several of his letters Paul is contradicting persons who have ideas about Judaism not known to have been held by first-century Jews, his comments may actually be responses to Gentile misperceptions of Judaism.[11] In other places Paul is contending with other Christian missionaries who insist on the circumcision of Gentiles and who may be playing on Gentile uncertainties about their status in the saved community.

Consequently, Paul's rhetoric does not stem from an intrinsic anti-Jewishness or rejection of the Torah. He is striving to counter Gentile infatuations with distorted ideas about Judaism. His attitude toward continued Torah-observance by Jews is, therefore, much more uncertain than previously thought, and it may well be that Paul countenanced such conformity.

The further observation that Paul may distinguish between the positive way in which the Torah is experienced by Jews who are within the Mosaic Covenant and the negative way in which Torah affects the Gentile nations who are outside that Covenant offers a new perspective on Paul's usage of "curse" language in respect to the Law.[12] The Law itself is not accursed, but it does act to condemn the Gentile nations by vividly revealing, rather like a giant spotlight, the full extent of their idolatry and immorality (N.B. Rom 1:18-32). These, of course, are the same pagan Gentiles whom Paul now feels called to save independently of the Law through God's new action in Christ. It should be noted that this perspective would serve to confirm the conclusion that Paul's rhetoric is embedded within the context of an inner-Jewish debate; an accurate conclusion even if the debating Jews are Jews "in Christ." Paul is not an apostate branding the Jewish Law as accursed. He is one Jew arguing with other Jews about the significance of the Law for Gentiles.

A danger with such intra-group writing is the potential for misconception if read by outsiders. "Paul's letters were composed in the context of a dialogue within Judaism, . . . [but] after his day, when his letters came to read by Gentiles who little understood Judaism, the misinterpretation of Paul became almost inevitable."[13] And so, while Paul's polemic regarding the Law was later read as an anti-Torah rejection of Judaism, such an understanding is probably wrong.

B. The Gospel of Mark

Although there are many debatable points in Marcan studies, there is widespread agreement that one of Mark's major aims is to insist that Jesus' identity as Son of God is discernible only by reckoning with his passion and death, an idea probably related to the evangelist's setting in a suffering or persecuted Church.[14]

As a subordinate theme in the Gospel, there are several passages which convey a negative attitude toward Judaism. These include the Marcan passion narrative and three passages which discuss sabbath observance (2:23-

28), purity (7:1-8), and kosher foods (7:18-19). Postponing consideration of the passion account for the moment, in all three of the other passages Jewish norms are downgraded or eliminated. The Son of Man is said to be master of the sabbath (2:28), purity practices are characterized as mere "human precepts" (7:7), and all foods are declared to be clean (7:19).

The topics addressed in these verses would seem to owe more to the evangelist's concerns around the year 70 C.E. than to problems arising during the ministry of Jesus in the early 30s. For instance, there is no evidence that either Jesus, his disciples, or any of their Jewish contemporaries seriously questioned the propriety of observing the sabbath or of eating kosher foods. Jews certainly debated what proper sabbath and dietary observances entailed, but there was no question of abandoning what is explicitly commanded in the Torah (e.g., Exod 20:8-11; Deut 14; Lev 11).

On the other hand, along with circumcision, the issues of kosher foods and of conformance to the sabbath were definitely controversial topics in the early Church (e.g., Gal 2:11-14, 4:10; Rom 14:1-6; Acts 10:9-16, 15:19-29, 21:17-26). The very existence of such debates indicates that Jesus himself spoke no definitive word on these matters. If Jesus had declared all foods clean, why was there a question about it later?

It seems that the debate over the ongoing legitimacy of Jewish practices arose in the process of defining the boundaries of the nascent Church, particularly after the admission of non-Jews. The fact that in the Marcan passages it is the disciples of Jesus and not Jesus himself who receive criticism suggests that it is followers of Jesus in Mark's day who are being censured for their un-Jewish conduct.

Further evidence of the influence of the evangelist's situation is seen in Mark's distant and not fully accurate editorial explanation of Jewish purity customs (7:3-4). The need of any explanation at all shows that Mark's intended readership is predominantly Gentile. As a matter of fact, all Jews did not observe these Pharisaic purity practices, nor does it appear that Pharisees demanded that their fellow Jews do so or think of them as sinners if they did not. In addition, the presentation of the Pharisees is somewhat stylized, a reflection of the evangelist's context. Pharisees did not patrol grainfields on the sabbath hoping to catch people plucking grain, nor did they inspect the cleanliness of the hands of non-Pharisees.[15]

All of these items, especially Mark's editorial assertion that "thus he declared all foods clean" (7:19), betray the perspectives of a largely Gentile church which defines itself as not bound by kosher, sabbath, or Pharisaic purity customs. In this, Mark differs from both Matthew and Luke. For example, Matthew omits the Marcan contention that Jesus declared all foods clean (15:10-20), while Luke has deleted the entire scene. Furthermore, Luke depicts the Apostolic Council in Jerusalem as requiring Gentile converts to observe some dietary restrictions (Acts 15:19-29), while Matthew deplores those who teach that any of the Law's provisions have been annulled (5:19).

Mark's attitude toward the Temple is consistent with his stance toward other Jewish practices. Jesus' cursing of a fruitless fig tree and its subsequent withering (11:12-14, 20-25) brackets the scene in which Jesus overturns tables in the Temple (11:15-19). The next two chapters show Jesus in mounting contention with Temple authorities, including a pointed parable about the caretakers of a vineyard whose murderous failure to produce fruit will result in the vineyard being given to others (12:1-12). Finally, at the instant of Jesus' death, the curtain of the Temple is torn asunder (15:38). This suggests both the eventual fate of the sacrificial cult (cf. 13:2) and the opening of access to the Divine Presence to the Gentile nations.

From all of these indications, it seems that Mark must represent the anti-Torah extreme of early Christian opinion about Torah observance and Gentile admission. He rejects Jewish food laws and sees no abiding significance in Jewish feasts or the cult of the Temple. For Mark, all of these are irrelevant in the Church, because "no one puts new wine into old wineskins" (2:22).

Mark's passion narrative, which stresses the role of the Jewish leadership in Jesus' death, also exhibits post-resurrectional colorations. For instance, the association of divinity with the Jewish honorific "Son of the Blessed," deemed by the High Priest to be blasphemous (14:61-64), smacks of later Christological disputes between the Church and the Synagogue (e.g., John 5:18).

Whether Mark intended his passion account to condemn Jews in general is doubtful. Literary criticism suggests that he may have wanted his readers to identify with the crowd, the disciples, and the women in order to move them to remorse.[16] Thus Mark's readers would identify with both the Marcan crowd's capricious support for Jesus and with Israel against the powers of the Roman Empire.[17] Such a view is consistent with a setting in which the Marcan Church is somehow being victimized by Romans.

In sum, Mark's attitude toward Judaism, expressed amid his primary stress on the suffering messiahship of Jesus, is typical of that segment of the early Church which took an extreme anti-nomian position on issues of boundary delineation and group membership. His passion narrative does highlight Jewish involvement, although not necessarily with malicious intent. The net result in subsequent Christian interpretation was that Mark's views accorded well with an anti-Torah reading of Paul and were compatible with even more negative Gospel passion accounts, such as those of Matthew and John.

C. The Gospel of Luke—Acts of the Apostles

The Acts of the Apostles repeatedly charges Jews with responsibility for the death of Jesus. For instance, Peter declares to a crowd in Jerusalem:

> You that are Israelites, listen to what I have to say: Jesus of Nazareth, a man attested to you by God with deeds of power, wonders, and signs that God did through him among you, as you yourselves know— this man, . . . you crucified and killed by the hands of those outside the law (Acts 2:22-23).[18]

Although there can be little doubt historically that the Romans must be assigned an important, if not the principal, role in the arrest and execution of Jesus,[19] Luke has focused and enlarged upon Jewish involvement. He has impugned not only the Jewish leadership, but the Jewish people at large.

There are two possible explanations. First, Luke may be tapping into recollections of early Christian preaching based on the Jewish tradition of prophetic self-criticism.[20] Early Jewish preachers of Jesus may have accused their fellow Jews of responsibility for his death in order to provoke a repentant sentiment and an acceptance of their message.[21] This pattern of condemnation coupled with a call for repentance is consistent with the prophetic tradition in the Hebrew Scriptures.[22] Therefore, Luke's condemnatory sermons can be seen as the consequence of one Jewish subgroup attempting to persuade other Jewish groups of the validity of its perspectives by means of typically Jewish prophetic language.

Second, Luke's emphasis on Jewish responsibility for Jesus' death is related to his effort to gain Roman favor for the Christian movement.[23] By having Roman authority repeatedly declare that Jesus is innocent of the charges brought against him (Luke 23:4, 14-16, 22, 47), Luke demonstrates that the empire has no reason to think of Christianity as a dangerous, revolutionary movement. By thus shifting responsibility away from Romans and onto Jews, Luke shares in a tendency visible in the other Gospels,[24] but he also succeeds in distancing the Church from those Jews who rebelled against Rome in 66 C.E. The Lucan practice of blaming Jews for Jesus' death, therefore, delineates boundaries between the Christian movement and Judaism in general.

While Luke has some interest in distancing the Church from Judaism, he also wants to assert that Christianity is the natural extension of Pharisaic Judaism.[25] He does this through the explicit claim that the Hebrew Scriptures foretold the coming and sufferings of Jesus Christ. While almost all the New Testament writers used the Hebrew Scriptures in their quest to understand their experience of Jesus,[26] Luke is perhaps the most blatant in his assertions about the Hebrew Scriptures, for example:

> Then [Jesus] said, "Oh, how foolish you are, and how slow of heart to believe all that the prophets have declared! Was it not necessary that the Messiah should suffer these things and then enter into his glory?" Then beginning with Moses and all the prophets, he interpreted to them the things about himself in all the scriptures (24:25-27).

> Then [Jesus] said to them, "These are my words that I spoke to you while I was still with you—that everything written about me in the law of Moses, the prophets, and the psalms must be fulfilled" (Luke 24:44; also see Acts 3:24; 10:43).

One purpose of these declarations is to authenticate the Church's reading of the Hebrew Scriptures in contrast to other Jewish interpretations. This serves to demarcate the boundaries between the Lucan community and the Jewish community at large.

It is important to note that Luke does not appear to hold that the Church has simply supplanted Judaism as the Chosen People.[27] Rather, he believes that Israel is being reconstituted, perfectly in accord with the Hebrew Scriptures, and is now composed of Jews who have responded to Jesus and the Gentiles whom they have converted.[28] In Luke's view, Jewish-Christians provide vital continuity with Judaism. Precisely because Luke holds them to be authentic Israel, they can authoritatively read about Jesus in the Law and the Prophets, and they can prophetically condemn their fellow Jews in an effort to persuade them of the Christian message. The polemical language in Luke-Acts, therefore, largely originates in the context of an inner-Jewish debate, although in Luke's case the Jewish members are now being supported by their Gentile allies.[29]

It is one thing for various competing Jewish factions to speak about culpability for the crucifixion or the Hebrew Scriptures as written to foretell Jesus. As will be seen below, it is quite another matter for such ideas to be read in the later context of an entirely Gentile Church.

D. The Gospel of Matthew

A similar dynamic is evident in the Gospel of Matthew. In his concluding chapters the evangelist unleashes a polemical assault on Jewish authority figures. In chapter 21 Jesus recounts the Matthean version of the Parable of the Tenants in the Vineyard, who successively slay the messengers sent by the owner of the vineyard to collect the harvest and ultimately kill the owner's son. The parable is found in one of Matthew's sources, the Gospel of Mark (12:1-2), but Matthew has added the conclusion, "Therefore, I tell you, the kingdom of God will be taken away from you and given to a people[30] that produces the fruits of the kingdom" (21:43). In addition, the Matthean account is addressed to the "chief priests and Pharisees . . . [who] realized that he was speaking about them"

(21:45). Since the Pharisees are not mentioned in Mark's version, a source for Matthew, it seems that Matthew is specially targeting them.

It is apparent from his recounting of the Parable of Guests Invited to a Feast that the evangelist believes that the corrupt leadership of the chief priests in Jesus' day was the cause of the Temple's destruction in 70 C.E. The Matthean narrative differs notably from the Lucan parallel in that after some of the invited guests had seized the king's servants and killed them, the king angrily "sent his troops, destroyed those murderers, and burned their city" (22:6-7). Under such leadership Jerusalem "kills the prophets" (23:37) and will act to kill Jesus as well.

An attack on corrupt leadership is also evident in Matthew 23 in which the Pharisees are the target of prolonged verbal invective. In seven "woes" directed against "the scribes and Pharisees, hypocrites!" (23:13, 15, 16, 23, 25, 27, 29), the Matthean Jesus berates his opponents, culminating in the accusation that they are lawless murderers, apparently not all that different from the chief priests.

As in Luke's Gospel, responsibility for Jesus' execution is deflected from Pilate, who, in Matthew's account, washes his hands of the whole affair (27:24). Furthermore, Matthew has the unscrupulous chief priests and elders (27:20) maneuver the Jerusalem crowd to convict itself of blood-guilt by inciting it to exclaim, "His blood be on us and on our children!" (27:25). The murderous designs of corrupt leaders have come full circle.

It should be noted that this "blood curse" language is typical of first-century polemical style. Although this passage has had particularly harmful consequences when read in later contexts, "we cannot view with the same seriousness the 'curse' laid on Jews by Matthew's Gospel when we recognize that curses were common coinage in those fights, and there were not many Jews or Gentiles who did not have at least one curse to deal with."[31] Even in Matthew's case, the guilty parties are punished by the destruction of Jerusalem (22:7). The evangelist in no way imagines that all Jews for all time are accursed.

Many scholars hold that this vituperative language reflects a polemical situation in the Matthean community; specifically that Matthew's Church is a predominantly Jewish-Christian assembly engaged in a bitter dispute with the local synagogue over authentic leadership of the Jewish community in the vacuum left by the Temple's destruction. Matthew argues that true Jews follow the Torah as definitively interpreted by Jesus, whereas the synagogue conforms to the nascent rabbinic tradition. Consequently, the Pharisees are especially criticized in Matthew's Gospel because they are emblematic of those with whom the evangelist is contending in the mid-80s.[32]

There is little doubt that as a Jewish-Christian Matthew understands himself to be in continuity with authentic Jewish tradition despite the contrary assertions of the leadership of the local synagogue (see, e.g., 5:17-20). His hostile words emerge from a Jewish-Jewish conflict and involves boundary delineation and attacks on the authority of his adversaries. Matthew's characteristically frequent recourse to "fulfillment passages" to demonstrate the authenticity of his understanding of Torah is another stratagem in an essentially Jewish debate.[33]

It should be noted that while both Lucan and Matthean polemics stem from the social dynamics of an intra-Jewish debate, they assume a much different tonality when read in a community which does not define itself as somehow Jewish. In other words, "the synoptic tradition, insofar as it was once addressed to Jews and Jewish Christians is not anti-Judaic; when it is read in a Gentile Christian context, speaking not *to* but *about* Jews, it tends to become so."[34]

This is perhaps particularly true for Matthew 27:25 which, because it was subsequently taken in tandem with 21:43 and 22:6-7 to refer to an eternal curse for the voluntary acceptance of guilt for the death of Jesus, "has been used more than any other New Testament passage to legitimate overt anti-Semitism."[35] Such an interpretation certainly exceeds Matthew's intentions, especially given his self-understanding as a "scribe trained for the kingdom of heaven" (13:52) enmeshed in a dispute with fellow Jews over authentic Jewish identity.[36]

E. The Gospel of John

The Fourth Gospel also contains negative polemic toward Jews and Judaism. Notable features include frequent references to "the Jews," usually in hostile tones (even though almost all of the Gospel's characters are Jews, including Jesus),[37] a clear effort to portray Jesus as replacing with his own person both important Jewish figures and sacred Jewish feasts and places,[38] and a remarkably heated altercation between Jesus and "Jews who had believed in him" (8:31) that climaxes with Jesus accusing his opponents of being offspring of the devil (8:44).

There is widespread scholarly agreement about the originating context of this perspective. The Johannine Church is a community which has recently experienced the trauma of having its Jewish members expelled from the local synagogue (see 9:22, 34; 12:42; 16:2).[39] The Gospel reflects the anger felt by Johannine Jewish-Christians at this ouster. The "Jews who had believed in him" (8:31) merit special wrath because they represent those Jews who had forsaken membership in the Johannine community in response to the threat of synagogue expulsion.[40]

This social context accounts for the Gospel's hostile references to "the Jews," for the intentional program of having Jesus supplant principal Jewish feasts and figures, and for certain similarities to the Gospel of Matthew, such as frequent negative references to Pharisees and an apostasizing exclamation by Jews while Pilate is mulling over Jesus' fate (19:15).

Johannine rhetoric can more properly be called "anti-Jewish" because the evangelist conceives of himself as outside the boundaries of Judaism. But while this out-group perspective may cause John to be more forceful than Matthew or Luke in claiming that salvation is possible only through Jesus (14:6), his anti-Jewish polemic shares with them a rootedness in disputes between the embryonic Church and nascent rabbinic Judaism, albeit further along in the process of separation. Boundary delineation and the definition of authentic membership criteria are major concerns of this evangelist.

F. The Letter to the Hebrews

Finally, while the Gospel of John's theme of replacement is expressed in hostile and angry tones, the Letter to the Hebrews more dispassionately conveys this assessment:

> But Jesus has now obtained a more excellent ministry, and to that degree he is the mediator of a better covenant, which has been enacted through better promises. For if that first covenant had been faultless, there would have been no need to look for a second one. God finds fault with them when he says, "The days are surely coming, says the Lord, when I will establish a new covenant with the house of Israel and with the house of Judah." . . . In speaking of "a new covenant," he has made the first one obsolete. And what is obsolete and growing old will soon disappear (8:6-8, 13).

This passage shows the clearest New Testament expression of a theological perspective now known as supersessionism, i.e., Christianity has superseded Judaism as God's Chosen People, the Old Testament has become outmoded with the dawning of the New.

So little is known about the origins of this letter that it is difficult to establish its social setting. It seems especially interested in the Jewish sacrificial cult of Jerusalem Temple,[41] but the precise reason for this interest is disputed.

It has been suggested that the letter was written between 75–90 C.E. by a Hellenist theologian to the Roman Church "when in whole or in part it has been seized by a nostalgia for the Israelite heritage—probably because the destruction of the Jerusalem Temple [70 C.E.] seemed to pave the way for Christianity to make its own that heritage."[42] The author of Hebrews, then, while not regarding Jewish cultic traditions as worthless, argues that they are inferior to the action of Christ and are consequently in the process of vanishing. He does this in order to counter what he deems to be an infatuation with things rendered secondary by Christ.

Others hold that Hebrews was written to console a Jewish-Christian community traumatized by the loss of the Temple. It is "simply an encouragement to the Jewish-Christians that all they have held dear in the Temple continues in Jesus and what he means for Jewish Christians."[43] This approach has the advantage of explaining the absence of polemic in the text. It also means that the author is not so much interested in asserting supersessionism as in providing continuity with the now defunct Temple tradition.

Still others understand the letter as a response to the deterioration of some Church community's faith because of the threat of persecution. The author presents a profound description of the Christian faith using the Jewish language of covenant and cult in order to inspire renewed commitment. In his emphasis on the excellence and finality of the new covenant in Christ, the High Priest, the author simultaneously critiques and relativizes the worth of the Jewish covenant.[44]

Whichever analysis is correct, Hebrews is situated in the context of a conversation between different Christian groups. The letter stresses the newness and finality of what has been done in Christ by delineating both the Church's continuity with and its distinctiveness from the traditions of Judaism. The author points out, without vituperation, the limitations of what he calls the "old" covenant. This indicates that the writer wants to accentuate the preferability of the practices and faith of the Christian covenant over those of the Jewish one. While this effort may or may not be a primary purpose of the letter, and even if it is impossible to determine the letter's originating social context, the language of Hebrews has contributed to a Christian conception of Judaism as superseded.

G. Summary

The above survey has highlighted the originating contexts of New Testament language which speaks of Jews or Judaism negatively. The various texts were seen to have emerged at various moments in the Church's gradual separation from Judaism. Paul, Mark, Luke-Acts, and Matthew come from a time when the Church was essentially another sub-group within Judaism, and their negative language must be understood as typical of the rhetoric of competing Jewish movements and not inherently "anti-Jewish." They also manifest the diversity of early Christian opinion on the nature of the relationship between the Church and Judaism. The latest work, the Gospel of John, dates from a period when a largely Jewish Church had been thrown out of a local synagogue. This expulsion caused the harsh invective found in the Gospel text. Thus, while it would be more proper to call John's rhetoric "anti-Jewish," its forcefulness is the consequence of what is in many ways still a conflict among Jews. The Letter to the Hebrews contains clear supersessionist sentiments arising from an unknown social context which involves a definition of Christian identity as preferable to Judaism.

Thus, it seems clear that New Testament negative remarks about Jews and Judaism are all related to the sociological processes involved in the birth, growth, and separation of a new movement from within a larger and ancient tradition. Concerns about identity, membership, and boundaries underlie all of the texts examined above. Although real theological differences between the Church and Judaism were developing, New Testament negativity toward Jews and Judaism is not a consequence of the Christian message per se, but resulted from sociological forces.

Furthermore, New Testament language hostile toward Jews is disjointed. Disparate negative ideas had not yet been combined into a unified and consistent stance toward Judaism. This process would not occur until the membership of the Church had become predominantly Gentile. Once that had occurred, earlier negative remarks were understood as referring not to other people sharing a common heritage but to outsiders, or to express it in the first person, as referring not to some of *us* but to *them*.

Abstracted from their originally intra-Jewish setting, the New Testament polemical motifs listed in Table 1 were to exert an enduring influence on subsequent Christian thought about Jews and Judaism.

Table 1
New Testament Anti-Jewish Polemical Motifs

- The Law enslaves people and is not meant for Christians.
- Jews are responsible for Jesus' death.
- Jerusalem was destroyed because it rejected Jesus.
- Jesus fulfilled what the prophets said about him.
- The Pharisees were hypocrites who hated Jesus.
- Jews are associated with the devil.
- The New Covenant has rendered the Old Covenant obsolete.

Notes

[1] The huge variety of thought and practice in first-century Judaism has led one author to speak of the Judaism*s* of the period. See Jacob Neusner, preface to *Judaisms and Their Messiahs at the Turn of the Christian Era,* ed. by Jacob Neusner, William S. Green, and Ernest Frerichs (New York: Cambridge University Press, 1987) ix–xiv.

[2] For examples of studies that apply sociological perspectives to the emergence of Christianity from Judaism, see Jerome H. Neyrey, *An Ideology of Revolt: John's Christology in Social-Science Perspective* (Philadelphia: Fortress, 1988); J. Andrew Overman, *Matthew's Gospel and Formative Judaism* (Minneapolis: Fortress, 1990); and Anthony J. Saldarini, "Delegitimation of Leaders in Matthew 23," *Catholic Biblical Quarterly* 54/4 (October 1992) 659–680.

[3] See Luke T. Johnson, "The New Testament's Anti-Jewish Slander and the Conventions of Ancient Polemic," *Journal of Biblical Literature* 108/3 (Fall 1989) 419–441.

[4] Ibid., 425.

[5] See the useful typology developed by Raymond E. Brown in his joint work with John P. Meier, *Antioch and Rome: New Testament Cradles of Catholic Christianity* (New York/Ramsey: Paulist, 1983) 2–8.

[6] Recent commentators include Lloyd Gaston, *Paul and the Torah* (Vancouver: University of British Columbia, 1987); Heikki Raisanen, *Paul and the Law* (Philadelphia: Fortress, 1986); E. P. Sanders, *Paul, the Law, and the Jewish People* (Philadelphia: Fortress, 1983); idem, *Paul and Palestinian Judaism* (Philadelphia: Fortress, 1977); Alan F. Segal, *Paul the Convert: The Apostolate and Apostasy of Saul the Pharisee* (New Haven: Yale University, 1990); Francis Watson, *Paul, Judaism, and the Gentiles: A Sociological Approach* (New York: Cambridge University, 1986); Stephen Westerholm, *Israel's Law and the Church's Faith: Paul and His Recent Interpreters* (Grand Rapids: Eerdmans, 1988).

[7] All biblical quotations are from the *New Revised Standard Version Bible* (Division of Christian Education of the National Council of Churches of Christ in the United States of America, 1989) unless otherwise indicated.

[8] Sanders, *Paul and Palestinian Judaism,* 33–58.

[9] Ibid., 59–436.

[10] Ibid., 75, 422.

[11] Gaston, "Paul and the Torah," in *Paul and the Torah,* 25.

[12] Ibid., 15–34.

[13] W. D. Davies, "Paul and the Law: Reflections on Pitfalls in Interpretation," in *Jewish and Pauline Studies* (Philadelphia: Fortress, 1984) 99.

[14] For example, Paul J. Achtemeier, *Mark* Proclamation Commentaries (Philadelphia: Fortress, 1975) 47, 90, 98–110; Ernest Best, *Disciples and Discipleship: Studies in the Gospel According to Mark* (Edinburgh: T & T Clark, 1986) 128–130, 225; Martin Hengel, *Studies in the Gospel of Mark* (Philadelphia: Fortress, 1985) 30, 44; Frank J. Matera, *What Are They Saying About Mark?* (New York/Mahwah: Paulist, 1987) 16–17, 54–55; Theodore J. Weeden, Sr., *Mark: Traditions in Conflict* (Philadelphia: Fortress, 1971) 159–168; and even C. S. Mann, *Mark* The Anchor Bible, vol. 27 (Garden City: Doubleday, 1986) 77–83, who holds the minority view that Mark post-dates Matthew and Luke.

[15] For the preceding four paragraphs I am indebted to the analyses in E. P. Sanders, *Jesus and Judaism* (Philadelphia: Fortress, 1985) 264–267; and Idem, *Jewish Law from Jesus to the Mishnah* (Philadelphia: Trinity, 1990) 6–41.

[16] Thomas E. Boomershine, "Intentionality and the Ethics of Interpretation: The Pilate Trial in Mark and Christian Anti-Semitism," Paper read at the annual meeting of the Society of Biblical Literature, Boston, December 7, 1987, 13.

[17] Ibid., 10–13.

[18] See also Acts 2:36; 3:15; 4:10, 27; 5:30; 7:53; 10:39; 13:28-29.

[19] See the discussion of the issue in Raymond E. Brown, *The Gospel According to John, XIII–XXI,* The Anchor Bible, vol. 29A (Garden City: Doubleday, 1970) 791-802.

[20] S. G. Wilson, "The Jews and the Death of Jesus in Acts," in *Anti-Judaism in Early Christianity,* vol. 1, *Paul and the Gospels,* ed. by Peter Richardson with David Granskou (Waterloo, Ont.: Wilfrid Laurier University Press, 1986) 159-60.

[21] N.B. Acts 2:38; 3:19; 5:31; 10:43; and 13:38. The presence of similar ideas in 1 Thessalonians 2:14-16, written in the early 50s, would lend support to this idea, provided that those verses are not a later interpolation.

[22] E.g., Jeremiah 2:1–4:2; Hosea 11; Isaiah 1:1-20.

[23] Joseph A. Fitzmyer, *The Gospel According to Luke, I–IX,* The Anchor Bible, vol. 28 (Garden City: Doubleday, 1981) 178.

[24] Joseph A. Fitzmyer, *The Gospel According to Luke, X–XXIV,* The Anchor Bible, vol. 28A (Garden City: Doubleday, 1985) 1363-1364.

[25] Fitzmyer, *Luke, I–IX,* 178.

[26] For a convincing argument that they were specifically seeking to comprehend the meaning of the crucified and raised one as Messiah, see Donald Juel, *Messianic Exegesis: Christological Interpretation of the Old Testament in Early Christianity* (Philadelphia: Fortress, 1988).

[27] *Contra* the arguments of Jack T. Sanders, *The Jews in Luke-Acts* (Philadelphia: Fortress, 1987).

[28] Jacob Jervell, "The Divided People of God," in *Luke and the People of God* (Minneapolis: Augsburg, 1972) 41–74; Joseph A. Fitzmyer, "The Jewish People and the Mosaic Law in Luke-Acts," in *Luke the Theologian: Aspects of His Teaching* (New York/Mahwah: Paulist, 1989) 175-202.

[29] The Lucan assertion that non-Jesus Jews are excluding themselves from membership in the People of God (Acts 3:23; cf. Deut 18:19) is quite comprehensible as an intra-Jewish dispute. Another Jewish group, the Essenes, also held that those Jews who did not accept their understanding of the scriptures had removed themselves from the covenanted community. See 1QS 3; 5 in Geza Vermes, *The Dead Sea Scrolls in English,* 3rd ed. (New York: Penguin, 1987) 64, 67.

[30] Note that the RSV had rendered *ethnos* as "nation," leading to a comparison between Israel who was losing the kingdom and the Gentiles who were receiving it. The NRSV more accurately translates *ethnos* as "people," preserving the essentially intra-Jewish sense of the verse. The issue here is between one group of Jews opposed to another, not Jews vs. Gentiles. See Overman, *Matthew's Gospel and Formative Judaism,* 148–149. See also the entry for *"ethnos"* in Henry George Liddell and Robert Scott, comps., *A Greek-English Lexicon,* 9th ed. (Oxford: Clarendon, 1940) 480.

[31] Johnson, "Anti-Jewish Slander," 441.

[32] E.g., O. Lamar Cope, *Matthew: A Scribe Trained for the Kingdom of Heaven,* The Catholic Biblical Quarterly Monograph Series, 5 (Washington: The Catholic Biblical Association of America, 1976) 124–130; Overman, *Matthew's Gospel and Formative Judaism,* 1–5, 141–149; Benno Przybylski, "The Setting of Matthean Anti-Judaism," in Richardson, *Anti-Judaism in Early Christianity,* 181–200; Anthony J. Saldarini, "The Gospel of Matthew and Jewish-Christian Conflict in Galilee," Paper to appear in the English and Hebrew Proceedings of the First International Conference on Galilean Studies in Late Antiquity, 1991; Clark M. Williamson and Ronald J. Allen, *Interpreting Difficult Texts: Anti-Judaism and Christian Preaching* (Philadelphia: Trinity, 1989) 42–45.

[33] See Matthew 1:22-23; 2:5-6, 14-15, 17-18, 23; 8:17; 12:17; 13:35; 21:4; 26:54-56; 27:9-35.

[34] Lloyd Gaston, "Anti-Judaism and the Passion Narrative in Luke and Acts," in Richardson, *Anti-Judaism in Early Christianity,* 151.

[35] Przybylski, "The Setting of Matthean Anti-Judaism," 182.

[36] Cope, *Matthew,* 129, 126-127.

[37] See, e.g., John 1:19; 2:18, 20, 5:10, 15, 16, 18; 6:41, 52; 7:1, 11, 13; 8:22, 48, 52, 57, 59; 9:18, 22; *et passim.* N.B. 4:9.

[38] Abraham—8:53; Jacob—4:12; Moses—1:19; 6:32, 49-50; the Temple—2:19-22; cf. 4:20-24; the Sabbath—5:1-47; Passover—6:1-71; Tabernacles—7:1-52; Dedication—10:22-42. See Raymond E. Brown, *The Gospel According to John, I–XII,* The Anchor Bible, vol. 29 (Garden City: Doubleday, 1966) 201–204.

[39] J. Louis Martyn, *History and Theology in the Fourth Gospel,* rev. and enl. ed. (Nashville: Abingdon, 1968); Raymond E. Brown, *The Community of the Beloved Disciple* (New York: Paulist, 1979) 22–24, 66-69; Neyrey, *An Ideology of Revolt,* 115-150; Rudolf Schnackenburg, *The Gospel According to St. John* (New York: Crossroad, 1982) 1:165-167.

[40] An aspect of the scholarly reconstruction of this expulsion scenario involves the *birkat ha-minim,* the "blessing against the heretics." Some have over-stressed the possibility of this prayer being used in a formal synagogue procedure against Jewish-Christians. See the discussion in Overman, *Matthew's Gospel and Formative Judaism,* 48–56.

[41] E.g., Hebrews 5:1ff.; 7-10.

[42] Raymond E. Brown, "The Roman Church in the Second Christian Generation," in idem and John P. Meier, *Antioch and Rome: New Testament Cradles of Catholic Christianity* (New York/Ramsey: Paulist, 1983) 155.

[43] Richard C. Lux, "Covenant Interpretation: A New Model for the Jewish-Christian Relationship," *Schola* 5/1 (1982) 47–48.

[44] Harold W. Attridge, *The Epistle to the Hebrews,* Hermeneia Commentary (Philadelphia: Fortress, 1989) 13–28, 225–226.

2

The Patristic Systematization
of Anti-Judaic Themes

While anti-Jewish expressions in New Testament times were primarily disjointed outbursts between rival Jewish movements, a very different social context in the patristic period (ca. 150–600 C.E.)[1] caused earlier negative themes to be combined and transmuted into a comprehensive anti-Jewish theology. This developing complex was augmented by new anti-Jewish arguments that arose in the various disputes of the time and which this chapter will outline. As in the New Testament period, it will be seen that political and social forces played crucial roles in the systematization of Christian anti-Jewish disputation.

A. The Socio-Political Context

For most of the patristic period, Christianity was engaged in a multi-faceted struggle for survival, respectability, and, ultimately, political power within the Roman Empire. The Church's initially vulnerable social position was further threatened by intense internal disputes over Christian teaching, especially Christological doctrine.

In contrast to Christianity's humble beginnings, Jews in the Roman Empire were a much more influential presence. In the first century the total number of Jews living throughout the Roman world has been estimated as between four and five million. This would represent a very significant fraction of about 7–10 percent of the total imperial population.[2]

The Jewish people seem to have recovered fairly quickly from the two devastating wars waged against Rome in 66–70 and 132–135. For most of the patristic period, Judaism remained an important presence in the imperial world, enjoying a social status which Christians would only gradually acquire. There were thriving Jewish communities throughout the Mediterranean region, and Jews were engaged in a wide variety of occupations on all levels of the economic spectrum.[3] As adherents of a religion legitimated in Roman law, Jews were recognized as Roman citizens in 212, a privilege not yet extended to Christians. It was also a time of enormous spiritual creativity in Judaism, as witnessed by the compilations of the Mishnah (ca. 200) and the Jerusalem and Babylonian Talmuds (ca. 400 and 550, respectively).[4]

The general prosperity of patristic Jewish communities has been demonstrated in recent archaeological discoveries. At Sardis in Asia Minor, a synagogue has been unearthed dating to the second and third centuries. It was 130 yards long, part of a grand gymnasium complex, decorated with fine marble and splendid mosaics, and situated on the town's main street. By contrast, the much smaller contemporary Christian church was in a less desirable location.[5]

In the town of Aphrodisias, also in Asia Minor, a memorial stone has been found commemorating a building project undertaken on the town synagogue in the third century. This in itself suggests a certain level of prosperity among local Jews. The stone also lists the names of contributors to the building fund, including about fifty-five Jews and fifty-two *theosebeis*. This latter group may represent Gentile God-fearers who were in some sort of formal association with the synagogue community. If so, the inscription demonstrates the attraction that Judaism had for some Gentiles and also the willingness of this synagogue to affiliate with them. These *theosebeis* were at least Gentile benefactors of the synagogue, an indication of the social standing enjoyed by the town's Jewish community.[6]

The Christian community, on the other hand, did not begin to rival seriously the Jewish presence in the Empire until the fourth century. Until that time, "on levels perhaps too deep to be fully articulated, [Christians] must have looked upon Jews with a certain amount of envy."[7] In addition to intermittent persecutions of varying geographical range and duration (such as those under the third-century emperors Decius and Diocletian), the Church had to defend itself against pagan critics who saw Christians as anti-social, godless, and unreasonable.[8]

Indeed, to pagan eyes Christianity had little to recommend it in comparison with Judaism. Impressed by the authority bestowed by antiquity, pagans tended to perceive in Judaism a venerability and respectability which Christianity plainly lacked. Furthermore, it was public knowledge that the Christian "Old Testament" books were really the ancient sacred writings of the Jews. Since Jews preserved these revered scriptures in their original languages, they were clearly the legitimate authorities to whom one should turn for their authentic interpretation. Christian claims that only they could really understand the Hebrew Scriptures seemed fantastic to pagans. The ritual veneration with which Jews handled their scrolls, and their chanting of them in a mysterious and ancient tongue, imparted to the synagogue an aura of the sacred and the awesome which greatly impressed both the average pagan and the typical Christian.[9]

Further compromising the situation for the patristic Church was a series of internal debates over Christian doctrine. On the one hand, supporters of Marcion argued for a radical discontinuity of the Church with Judaism, while on the other, some Christian communities held that belief in Christ did not invalidate observance of the Mosaic Law, and they worshipped and read the scriptures in Hebrew.[10] Various types of Gnostic and docetic movements also abounded, and in the fourth century the Arian controversy threatened to divide the Church completely. Although authoritative ecclesiastical councils were held, they seldom put an end to bitter internal debates. Fifty years after the Council of Nicea (325), for example, there were in Antioch four rival "Christian" leaders—one Arian bishop, two Nicene bishops, and one Apollinarian bishop.[11] Despite this confusion, the political and social situation for the Church had begun to improve around the year 300. Reforms started by the Emperor Diocletian had instituted a new bureaucratic aristocracy which gave Christians increasing opportunities to advance their political stature. Although the details remain unclear, the number of Christians holding governmental positions increased swiftly. By "the late fourth century Christians and Jews were competitors for power and influence in the new society of the eastern empire, and the advantage of the Christians brought the direct decline of the Jews."[12]

The accession of the first Christian emperor, Constantine I, in 312 and the establishment of Christianity as the official imperial religion by the Emperor Theodosius I in 380 gave Christianity unprecedented political clout. The enhanced position of the Church is apparent in contemporary Jewish literature. Whereas earlier works, such as the Mishnah, betray scant awareness of the Church's existence, Christianity's growing power in the late fourth century provoked Jewish theological responses to the Church's claims in the Jerusalem Talmud, Genesis Rabbah, and Leviticus Rabbah.[13]

To Christians living at this time, however, it was by no means apparent that a new Christian Age had begun. The brief reign of the pagan Emperor Julian (361–363) demonstrated what could happen when an enemy of Christianity exploited the continuing dynamic presence of Judaism for his own purposes. As will be discussed below, Julian's religio-political activities and assertions were to have an enormous influence on the Jewish-Christian relationship. Christian uncertainties were further compounded by the rule of the eastern Emperor Valens (364-378) who was a dedicated Arian.[14]

All of these complex factors motivated the Church Fathers to articulate a comprehensive presentation of the Christian faith which incorporated a negative theological attitude toward Judaism. The need for the Church to defend itself from Roman charges that Christianity was a heretical deviation from Judaism, the continuing appeal of Jewish customs for many Christians, and the vibrant presence of numerous synagogue communities caused the developing Christian tradition to assert its legitimacy as a religious group by denying spiritual value to Judaism.

Naturally, this denial was expressed according to the rhetorical norms of Graeco-Roman culture. Patristic anti-Jewish polemic (and rhetoric against deviant Christian groups as well) is characterized by the standard contemporary conventions of invective speech: "the use of half-truths, innuendo, guilt by association, abusive and incendiary language, malicious comparisons, and in all, excess and exaggeration."[15] A fourth-century audience would automatically recognize such speech as overstated, argumentative, and even entertaining. But patristic anti-Jewish rhetoric would assume a more pernicious character in later historical contexts, repeating on a grander scale the non-contextualized reading of New Testament polemic.

B. The Debate with Marcion

The Church's quarrel with Marcion in the mid-second century illustrates several features of the emerging anti-Jewish tradition. Marcion (ca. 85–ca. 165) was rejected by the Church in Rome after teaching that humanity had been created by a wrathful deity who had subjugated it to the harsh Law of Moses. Jesus, the Son of a new and previously unknown God, came and liberated humankind from the dominance of the oppressive creator deity. The "Old Testament" existed as a witness to the power of that merciless creator, but held no authority for Christians. Of what became the New Testament, Marcion accepted only parts of Paul's letters and an edited version of Luke's Gospel.

Christian writers such as Justin Martyr (ca. 105–ca. 165), Irenaeus (ca. 125–202), Tertullian (ca. 125–ca. 222), and Origen (ca. 185–254) responded to Marcion with several arguments. Confronted with the challenge of maintaining continuity with the Hebrew tradition in a way that did not further enhance the lofty status of their Jewish contemporaries, they developed themes that demeaned Jews while shifting the venerability of the Jewish tradition onto the Church.

They argued that the Law of Moses was oppressive, not because it was devised by an oppressive God, but because it was needed to control the constantly sinful and wayward Jews. Moreover, Christ's coming was not unexpected. It had been foretold for ages in the Hebrew Scriptures. Even the Gentiles' replacement of the Jews because of the Jewish rejection of Christ had been predicted. Thus, Marcion's assertion of the radically unanticipated novelty of Christ was unwarranted. He was wrong to declare that some new God had been revealed in Christ. The same God is both the creator and the destroyer of the Jews' Temple. In the opinion of Origen, Marcion was just as bad as the Jews because he read the Hebrew Scriptures on a mere literal level and failed to see their spiritual significance in Christ. A consequence of these various anti-Marcionite arguments was the emergence of the idea that God, Christ, and the Bible all stand in opposition to the Jews.[16]

C. The Debate with Pagans

The patristic Church's debate with non-Christian Gentiles also catalyzed the development of anti-Judaic concepts. Celsus, for example, noting that Christianity claimed to be the sole and legitimate heir to the Jewish tradition, asked why Christians repudiated the God-given Law of Moses which the Jewish People continued to revere.[17] Origen responded to Celsus in this way:

> One of the facts which show that Jesus was some divine and sacred person is just that on his account such great and fearful calamities have now for a long time befallen the Jews. . . . For they committed the most impious crime of all, when they conspired against the Savior of mankind, in the city where they performed to God the customary rites which were symbols of profound mysteries. Therefore that city where Jesus suffered these indignities had to be utterly destroyed. The Jewish nation had to be overthrown, and God's invitation to blessedness transferred to others, I mean the Christians, to whom came the teaching about the simple and pure worship of God. And they received new laws which fit in with the order established everywhere. Those which had previously been given were intended for a single nation ruled by men of the same nationality and customs, so that it would be impossible for everyone to keep them now.[18]

By thus combining several New Testament themes, Origen argued that Christian abandonment of the Mosaic Law was in simple obedience to the God who had punished the murderous Jews by removing their chosen status and laws, and who had established new laws and a new chosen people.

Of particular interest is Origen's appeal to recent history to justify his assertions. The destruction of the Temple in Jerusalem was cited by Christians as proof of God's rejection of Israel. Prior to the improvement in their socio-political rank in the fourth century, it was one of the few ostensibly legitimating events to which Christians could refer. In addition, the Temple's destruction was advanced as proof of Christ's power and divinity. Citing such New Testament passages as Matthew 24:2, Christians claimed that Christ had predicted the Temple's fall. Did not this display his divine foreknowledge? Was it not divine power which destroyed the Temple and prohibited its rebuilding?[19]

This logic is what made the reign of the Emperor Julian (361–363) so frightening for Christians. Committed to the restoration of pagan religious observances, and a former Christian himself, Julian was well aware of Christian vulnerability concerning its origins in Judaism. In a treatise against Christianity he repeated some earlier pagan charges. Christianity was a heretical deviation from Judaism. It had erroneously ceased to follow the Mosaic Law still observed by faithful Jews. This was because the Church's preaching had perversely deified a man who had simply called for more sincere worship of the God of Israel.

Julian reasoned that if the Temple were to be rebuilt two lethal blows would be struck at the Church. First, the restoration would prove that Jews were not rejected by God. Consequently, Christians would have to admit that they were wrong in disavowing the Torah. Second, it would prove that Jesus' prediction was in error, and, therefore, he could not be divine. Being the emperor, Julian had it within his power to order the reconstruction of the Temple in Jerusalem.[20]

The work of rebuilding commenced, but in 363 some sort of on-site disaster, a fire or an earthquake, halted the project. It was completely abandoned following the death of Julian in battle shortly thereafter.

Christians, of course, interpreted these events as evidence of divine intervention to thwart an evil plot. But an extreme vulnerability in Christian argumentation had been exposed. What was to stop some other emperor from attempting the same deed to the detriment of the Church's credibility? As a result of Julian's actions, Christian rhetoric against the Jews intensified. It became even more urgent to proclaim the divine rejection of Jews as a consequence of their rejection and slaying of Christ. The linkage between the divinity of Christ, the destruction of the Temple, and the termination of the Law was also intensified, with repercussions for those Christians who were still Torah-observant. Perhaps the most lasting effect of the Julian affair for the long-term relationship between Judaism and Christianity was the enshrining in the Christian mind of the notion that "the truth of one religion [was] dependent on the invalidity of the other."[21]

Even without the rebuilding of the Temple, the obvious prospering of the Jewish people in patristic times weakened the Church's assertions about their divine rejection and continued to provide ammunition for pagan attacks on Christianity. Several Church Fathers developed similar responses to this critique, but that of Augustine of Hippo (354–430) provides a convenient and influential summary. In his effort to explain how obsolete and divinely spurned Judaism still thrived, Augustine developed parallels between the Jews of his day and the biblical story of Cain, the murderer of Abel:

> Here no one can fail to see that in every land where the Jews are scattered they mourn for the loss of their kingdom, and are in terrified subjection to the immensely superior number of Christians. . . . [Like Cain, Jews may not be killed] for whoever destroys them in this way shall suffer sevenfold vengeance, that is, shall bring upon himself the sevenfold penalty under which the Jews lie for the crucifixion of Christ. So to the end of the seven days of time, the continued preservation of the Jews will be a proof to believing Christians of the subjection merited by those who, in the pride of their kingdom, put the Lord to death.[22]

Jews endured, then, as a warning to Christians of the evils that befall the faithless. Bereft of the land of Israel, Jews were doomed to wander the earth as the penalty for the crucifixion.[23]

It should be noted that stress on the theme of God's rejection of Judaism, shown by the loss of the Temple and the Jewish state, resulted more from pagan denunciations of Christianity than from Jewish criticisms. This is perhaps seen in Augustine's allegorical application of the Cain and Abel story to prohibit the slaying of Jews. His interest is in delegitimizing the use of the Jewish tradition to undercut Christianity, not in encouraging attacks upon Jews. Of course, in a different context in which Christians vastly outnumbered Jews, such arguments could promote exactly that violent response.

D. The Debate with Jews

There is evidence of ongoing direct disputation between Jews and Christians in the patristic period. Most of this exchange centered on the proper interpretation of the Hebrew Scriptures. The presence of an organized and vital alternative interpretative tradition forced Christian thinkers to devise their own approach to the biblical texts to justify Christian practice and belief. This imperative could be described as an effort to delineate the relationship between the Hebrew Scriptures and the Christian "New Testament."[24]

In the second and third centuries, The Epistle of Barnabas, Justin Martyr, Origen, and Tertullian all responded to Jewish questions about the non-appearance of universal messianic peace by claiming that the Hebrew Bible had to be read "spiritually" or Christologically. In the words of Origen, the reason why Jews "hold false opinions and make impious or ignorant suggestions about God appears to be nothing else than this, that scripture is not understood in its spiritual sense, but is interpreted according to the bare letter."[25] It should be observed that this Christian charge of Jewish exegetical literalism is inaccurate. Both Jews and Christians utilized allegory and typology in interpreting the biblical texts. It was not a methodological disparity that was at issue, but rather the contrary evaluations of the significance of Christ in the process. Jews read their scriptures without reference to Christ. Origen felt that this was like reading the Bible while under a veil.[26]

This emphasis on a spiritual approach to the text is likewise found in the later writings of Augustine of Hippo (354–430). His writings also manifest the influence of Manichaean dualism:

> And so [Christ] made manifest a new covenant of the everlasting inheritance, wherein man, renewed by the grace of God, might lead a new life, that is the spiritual life; and that He might show the first covenant to be antiquated, wherein a carnal people living after the old man (with the exception of a few, Patriarchs and Prophets and some unknown saints, who had observed it), and leading a carnal life, eagerly desired of the Lord carnal rewards and received them as a symbol of spiritual blessings. And therefore, I say, did Christ the Lord, made man, despise all the good things of the earth, that He might show us that these things are to be despised; and endured earthly ills that He taught must be endured; so that neither might happiness be sought in the former, nor unhappiness feared in the latter.[27]

It can be seen that Jews and Judaism are categorized as carnal and earthly, in opposition to the spiritual and heavenly realities which Christ revealed. Notably, the patriarchs and prophets are thought of as "hidden" Christians, and are elsewhere described as "saved by believing that He would come"[28] and "who thought on the rest to come and sought a heavenly home."[29]

This approach to the prophets, combined with the argument that the Hebrew Scriptures must be read in their spiritual/Christological sense, resulted in a reading of the Hebrew Scriptures that classified negative comments as references to Jews and positive statements as foreshadowings of the spiritual perfection now realized in the Church. Seeing the prophets as retroactive Christians enabled the tradition of Jewish prophetic self-criticism to become a biblical assault on Judaism itself.[30]

In the fifth century Cyril of Alexandria undertook a campaign to destroy the influence of the Jewish minority in that city. His reaction to Jewish biblical interpretation strongly affected his exegetical and Christological writings. Stressing such themes as worship in spirit and truth, the New Creation, Christ as the Second Adam and the New Man, Christ as bringer of life in contrast to Moses the minister of the Law of death, Cyril developed a Christological approach in which Judaism functioned as a foil for Christian theology.[31]

The patristic response to the ongoing vitality of Judaism, then, had consequences for both biblical interpretation and Christology. Indeed, "the overwhelming impression from the study of Cyril is that Christian beliefs are so deeply rooted in attitudes toward Judaism that it is impossible to disentangle what Christians say about Christ and the Church from what they say about Judaism."[32] Clearly, the consequences of the social and theological rivalry with Judaism during Christianity's formative centuries were extensive and long-lasting.

E. The Debate with "Judaizing" Christians

The convoluted social and theological dynamics between Christians, Jews, and pagans in patristic times were further complicated by the activities of some Christians, who are, perhaps unfortunately, referred to as the "Judaizers." To be distinguished from Jewish types of Christianity, Judaizers disrupted Gentile churches by actions and assertions which challenged the authority of Christian teaching.[33]

As mentioned above, Christians and Jews were in close social contact in many cities and towns in the empire, and Judaism was attractive to Christians for a variety of reasons. The aura of holiness surrounding the synagogue which housed the sacred Jewish writings, the mysterious language employed in Jewish worship, the highly visible celebration of Jewish festivals, the distinctive lifestyle enjoined by the Mosaic Law, and the undeniable venerability bestowed by the antiquity of the Jewish faith, all were powerfully appealing to pagans and Christians alike. As members of a community so closely related to Judaism, Christians were especially inclined toward Jewish rites and spirituality.

Christians who became deeply associated with Jewish services might absent themselves from Christian liturgies during Jewish high holy days. They might close their businesses in conformity with the Jewish sabbath on Saturday instead of the Christian one on Sunday. They might celebrate Passover instead of Easter or observe Easter according to the Passover calendrical calculations of the rabbis. They might insist on observing the Mosaic Law to varying degrees. They might be fasting on days when their fellow Christians were feasting. And most importantly, they might urge their fellow Christians to act in similar fashion and would challenge Church leaders with such arguments as, "Jesus observed the Law and condemned those who minimized the Law (citing Matt 5:17-19), we must, therefore, observe the Law of Moses, too."[34]

It should be stressed that such matters as the liturgical calendar and attendance at religious rites defined and declared one's religious identity. By aligning themselves with Jewish practices, these Judaizing Christians threatened the authority of Church leaders and challenged the credibility of Christian teaching, particularly its claims that Judaism had no abiding significance. Their public actions made it clear that they held Jewish praxis to be more valid. When Christians left churches empty while praying in synagogues, this was quickly known throughout small cities, and suggested that God was present in greater power in Judaism than in Christianity.

From another perspective, the Judaizing Christians seemed "to reflect, in inchoate form, a different type of Christianity, which claimed to receive its authority from Judaism and from the example of Jesus, not from the apostolic tradition as interpreted by the great Church. This is why they could not be ignored."[35]

In response to this situation, Christian leaders felt compelled to demean Judaism in the eyes of their congregations in order to discourage their flirtations with the Church's rival. Preaching according to the conventions of Hellenistic rhetoric discussed above, these anti-Jewish declamations reached a new level of invective and vituperation. For example, Cyprian (ca. 200–258) alleged that since only Christians could legitimately address God as "our Father," when a Christian utters the Lord's Prayer, he or she

> . . . reproaches and condemns the Jews, because they not only faithlessly spurned Christ . . . but also cruelly slew him; who now cannot call the Lord "Father," since the Lord confounds and refutes them, saying, "You are born of the devil as father, and you wish to do the desires of your father [citing John 8:44]."[36]

Most vitriolic in his rhetoric, however, was the Antiochean presbyter, John Chrysostom (347–407). In eight sermons delivered over a two-year span, Chrysostom attempted to thwart Christian Judaizers and counter the appeal of the synagogue. For instance,

> Didn't you hear the argument in my earlier sermon which proved clearly that the demons inhabit the very souls of the Jews, as well as the places where they gather? Tell me, how do you dare to return to the congregation of the apostles after you have cavorted with demons? After you have gone off and joined those who shed Christ's blood, how can you keep from trembling when you return and eat from this holy Table and drink this precious blood? Does it make you shudder? Doesn't such lawlessness appall you with terror?[37]

Chrysostom's diatribes were typical according to the standards of argumentation of the time, and even provided entertainment for people used to such debate. Ironically, his efforts seem to have backfired and only encouraged Christians to visit the synagogue to see what all the fuss was about.[38]

However, as has already been seen, "religious works from antiquity have double lives, a life in the time in which they were first composed and a second life as they were read, studied, and used by later generations.''[39] Chrysostom's sermons were to be highly influential in subsequent Christian history, injecting a hateful sentiment into the Christian view of Judaism, and contributing directly to persecutions and pogroms against Jews.[40]

F. The Debate in Imperial Legislation

When in the fourth century Christianity became more politically powerful, it acquired the capacity to use the Roman legal system to restrict the influence of Jews. The legislation of the time thus provides further insights into the gradual domination of Judaism by Christianity.

Throughout the fourth century Judaism prospered as a licit religion protected by Roman law. However, as the next century began the empire tended to classify Judaism with religions and sects limited by law and to impose on Jews restraints previously applied only to undesirable groups.[41] In a similar progression, legislation pertaining to Jewish involvement in municipal life passed through three phases: a privileged status for Jews in the early fourth century, to equalization of their status with the population at large in fourth and fifth centuries, and finally to Jews as the subjects of legal discrimination in the sixth century.[42] As might be expected, the greatest number of laws enacted in this period were concerned with conversions to and from Judaism and with Christian association with Jews. The large number of such laws also suggests that ''the authorities were not completely successful in their attempt to resolve [conversion] problems in the manner advocated by the Church.''[43]

The Council of Elvira (ca. 300) forbade Christian girls to marry Jews, disallowed Jews to bless Christian crops, and excommunicated Christians who ate with Jews. In 329 the Emperor Constantine decreed that Jews who assaulted Jewish converts to Christianity were liable to capital punishment. The prohibition of Jewish-Christian intermarriage was repeated in a law of the Emperor Constantius in 339. At the same time, the emperor forbade Jews to purchase Christian slaves and ordered the execution of a Jew who circumcised his slaves. In 426 Valentinian III prevented Jews from disinheriting their children who had forsaken their faith.[44]

All of these laws sought to diminish the likelihood of Christians becoming Jews, either by intermarriage, by association with Jews, or by being owned by Jewish masters. The reverse was not the case; Jews could become Christians more easily. While it is impossible to measure the degree to which such legislation was enforced, it is noteworthy that the penalties for violating such intergroup restrictions gradually increased.[45]

A revealing incident occurred in 388 when the Emperor Theodosius ordered a bishop in Asia Minor to rebuild a synagogue that had been burned down by a mob at the bishop's instigation. Ambrose, bishop of Milan, intervened and wrote to Theodosius to rescind the order, asking, "Which, then, is of greater importance, the show of legal discipline or the cause of religion? It is needful that legal censure should yield to religion."[46] After asserting that a synagogue is "a home of unbelief, a house of impiety, a receptacle of folly which God himself has condemned,"[47] and after refusing to celebrate Mass for the emperor until the order was rescinded, Ambrose succeeded in having the reconstruction stopped.[48] However, Theodosius issued a law in 393 which declared that "the sect of the Jews is prohibited by no law," and ordered local officials to "repress with due severity the excess of those who presume to commit illegal deeds under the name of the Christian religion and attempt to destroy and despoil synagogues."[49]

This episode conveys the state of affairs at the end of the fourth century. Christian attacks on synagogues occurred.[50] Christian authorities could pressure Christian emperors to turn a blind eye to such events. Roman legal precedent and custom provided Jews with continued legal recourse.

The fact that Jews were more and more frequently associated with pagans in Roman legislation shows a principal means by which Christians were able to acquire legal power over Jews. Christians succeeded in guiding imperial legislators into categorizing Jews among groups the empire considered marginal. This was a somewhat risky tactic in that Christians themselves were in a sense "heretics" during the fourth-century imperial reigns of the Arians Constantius and Valens. But under Christian emperors, the tendency was to marginalize those who rejected (Nicean) Christian doctrine, a strategy that was exercised against pagans and heretics as well as Jews.[51]

As the fifth century unfolded, the empire's religious and political ties to the Church became more apparent in imperial law, to the obvious disadvantage of Jews. In 439 Emperor Theodosius II issued a law which prevented Jews from holding civil offices or to act as judges in cases involving Christians because "we believe it sinful that the enemies of the heavenly majesty and of the Roman laws should become the executors of our laws. . . ."[52] The same set of ordinances also forbade the construction of new synagogues.[53] The Emperor Justinian decreed in 531 that those "who cherish the Jewish superstition" could not offer testimony against Christians in court.[54]

In 452 two edicts were issued by the Emperor Marcian among several laws designed to enforce the decisions of the Council of Chalcedon, a council which Marcian himself had convened. The following is an excerpt from the second decree, which was apparently promulgated after the first one had proven to be ineffective.

> For the most devout bishops came to Chalcedon on our commands, and taught in clear definition what must be observed in religion. . . . Anyone, therefore, who discusses something further after the truth has been discovered, looks for falsehood. No one, therefore, either cleric or public official or of whatever other rank shall try in the future to treat of the Christian faith in public to crowds assembled and listening, looking thus for pretense for tumult and perfidy. For if someone strives to reopen and discuss in public what have been once judged and rightfully settled he commits injury to the verdict of the . . . council. . . . Punishment against those [disregarding] this law shall not be lacking, because they not only go out against the well established faith, but also profanate by this contention the venerable mysteries in front of Jews and pagans.[55]

This and similar legislation shows the extent of the empire's identification with the Church by the mid-fifth century. Legal efforts were being made to establish a uniformity of Christian belief and to restrict the influence of Jews and pagans. These groups were still seen as something of a threat to the emerging Christian state.

In summary, the imperial legal enactments of the third through fifth centuries illustrate the gradual demise of Jewish political influence. Early laws whose main purpose was to defend the group boundaries of the Church against Jewish influence set the stage for laws which increasingly restricted Jewish activities. This precedent was to lead to more intense legal discrimination against Jews in the following centuries now that they had been identified as foes of the state as well as opponents of Christianity.

By the time of the papacy of Gregory the Great (590–604), the protective influence of Roman legislation had deteriorated to the point that Gregory on several occasions exerted papal authority in an effort to stop attacks on synagogues. While such assaults undoubtedly sprang from socio-political as well as theological motives, Gregory's repeated insistence that "just as Jews ought not to be allowed in their synagogues more than is decreed by law, so neither ought what the law concedes them suffer any curtailment,"[56] demonstrates that Jewish freedom was vulnerable and minimally tolerated according to the letter of the law. In the later Middle Ages their status would be further jeopardized under less judicious leadership than Gregory's.

G. Summary

As a result of a complex social and political dynamic involving Jews, Christians, pagans, and Christian Judaizers, the patristic era witnessed the reversal of the relative status and influence of Judaism and Christianity. In the process of defending itself against pagan criticisms and persecutions, the powerful attractiveness of a dynamic Jewish community, the internal disputes over a wide range of doctrines and practices, and the unsettling activities of Christian Judaizers, the Church was impelled to develop a comprehensive anti-Jewish theology. It did this by joining originally disparate New Testament polemic into a unified system and by incorporating contemporary rhetorical styles with assertions about recent history and the proper approach to the sacred scriptures.

This consolidated anti-Jewish theology thus emerged in tandem with developing foundational beliefs regarding Christology, biblical interpretation, and Christian self-identity. Together with attendant political and economic advantages, it provided the rationale for legal restrictions against Jews once Christianity had gained sufficient influence in the empire. It defined the Church's stance toward Judaism for the next millennium and a half.[57] This does not mean that there were no truly theological differences between Christianity and Judaism, only that such differences were articulated by Christians in ways that shaped Christian self-identity and which would engender lasting contempt. Table 2 presents the broad outlines of this anti-Jewish framework, whose influence was apparent in Catholic religion textbooks as recently as the 1960s.

It is beyond the scope of this study to detail the elaboration of these ideas which occurred in the social context of the Middle Ages, when Jews were a tiny minority in Christian Europe.[58] It is sufficient to observe that with the passing of the patristic period, the basic pattern of Christian theological anti-Judaism had been established. While it is true that over the

---

Table 2
Elements of the Patristic Anti-Jewish Theology

- The strict Law of Moses was given to the Jews by God in a futile effort to control Jewish sinfulness. It was always intended to be temporary.

- God revealed to the prophets the divine plan to send Jesus who would bring the new Law of love and mercy. These prophets constantly chastised the Jews for their sinfulness and hard-heartedness.

- The true, spiritual meaning of the Hebrew Bible is to be discerned by reading it in reference to Christ and the Church.

- The Jews killed Jesus. Consequently, they were rejected by God and their Temple and nation were forever destroyed.

- Although replaced in God's favor by the Church, God permits the Jews to endure as a people in hopeless wandering as a sign of the results of faithlessness. Christians must not do violence to the Jews, but must be on guard against their errors.

- Jewish obstinacy in rejecting the truth is related to their association with the demonic.

centuries various ecclesial leaders and councils mitigated diverse elements of this tradition of anti-Judaism,[59] it was nevertheless not until the twentieth century that the comprehensive anti-Jewish framework was subjected to enough critique and reform to begin to impact upon the popular Christian consciousness.

Notes

[1] The patristic period has ambiguous and somewhat arbitrary boundaries. It is generally understood as the time span between the end of the New Testament period and the beginnings of Scholasticism with John Scotus Erigena in the middle of the ninth century. [See Richard P. McBrien, *Catholicism* (Minneapolis: Winston, 1980) 2:xxx; and W. L. Reese, *Dictionary of Philosophy and Religion: Eastern and Western Thought* (Atlantic Highlands, N.J.: Humanities Press, 1980) 416.] However, for our purposes it is convenient to see the papacy of Gregory the Great (590-604) as straddling the patristic period and the Middle Ages.

[2] Robert L. Wilken, *Judaism and the Early Christian Mind: A Study of Cyril of Alexandria's Exegesis and Theology* (New Haven: Yale University Press, 1971) 9.

[3] Wayne A. Meeks, *The First Urban Christians: The Social World of the Apostle Paul* (New Haven: Yale University Press, 1983) 39.

[4] For discussions of the status of Jews in the second through fifth centuries see Robert L. Wilken, *John Chrysostom and the Jews: Rhetoric and Reality in the Late Fourth Century* (Berkeley: University of California Press, 1983) 34-65; and Idem, *Judaism and the Early Christian Mind,* 9-53.

[5] John. G. Gager, *The Origins of Anti-Semitism: Attitudes Toward Judaism in Pagan and Christian Antiquity* (New York/Oxford: Oxford University Press, 1985) 99-100; Marc Saperstein, *Moments of Crisis in Jewish-Christian Relations* (Philadelphia: Trinity, 1989) 6.

[6] Joyce Reynolds and Robert Tannenbaum, *Jews and Godfearers at Aphrodisias* (Cambridge, England: Cambridge Philological Society, 1987); Meeks, *The First Urban Christians,* 208, n. 175. See also Louis H. Feldman, "Proselytes and 'Sympathizers' in the Light of the New Inscriptions from Aphrodisias," *Revue des Etudes Juives* 148 (March-April, 1989) 265-305.

[7] Saperstein, *Moments of Crisis,* 5.

[8] See Robert L. Wilken, *The Christians as the Romans Saw Them* (New Haven: Yale University Press, 1984).

[9] Idem, *John Chrysostom and the Jews,* 79-83. Feldman, "Proselytes and 'Sympathizers,'" enumerates twenty-eight reasons for Judaism's appeal in the patristic era.

[10] Wilken, *John Chrysostom and the Jews,* 68-73.

[11] Ibid., 13.

[12] Wayne A. Meeks and Robert L. Wilken, *Jews and Christians in Antioch in the First Four Centuries of the Common Era* (Missoula: Scholars Press, 1978) 27. See also 25-30.

[13] Jacob Neusner, ed. and trans., *Scriptures of the Oral Torah* (San Francisco: Harper & Row, 1967) 20-30.

[14] Wilken, *John Chrysostom and the Jews,* 29-33.

[15] Ibid., 116.

[16] David P. Efroymson, "The Patristic Connection," in *AntiSemitism and the Foundations of Christianity,* ed. by Alan T. Davies (New York: Paulist, 1979) 100–108.

[17] Wilken, *Christians as the Romans Saw Them,* 198.

[18] Henry Chadwick, *Origen: Contra Celsum* (Cambridge: Cambridge University Press, 1965) IV, 22, quoted in Efroymson, "Patristic Connection," 111–112.

[19] Wilken, *John Chrysostom and the Jews,* 131.

[20] Ibid., 138–144.

[21] Ibid., 148.

[22] Augustine, "Reply to Faustus the Manichaean," quoted in *Disputation and Dialogue: Readings in the Jewish-Encounter,* ed. by Frank Ephraim Talmage (New York: KTAV, 1975) 31.

[23] The pervasive influence of Augustine's argument is apparent in the still current practice of referring to a common houseplant as a "wandering Jew."

[24] Wilken, *Judaism and the Early Christian Mind,* 12–21, 36–38. This is not meant to suggest that all patristic writings on this subject were directly addressed to Jews. Some show signs of having been written to Christians in order to provide them with arguments to use in discussion with Jews. In the words of Wilken, "even if the works against the Jews are not themselves addressed to the Jewish community, they seem to give evidence that Christians had to contend with Jews during the period under discussion" [Ibid., 19].

[25] Ibid., 16.

[26] Ibid., 45–46.

[27] Augustine, *De Catechizandis Rudibus,* trans. Joseph Patrick Christopher (Washington: Catholic University of America, 1926) 97.

[28] Ibid., 77.

[29] Ibid., 85.

[30] Rosemary Ruether, *Faith and Fratricide: The Theological Roots of Anti-Semitism* (Minneapolis: Seabury, 1974) 163.

[31] Wilken, *Judaism and the Early Christian Mind,* 54–230.

[32] Ibid., 229.

[33] Wilken, *John Chrysostom and the Jews,* 72–73.

[34] Ibid., 68–94.

[35] Ibid., 94.

[36] *Saint Cyprian: Treatises,* trans. Roy J. Deferrari (New York: Fathers of the Church, Inc., 1958) 134–135.

[37] John Chrysostom, *Eight Orations against the Jews,* II, 3, quoted in Ruether, *Faith and Fratricide,* 179.

[38] Wilken, *John Chrysostom and the Jews,* 75.

[39] Ibid., 161.

[40] Ibid., 161–162.

[41] Amnon Linder, *The Jews in Roman Imperial Legislation* (Detroit: Wayne State University Press, 1987) 63.

[42] Ibid., 76.

[43] Ibid., 79.

[44] Ibid., 79; Jacob R. Marcus, ed., *The Jew in the Medieval World: A Source Book: 315–1791* (New York: Atheneum, 1938) 101–102, 4–5.

[45] Linder, *Jews in Roman Imperial Legislation,* 81.

[46] "Ambrose, Bishop, to the Most Clement Prince, and Blessed Emperor, Theodosius the Augustus. . . ." quoted in Marcus, *The Jew in the Medieval World,* 108.

[47] Ibid.

[48] Ibid., 109–110.

[49] Linder, *Jews in Roman Imperial Legislation,* 190.

[50] Between 373 and 423 six laws were passed to stop such assaults. [Edward H. Flannery, *The Anguish of the Jews: Twenty-Three Centuries of Anti-Semitism,* rev. ed. (New York/Mahwah: Paulist, 1985) 60–61.]

[51] James Parkes, *The Conflict of the Church and the Synagogue: A Study in the Origins of Antisemitism* (New York: Atheneum, 1969) 183–184.

[52] Ibid., 5.

[53] Ibid.

[54] Ibid., 6–7.

[55] Linder, *Jews in Roman Imperial Legislation,* 344.

[56] Flannery, *Anguish of the Jews,* 73.

[57] The pervasive influence of the patristic Church's rivalry with Judaism is sadly ignored in a recent Vatican instruction which urges greater study of the Church Fathers in priestly seminary training. The fact that the patristic writers "profoundly influenced subsequent ages and, in particular, the whole spiritual, intellectual and social life of the Middle Ages" [Congregation for Catholic Education, "Study of the Fathers of the Church" (1990) II,3,b], has a darker side in terms of Christian attitudes toward Jews which should not be overlooked in current patristic studies. The problem is explicitly recognized in another 1990 statement issued in collaboration with a different Vatican commission that "certain traditions of Christian thought, teaching, and practice in the patristic period and the Middle Ages contributed to the creation of anti-Semitism in Western society" [Int. Cath.-Jew. Liaison Com., "Uprooting Anti-Semitism" (1990) 235]. The contrast between these two quotations illustrates a certain unevenness in sensitivity to Jewish-Christian issues among various Vatican congregations, as will be discussed in the following chapter.

[58] Medieval allegations included the "blood libel" or "ritual murder" charge, according to which Jews supposedly kidnapped Christian children at Passover time in order to crucify them and use their blood in the making of matzoth; the "host desecration" charge which accused Jews of stealing hosts for the purpose of either committing sacrilege or to use them in sorcerous potions; and being involved in satanic plots to destroy Christendom by poisoning wells or spreading the Black Plague. See Marcus, *The Jew in the Medieval World,* 43–48, 121–136, 155–158; Joshua Trachtenberg, *The Devil and the Jews: The Medieval Conception of the Jew and Its Relation to Modern Anti-Semitism* (Philadelphia: Jewish Publication Society, 1944).

[59] For example, the Catechism of the Council of Trent (Part 1, Ch. 5, Question 9) taught that "Christian sinners are more responsible for the death of Christ in comparison with certain Jews who participated in it. The latter really 'did not know what they did,' whereas we know only too well." [Cited in Polish Bishops, "Jewish-Catholic Relations" (1990) 594.]

3

The Modern Church's Renunciation of Anti-Judaism

In 1964 the Second Vatican Council in its Dogmatic Constitution on the Church (*Lumen Gentium*) declared that "on account of their fathers, this [Jewish] people remains most dear to God, for God does not repent of the gifts [God] makes nor of the calls [God] issues (cf. Rom 11:28-29)."[1] In a single phrase the Roman Church reversed at least sixteen centuries of popular Christian teaching, typified by Chrysostom's, "God hates them and always hated them."[2] The Council went even further the next year when it issued a Declaration on the Relationship of the Church to Non-Christian Religions (*Nostra Aetate*). Both of these documents contradicted the foundational anti-Jewish teachings of the Church Fathers. As will be seen below, *Nostra Aetate* in particular was a pivotal event in Church history, striking as it did at the heart of the ancient anti-Jewish tradition.

What could have triggered such a reversal? While simplistic answers are to be avoided, there can be little doubt that two twentieth-century events played a major role in setting the stage for *Nostra Aetate*. The systematic torture and genocide of six million Jews during the *Shoah*,[3] in a part of the world long associated with Christianity, obliged the Church to confront its history of anti-Jewish teaching. One participant in the writing of *Nostra Aetate* believes that Pope John XXIII instructed the Secretariat for Promoting Christian Unity to prepare the draft of what eventually became the declaration because of his own experiences during the *Shoah*.[4]

The founding of the State of Israel in 1948 also defied standard Christian ideas about Jews. Augustine's theory about the perpetually "wandering Jew" was refuted by the existence of a Jewish state that had successfully repelled invading armies.

The promulgation of *Nostra Aetate* sparked a series of declarations and instructions from official bodies throughout all the Christian Churches.[5] They have extended the process begun by *Nostra Aetate* of dismantling the Church's anti-Jewish heritage. Thus, a discussion of *Nostra Aetate* should also consider the developing documentary tradition which it has generated.

Moreover, the advent of biblical criticism,[6] with its stress on determining the intentions of the sacred writers, relativized the authority of scriptural polemics. It was no longer acceptable to absolutize New Testament debates into eternal anti-Jewish principles. The use of critical tools by Roman Catholics was first required by Pius XII's 1943 encyclical *Divino Afflante Spiritu*. His call for critical biblical study was reinforced by Vatican II's *Dei Verbum* (1965) and furthered by a series of instructions from the Pontifical Biblical Commission.

Since this study examined Roman Catholic textbooks, this chapter considers only Catholic documents. This developing Catholic documentary tradition concerning Jews and Judaism includes both Vatican and papal statements and the instructions issued by national bishops' conferences and their various sub- committees. This body of literature provides the criteria with which Catholic teaching materials can be assessed. Table 3 lists the Catholic documentation that was used in this analysis.

A. Nostra Aetate (1965)

The Second Vatican Council's major treatment of the Church's stance toward Judaism occurs in the fourth section of an essay on the "Relationship of the Church with Non-Christian Religions." This format may be misleading. *Nostra Aetate's* emphasis on the "spiritual ties which link the people of the New Covenant to the stock of Abraham"[7] clearly indicates that the relationship of the Church to Judaism is much closer than its connection with, say, Buddhism. Indeed, a stress on the Church's spiritual solidarity with Judaism is one of the text's most prominent features. While intended at first to be an independent declaration, the statement on Judaism finally appeared in the perhaps unfortunate context of an essay on non-Christian religions because of a complex process of composition and conciliar approval.[8]

The statement emphasizes the Church's origins in Judaism, the Jewish backgrounds of Jesus, Mary, and the apostles, and the Church's ongoing nourishment "from that good olive tree" of the Jewish tradition onto which the Church has been grafted. This image is drawn from Romans 11:16-24, but the Council applies the metaphor to Judaism at large and not to Jewish-Christians as may have been the case in the original Pauline setting.

A most significant use of Pauline language occurred in the Council's citing of Romans 9:4-5, which rendered a disputed passage in the present tense:

> Likewise the Church keeps ever before her mind the words of the apostle Paul about his kinsmen: "they *are* the Israelites, and to them *belong* the sonship, the glory, the covenants, the giving of the law,

---

Table 3
Roman Catholic Ecclesial Documents
Contributing to a Renunciation of Anti-Judaism

Vatican Council II
  Lumen Gentium (1964)
  Dei Verbum (1965)
  Nostra Aetate (1965)

John Paul II
  addresses and letters (1979–present)

Vatican Offices
  Commission for Religious Relations with the Jews:
    "Guidelines on Implementing *Nostra Aetate*" (1974)
    "Notes on the Correct Way to Present Jews and Judaism" (1985)
  Internation Catholic-Jewish Liaison Committee:
    "Uprooting Anti-Semitism" (1990)
  Pontifical Biblical Commission:
    "Historical Truth in the Gospels" (1964)
    "The Bible and Christology" (1984)
  Pontifical Justice and Peace Commission:
    "The Church and Racism" (1988)

National Conference of Catholic Bishops [and sub-committees]
  "Guidelines for Catholic-Jewish Relations" (1967)
  "Statement on the Middle East" (1973)
  "Statement on Catholic-Jewish Relations" (1975)
  "Guidelines for Catholic-Jewish Relations" (1985)
  Within Context (1987)
  Criteria for the Evaluation of Dramatizations of the Passion (1988)
  God's Mercy Endures Forever (1988)
  "Toward Peace in the Middle East" (1989)

Notable Documents by Other Episcopal Conferences
  French Bishops (1973)
  West German Bishops (1980)
  Bishops of West Germany, Austria, and Berlin (1988)
  Polish Bishops (1990)

the worship, and the promises; to them *belong* the patriarchs, and
of their race, according to the flesh, is the Christ."[9]

The clear implication of this phraseology is that Jews remain in relationship with God, that they worship God legitimately, and that their continued observance of the Torah is a sign of ongoing fidelity to God.[10]
Combined with the statement in the declaration's next paragraph that "the
Jews remain very dear to God" (citing Rom 11:28-29), it is evident that
the Council has contradicted the patristic axiom that Jews had been rejected by God. On the contrary, the Council implicitly declared that Jews
abide in relationship with God independently of the Church's belief in
Christ. This pivotal teaching would be clarified and made explicit in subsequent Catholic documents.

Another concept introduced by *Nostra Aetate* was the thought that
"the Church awaits the day, known to God alone, when all peoples will
call on God with one voice and 'serve [God] shoulder to shoulder' (Zeph
3:0)."[11] This impulse toward a more future-oriented eschatology would
intensify in ensuing ecclesial statements concerning Jewish-Christian relations.

An important difference in the attitude toward Jews evident in *Nostra
Aetate* in contrast to the earlier anti-Jewish tradition was the Council's
call for ongoing conversation between Jews and Catholics. Again calling
attention to their "common spiritual heritage," the Council sought to encourage "mutual understanding and appreciation . . . especially by way
of biblical and theological enquiry and through friendly discussions."[12]

The Council explicitly condemned the charge that "the Jews" in all
times and places were liable for the death of Jesus. It then went on make
the following crucial statement:

> Although the Church is the new people of God, the Jews should not
> be presented as repudiated or cursed by God, as if such views fol-
> lowed from the holy Scriptures. All should take pains, then, lest in
> catechetical instruction and in the preaching of God's Word they teach
> anything out of harmony with the truth of the gospel and the spirit
> of Christ. The Church . . . deplores the hatred, persecutions, and
> displays of anti-Semitism directed against the Jews at any time and
> from any source.[13]

This direct rejection of the ancient polemical claim that the New Testament teaches that God has spurned the Jews was thus linked by the Council
to a concern for accuracy in Catholic preaching and teaching. A stress
on religious education would also characterize later documents inspired
by *Nostra Aetate*. Furthermore, the Council articulated a significant hermeneutical principle regarding New Testament texts: reading scriptural

polemics (e.g., Matt 27:25) so as to assert that Jews are accursed is a misreading of the Bible and is non-revelatory.[14]

In summary, *Nostra Aetate* rejected key elements of the ancient anti-Jewish tradition. "The Jews" were not guilty of the crucifixion, had not been renounced by God, were not under a wandering curse, and their covenantal bond with God endured.

However, the declaration did have its flaws. Being a committee-composed and a conciliarly-approved work, it was inevitable that certain sentences would be in tension or even in apparent contradiction with other passages of the document.[15] Similarly, some major issues were not mentioned, such as the significance of the Land of Israel (*Eretz Yisrael*) or the ongoing spiritual vitality of Judaism. Other topics were ambiguously treated.[16]

Nonetheless, the declaration was a historic turning point in Christian attitudes toward Judaism. It initiated an unprecedented and lasting process of Christian rapprochement with Judaism, as witnessed by developments in subsequent ecclesial documents and by continuing scholarly theological reflection.[17]

B. The Vatican "Guidelines" (1974)

On December 1, 1974, the Vatican Commission for Religious Relations with the Jews issued a series of "Guidelines and Suggestions for Implementing the Conciliar Declaration *Nostra Aetate* (no. 4)." As the title implies, the document was intended to "offer some first practical applications" of *Nostra Aetate's* principles in order to promote "sound relations between Catholics and their Jewish brothers."[18] Thus, the commission saw its comments as only the initial steps in an extensive process. Moreover, implementing the Vatican Council's call for dialogue, the statement suggested that its recommendations were the result of nine years of dialogical experience which made it "easier to distinguish the conditions under which a new relationship between Jews and Christians may be worked out and developed."[19]

The "Guidelines" both expanded on topics first raised in *Nostra Aetate* and also introduced new ideas. They repeated the Council's condemnation of anti-Semitism, rejecting it "as opposed to the very spirit of Christianity."[20] They also echoed *Nostra Aetate's* emphasis on the "spiritual bonds and historical links binding the Church to Judaism" and on the consequent demand for "better mutual understanding and renewed mutual esteem."[21]

The "Guidelines" added a significant new idea by calling for Christians to "strive to learn by what essential traits the Jews *define themselves in the light of their own religious experience.*"[22] It was not enough for

Catholics to comprehend Judaism using Christian categories. Rather, due to the inherent validity of their own experiences of God, Jewish self-understanding must be the basis of Christian images of Judaism.

This esteem for the Jewish religious experience recurred in the "Guidelines' " insistence on respect for one another's traditions and for personal religious liberty.[23] Those involved in Jewish-Catholic dialogue were cautioned to be aware of their own prejudices which only add to a "widespread air of suspicion, inspired by an unfortunate past."[24] This last item hints at a recognition of the historic Christian perpetuation of anti-Jewish attitudes, a theme which would be made explicit in later documents. The statement's respect for Jewish traditions extended to the theological foundations of both communities, for the "Guidelines" urged Catholics "to strive to understand the difficulties which arise for the Jewish soul—rightly imbued with an extremely high, pure notion of divine transcendence—when faced with the mystery of the incarnate Word."[25]

The "Guidelines" took important steps in extending the thought of *Nostra Aetate* in several areas. First, they referred explicitly to the richness of post-biblical Judaism: "The history of Judaism did not end with the destruction of Jerusalem, but rather went on to develop a religious tradition. And, although we believe that the importance and meaning of that tradition were deeply affected by the coming of Christ, it is nonetheless rich in religious values."[26] The expression "deeply affected by the coming of Christ" has an unhappy and potentially troublesome ambiguity. Is the coming of Christ a reference to "Christ as the culmination of God's promise to Abraham? If so, it is, once again, the teaching of contempt. Or is it a reference to Christian persecution of Jews?"[27] This lack of clarity aside, the "Guidelines" are significant for their definite, even if qualified, recognition of the spiritual worth of post-biblical Judaism, as typified by this sentence: "The idea of a living community in the service of God, and in the service of [people] for the love of God, such as it is realized in the liturgy, is just as characteristic of the Jewish liturgy as it is of the Christian one."[28]

Another emerging theme in the "Guidelines" concerned the Hebrew Scriptures. It was made clear that "an effort will be made to acquire a better understanding of whatever in the Old Testament retains its own perpetual value (cf. *Dei Verbum,* 14–15), since that has not been canceled by the later interpretation of the New Testament."[29] Although the statement went on to repeat the Augustinian idea that "New Testament brings out the full meaning of the Old,"[30] a major new element had appeared. A Christological reading of the Hebrew Scriptures is not the only legitimate approach. Those sacred texts maintain a "perpetual value" irrespective of Christian readings. Precisely what principles should guide such non-Christological readings of the Hebrew Scriptures were not addressed.

Presumably, the emphasis in Vatican II's *Dei Verbum* on the "meaning the sacred writer really intended" would be the guiding norm.[31]

The "Guidelines" went on to state that "the Old Testament and the Jewish tradition founded upon it must not be set against the New Testament in such a way that former seems to constitute a religion of only justice, fear, and legalism, with no appeal to the love of God and neighbor."[32] This prohibition rejects what had been standard Christian practice since the patristic era.

A final comment on the relationship between the Hebrew Scriptures and the New Testament occurred in the context of calling for an emphasis in the Christian liturgy on the "continuity of our faith with that of the earlier Covenant." The Commission declared that "we believe that [Torah] promises were fulfilled with the first coming of Christ. But it is nonetheless true that we still await their perfect fulfillment in His glorious return at the end of time."[33] Echoing *Nostra Aetate's* allusion to a future-oriented eschatology, this statement set the stage for a sophisticated treatment of typological readings of the Bible in the later Vatican "Notes" (1985).

The "Guidelines" also heightened *Nostra Aetate's* concern for education. The document declared that the Christian people must receive instruction regarding liturgical readings "which seem to show the Jewish people as such in an unfavorable light." It also drew attention to the need for "particular attention" in liturgical translations to problematic and potentially prejudicial phrases, such as "the Jews" in John's Gospel and the pejorative use of the term "the Pharisees."[34] The "Guidelines" further called for education on Jewish-Christian issues "at all levels of Christian instruction," with special cognizance given to "catechisms and religious textbooks, history books, the mass media . . . training schools, seminaries, and universities."[35]

The "Guidelines" also extended the thought of *Nostra Aetate* by recommending that Christians and Jews "work willingly together . . . in the spirit of the prophets . . . [to seek] social justice and peace at every level."[36] It could be argued that this call for collaboration on contemporary issues was related to the statement's emphasis on both the ongoing spiritual legitimacy of Judaism and on the common religious heritage of Jews and Catholics. This commonality was mentioned in the document's final words: when the Church ponders its own mystery, it "encounters the mystery of Israel," and in this encounter with the "earlier Covenant" the Church is aided in its search for Christ.[37]

C. The Vatican "Notes" (1985)

On June 24, 1985, the Vatican Commission for Religious Relations with the Jews issued "Notes on the Correct Way to Present Jews and Judaism in Preaching and Catechesis in the Roman Catholic Church." The commission saw itself as furthering earlier calls for precise education on Jews and Judaism, but recognized by the use of the word "Notes" (in the original Italian, *sussidi,* = "aids" or "helps") that the Church was still only in the beginning stages of its new dialogue with Judaism.[38]

Accurate and thorough religious education about Jews and Judaism was the major theme of the document:

> Religious teaching, catechesis, and preaching should be a preparation not only for objectivity, justice, [and] tolerance but also for understanding and dialogue. Our two traditions are so related that they cannot ignore each other. Mutual knowledge must be encouraged at every level. There is evident in particular a painful ignorance of the history and traditions of Judaism, of which only negative aspects and often caricature seem to form part of the stock ideas of many Christians. That is what these notes aim to remedy.[39]

It was acknowledged that such an educational objective was required not only by the now familiar recognition of the close ties between Christianity and Judaism, but also because of the continuing threat of religious and ethnic prejudice:

> The urgency and importance of precise, objective and rigorously accurate teaching on Judaism for our faithful follows . . . from the danger of anti-Semitism which is always ready to reappear under different guises. The question is not merely to uproot from among the faithful the remains of anti-Semitism still to be found here and there, but rather to arouse in them, through educational work, an exact knowledge of the wholly unique "bond" (*Nostra Aetate,* 4) which joins us a church to the Jews and Judaism.[40]

The "Notes" further indicated that "Jews and Judaism should not occupy an occasional and marginal place in catechesis: Their presence is essential and should be organically integrated."[41]

These educational observations reiterated the earlier concerns of *Nostra Aetate* and the "Guidelines," but in a more developed manner. For instance, it would seem that the growing realization of the depth of the inherent connection between Jews and Christians contributed to the insight that education on Judaism was not tangential to catechesis, but at its heart. With this conviction, the "Notes" proceeded to a number of catechetical topics.

On the subject of the relationship between the Hebrew Scriptures and the New Testament, the "Notes" made several significant points. It acknowledged a growing uneasiness with the conventional Christian phrase "Old Testament" because it suggested the obsolescence of the Hebrew Scriptures:

> We continue to use the expression "Old Testament" because it is traditional (cf. already 2 Cor 3:14), but also because "old" does not mean "out of date" or "outworn." In any case, it is the permanent value of the Old Testament as a source of Christian revelation that is emphasized here (*Dei Verbum,* 3).[42]

The "Notes" went on to discuss biblical typology, marking the first treatment of that issue in ecclesial documents concerning Jews and Judaism. Typology was understood as "reading the Old Testament as preparation and, in certain aspects, outline and foreshadowing of the New [Testament]. . . . Christ is henceforth the key and point of reference to the Scriptures."[43] The "Notes" recognized, however, "that typology . . . makes many people uneasy and is perhaps the sign of a problem unresolved."[44] The apparent difficulty is the danger that a purely Christological reading of the Bible tends to deny validity to any other approach, as it did in the patristic period. The "Notes" explored the subject in two remarkable paragraphs:

> It is true, then, and should be stressed, that the Church and Christians read the Old Testament in the light of the event of the dead and risen Christ and that on these grounds there is a Christian reading of the Old Testament which does not necessarily coincide with the Jewish reading. Thus Christian identity and Jewish identity should be carefully distinguished in their respective reading of the Bible. But this detracts nothing from the value of the Old Testament in the Church and *does nothing to hinder Christians from profiting discerningly from the traditions of Jewish reading.*
>   Typological reading only manifests the unfathomable riches of the Old Testament, its inexhaustible content and the mystery of which it is full, and should not lead us to forget that *it retains its own value as revelation that the New Testament often does no more than resume* (cf. Mark 12:29-31). Moreover, the New Testament itself demands to be read in the light of the Old. Primitive Christian catechesis constantly had recourse to this (cf. e.g., 1 Cor 5:6-8; 10:1-11).[45]

These words made it clear that typological readings were not the only legitimate interpretative approach to the Bible.[46] Christians would benefit from familiarity with Jewish understandings. The value of the Hebrew Scriptures was emphasized by highlighting its richness, and by noting that in some respects it is more comprehensive than the New Testament.

The "Notes" also offered a new perspective on the workings of typology by utilizing the movement toward a future-oriented eschatology present in *Nostra Aetate* and the "Guidelines":

> Typology further signifies reaching toward an accomplishment of the divine plan, when "God will be all in all" (1 Cor 15:28). This holds true also for the Church which, realized already in Christ, yet awaits its definitive perfection as the body of Christ. The fact that the body of Christ is still tending toward its full stature (cf. Eph 4:12-19) takes nothing from the value of being a Christian. So also the calling of the patriarchs and the Exodus from Egypt do not lose their importance and value in God's design from being at the same time intermediate stages (cf. e.g., *Nostra Aetate,* 4).[47]

By referring to the unrealized aspects of salvation and to the future eschaton, the "Notes" put typological approaches into a new context. In ordinary typological readings, portions of the Hebrew Scriptures were read as types of Christ's death and resurrection and of the Church. The Church and Christ, then, functioned as "antitypes," the person or things signified or foreshadowed by an earlier "type" or symbol. The "Notes" proposed a typological approach which conceived of the Hebrew Scriptures, the Christ-event, and the life of the Church as all types of the great eschatological antitype in the future, when, in the Christian view, "the fulfillment of God's design [will find] its final consummation with the return of Jesus as Messiah."[48] This procedure significantly relativized typology's power to limit revelatory authority to one hermeneutical approach. In the words of Eugene Fisher,

> . . . the "Notes" open up a startling new angle on the Church's own self-understanding. Both the New Testament and the Church's own sacraments are, "with respect to the last things," typological themselves, no less than are the Hebrew Scriptures and Rabbinic Judaism. Neither the Church, nor the Jewish people, the "Notes" maintain, exist for themselves but are called to sense God's ultimate purpose.[49]

Such a futurist eschatological perspective enabled the "Notes" to stress a major confluence of the Hebrew and Christian Scriptures; namely, their capacity to generate social action and collaboration:

> Furthermore, in underlining the eschatological dimension of Christianity we shall reach a greater awareness that the people of God of the Old and New Testaments are tending toward a like end in the future: the coming or the return of the Messiah—even if they start from two different points of view. It is more clearly understood that the person of the Messiah is not only a point of division for the people of God but also a point of convergence. . . . Attentive to the same

God who has spoken, hanging on the same word, we have to witness to one same memory and one common hope in [the One] who is the master of history. We must also accept our responsibility to prepare the world for the coming of the Messiah by working together for social justice, respect for the rights of persons and nations and for social and international reconciliation. To this we are driven, Jews and Christians, by the command to love our neighbor, by a common hope for the kingdom of God, and by the great heritage of the prophets. Transmitted soon enough by catechesis, such a conception would teach young Christians in a practical way to cooperate with Jews, going beyond simple dialogue (cf. "Guidelines," IV).[50]

Thus, the document's treatment of the scriptures made several important points: (1) There is more than one legitimate way to read the Bible, (2) Christians would benefit from knowledge of Jewish interpretations, (3) typological readings, while perhaps problematic, can be especially helpful if grounded in a futurist eschatological perspective, (4) there is a richness and profundity to the Hebrew Scriptures that is of tremendous revelatory value, and (5) Jews and Christians are both called by God to collaborate in the pursuit of justice and peace.

In regard to the subject of Christianity's Jewish roots, the "Notes" provided significant new educational guidelines as well. The statement affirmed that Jesus was a Jew whose ministry was "deliberately limited" to his Jewish contemporaries. He was "fully a man of his time and environment—the Jewish Palestinian one of the first century, the anxieties and hopes of which he shared."[51] He was obedient to the Torah, celebrated Jewish festivals, and taught in local synagogues.[52]

The "Notes" were the first Vatican document to explore the relationship between Jesus and the Pharisees. The document cited positive interactions between them[53] and observed the lack of Pharisaic involvement in Jesus' death.[54] Parallels in the thought of Jesus and the Pharisees were also noted:

> Jesus shares, with the majority of Palestinian Jews of that time, some pharisaic doctrines: the resurrection of the body; forms of piety like almsgiving, prayer, [and] fasting (cf. Matt 6:1-18) and the liturgical practice of addressing God as father; [and] the priority of the commandment to love God and our neighbor (cf. Mark 12:28-34). . . . Jesus [also] used methods of reading and interpreting Scripture and of teaching his disciples which were common to the Pharisees of [the] time. This applies to the use of parables in Jesus' ministry. . . .[55]

This consideration of Jesus and the Pharisees concluded with two important points: (1) "An exclusively negative picture of the Pharisees is likely to be inaccurate and unjust,"[56] and (2) "if Jesus shows himself severe toward the Pharisees, it is because he is closer to them than to other contemporary Jewish groups."[57]

The last item is related to the document's discussion of anti-Jewish polemic in the Gospels. Referring to the exegetical principles elaborated in *Dei Verbum* and the "Instruction on the Historical Truth of the Gospels" (see section E below), the "Notes" pointed out that:

> The Gospels are the outcome of long and complicated editorial work. . . . Hence it cannot be ruled out that some references hostile or less than favorable to the Jews have their historical context in conflicts between the nascent Church and the Jewish community. Certain controversies reflect Christian-Jewish relations long after the time of Christ. . . . All of this should be taken into account when preparing catechesis and homilies for the last weeks of Lent and Holy Week.[58]

This concern for the potentially harmful effects of polemical passages in the Gospel passion narratives was reflected in the document's reiteration of particular points made by *Nostra Aetate* and the "Guidelines" about responsibility for the crucifixion. The "Notes" added to their rejection of universal Jewish culpability by recalling the teaching of the Council of Trent "that Christian sinners are more to blame for the death of Christ than those few [unwitting] Jews who brought it about."[59]

After calling for greater Christian familiarity with Jewish liturgical practices, both past and present,[60] the "Notes" went on to discuss the meaning of Judaism in human history:

> The history of Israel did not end in 70 A.D. . . . It continued, especially in a numerous Diaspora which allowed Israel to carry on to the whole world a witness—often heroic—of its fidelity to the one God and to "exalt him in the presence of all the living" (Tb 13:4), while preserving the memory of the land of their forefathers at the heart of their hope (Passover seder).
>
> Christians are invited to understand this religious attachment which finds its roots in biblical tradition. . . . The existence of the state of Israel and its political options should be envisaged not in a perspective which is in itself religious, but in reference to . . . international law.
>
> The permanence of Israel (while so many ancient peoples have disappeared without trace) is a historic fact and a sign to be interpreted within God's design.[61]

These remarks broached issues which had not been addressed in earlier Vatican documents, such as the witness of post-biblical Jews and the meaning of the State of Israel. Catholics were urged to comprehend Judaism's love of the Land of Israel, but were cautioned that the State of Israel should not be conceived of theologically, but in accordance with standard diplomatic principles.

Of great import was the document's comment that the ongoing existence of the Jewish people has revelatory meaning as a "sign . . . within God's design." "While it would perhaps be premature for the Church to define more precisely the significance of that 'sign,' the *fact* that Judaism is a spiritual sign (one might say 'sacrament' here) of the encounter with God is established as an essential element of Catholic catechesis."[62] This perspective creates the possibility of venerating Jews killed by the Crusaders as true martyrs to covenantal fidelity and of characterizing the rise of rabbinic Judaism as a divinely-sanctioned development.[63]

Perhaps owing to its recognition of such revelatory potential, the commission stressed that Catholics needed to become aware of the enduring spiritual richness of Judaism. "We must remind ourselves how the permanence of Israel is accompanied by a continuous spiritual fecundity in the rabbinical period, in the Middle Ages, and in modern times, taking its start from a patrimony which we long shared. . . ."[64]

This call for historical awareness was also linked with the Church's tradition of anti-Judaism, particularly in reference to the ancient allegation of the divine rejection of Jews:

> We must in any case rid ourselves of the traditional idea of a people *punished,* preserved as a *living argument* for Christian apologetic. [Israel] remains a chosen people. . . . We must remember how much the balance of relations between Jews and Christians over 2,000 years has been negative.[65]

Specifically, the "Notes" encouraged catechesis on the *Shoah* as part of its educational objective to promote an accurate historical and theological awareness of the Jewish-Christian relationship.[66]

The 1985 "Notes," then, marked a significant step in the developing documentary tradition concerning Catholics and Jews. Educational, scriptural, liturgical, and historical topics were addressed to an extent not previously achieved in earlier Vatican instructions. Indeed, certain issues (such as the need for Christians to appreciate Jewish attachment to the Land, the meaning of the State of Israel, and the necessity for education on the *Shoah*) were raised for the first time, albeit in a preliminary way that some deemed not to be fully adequate. The "Notes" were also criticized for not fulfilling the axiom of the "Guidelines" that Catholics should seek to comprehend Judaism on its own terms and not in purely Christian categories, and for occasionally using terminology that smacked of the old anti-Jewish tradition.[67]

Nonetheless, the new elements which appeared in the "Notes," such as the urgency placed on thorough and pervasive religious education on

Jews and Judaism, the discussion of biblical hermeneutics and typology, and the stress put on the faithfulness of Jewish witness in history, were all signs of the continuing vitality of the process initiated by *Nostra Aetate.*

D. Pope John Paul II

Throughout his papacy John Paul II has spoken frequently and with eloquence about Jewish-Christian matters.[68] Indeed, he seems to regard the Church's relationship with Judaism as one of his top priorities: "It is the task of every local church to promote cooperation between Christians and Jews. As the successor of St. Peter, I have a special concern for all the churches and am therefore committed to furthering such a policy throughout the world."[69] His often creative and vigorous extensions of the principles of *Nostra Aetate* have proven to be influential. His comments, for example, were frequently cited in the text of the Vatican "Notes."[70]

The Pope focuses on three themes: (1) the permanency of God's covenant with the Jewish people, (2) the spiritual link between Jews and Christians, and (3) the meaning of the *Shoah.*

By referring to Jews as "the people of God of the Old Covenant, never revoked by God,"[71] as "the present-day people of the covenant concluded with Moses,"[72] and as partners in "a covenant of eternal love which was never revoked,"[73] the Pope has unequivocally articulated a belief in the perpetual relationship of God with the Chosen Jewish People. The heritage of Judaism is above all "a living heritage, which must be understood and preserved in its depth and richness by us Catholic Christians."[74]

This explicit emphasis has perhaps given rise to some other notable features of papal statements. First, the Torah is described in positive terms and on a par with the prophets. Previous Christian thinking had tended to denigrate the value of the Law because of a stress on the prophets as the foretellers of Jesus' coming. John Paul II, however, alludes to "the covenant of eternal love . . . [that was] confirmed by the gift of the Torah to Moses, opened by the prophets to the hope of eternal redemption and to the universal commitment for justice and peace."[75] Moreover, the "common heritage [of Jews and Catholics] drawn from the Law and the Prophets . . . [is] the *shalom* hoped for by the lawmakers, prophets, and wise men of Israel."[76] This last phrase parallels the Jewish division of the Tanakh into the Torah, the Prophets, and the Writings.

Another result of the Pope's conviction that the Election of the People of Israel is permanent might be seen in his eventual use of the terms "Hebrew and Christian Scriptures."[77] This formulation, it might be recalled, was not employed only a year earlier in the Vatican "Notes." The appearance of alternative phraseology in a later papal address, therefore, is an indication of ongoing development in Catholic thought about the relationship between the covenants.[78]

John Paul II has also made numerous statements about the relationship between Judaism and Christianity. Holding from early in his papacy that "our two religious communities are connected and closely related at the very level of their respective religious identities,"[79] the Pope's remarks are occasionally quite striking:

> The Church of Christ discovers her "bond" with Judaism by "searching into her own mystery" (cf. *Nostra Aetate*). The Jewish religion is not "extrinsic" to us, but in a certain way is "intrinsic" to our own religion. With Judaism therefore we have a relationship which we do not have with any other religion. You are our dearly beloved brothers and, in a certain way, it could be said that you are our elder brothers.[80]

These words declare that a unique and intense intimacy, "founded on the design of the God of the Covenant,"[81] marks the Jewish and Christian relationship. This relationship is seen by the Pope to be similar to that "between the first and second part of [the Church's] Bible," and should, therefore, be marked by "reciprocal enlightenment and explanation."[82] The relationship must also be founded upon a profound respect, "based on the mysterious spiritual link which brings us close together, in Abraham and, through Abraham, in God who chose Israel and brought forth the Church from Israel."[83]

One aspect of the Pope's focus on the depth of the Jewish-Christian "link" is his frequent use of familial language: "The Catholic faith is rooted in the eternal truths of the Hebrew Scriptures and in the irrevocable covenant made with Abraham. We, too, gratefully hold these same truths of our Jewish heritage and look upon you as our brothers and sisters in the Lord."[84] Such words were once used only *within* the Christian community. By including Jews within the Christian "family circle," the commonality of faith uniting Christians and Jews is stressed.[85]

This religious kinship has also led the Pope to observe that Christians have much to learn from Jews:

> Our common spiritual heritage is considerable. Help in better understanding certain aspects of the Church's life can be gained by taking an inventory of that heritage, but also by taking into account the faith and religious life of the Jewish people as professed and lived now as well.[86]

Finally, John Paul II's thoughts regarding the effects of the *Shoah* have also been significant. In addition to asserting "in the strongest possible way that hostility and hatred against Judaism are in complete contradiction to the Christian vision of human dignity,''[87] the Pope has insisted upon educational programs that ''will truly promote mutual respect and teach future generations about the Holocaust so that never again will such a horror be possible.''[88]He has also reflected on the meaning of the *Shoah* in theological and geo-political terms:

> One might say that you suffered [the *Shoah*] also on behalf of those who were likewise to have been exterminated. We believe in the purifying power of suffering. The more atrocious the suffering, the greater the purification. The more painful the experiences, the greater the hope. I think that today the nation of Israel . . . finds itself at the center of the attention of the nations of the world, above all because of this terrible experience, through which you have become a loud warning voice for all humanity, for all nations, all the powers of this world, all systems, and every person. More than anyone else, it is precisely you who have become this saving warning. I think that in this sense you continue your particular vocation, showing yourselves to be still the heirs of that election to which God is faithful. This is your mission in the contemporary world before the peoples, the nations, all of humanity, the church. And in this church all peoples and nations feel united to you in this mission. . . . [Our meeting] helps me and all the church to become even more aware of what unites us in the disposition of the divine covenant.[89]

Here the Pope has sought, in a preliminary way, to understand the permanent divine call of the Jewish people in relationship to both the *Shoah* and the State of Israel. Comprehending that mission in terms of an unceasing quest for universal human dignity, he aligns the Church with the Jewish people in its pursuit.

He does this with an awareness of Christian complicity in the *Shoah*. But this sparks only added resolve to seek justice:

> There is no doubt that the sufferings endured by the Jews are also for the Catholic Church a motive of sincere sorrow, especially when one thinks of the indifference and sometimes resentment which, in particular historical circumstances, have divided Jews and Christians. Indeed this evokes in us still further resolutions to cooperate for justice and peace.[90]

This renewed commitment to the pursuit of justice is also evident in papal comments about the State of Israel. John Paul II has asserted the Jewish people's right to a homeland with its security guaranteed according to international legal principles. Simultaneously, he has called for the same rights to be honored for Palestinians.[91]

The Pope has also discussed other questions prompted by reflections on the *Shoah*: ''How can we go on living after Auschwitz? . . . Is it still possible to speak about God after Auschwitz?''[92] As in his other remarks, these profound questions seem to produce in him an intensified commitment to ''the inalienable dignity that comes to [humanity] from being created in the image and likeness of God.''[93]

To summarize, the statements of John Paul II have contributed to the Christian renunciation of its anti-Judaic past. His insistence on the permanence of the Jewish covenantal bonding with God, on the intimacy of the Jewish and Christian relationship, and on the need for a renewed dedication to global peace and justice because of the *Shoah* have all given added impetus to the process begun by *Nostra Aetate.*

E. Other Vatican Documents

In addition to *Nostra Aetate,* the ''Guidelines,'' and ''Notes,'' a number of other Vatican statements have been issued that have also added to the demise of the Christian theological anti-Jewish tradition. These include instructions on the Bible and recent declarations on racism and anti-Semitism.

1. *DEI VERBUM* (1965)

As mentioned earlier, Vatican II's Dogmatic Constitution on Divine Revelation called for a critical approach to the Bible which seeks to discern the sacred authors' intentions and which recognizes those authors' historical-cultural settings:

> Seeing that, in sacred Scripture, God speaks through [people] in human fashion, it follows that the interpreter of sacred Scriptures, if he [/she] is to ascertain what God has wished to communicate to us, should carefully search out the meaning that the sacred writers really had in mind, that meaning which God had thought well to manifest through the medium of their words. . . . Rightly to understand what the sacred author wanted to affirm in his [/her] work, due attention must be paid to the customary and characteristic patterns of perception, speech, and narrative which prevailed at the age of the sacred writer, and to the conventions which the people of [that] time followed in their dealings with one another.[94]

This crucial statement asserted that authentic understanding of the scriptural text is to be found in the intentions of the biblical writer. The revelation ''which God intended to communicate'' is mediated through the human authors' personal skills and perceptions, is immersed in specific historical and cultural circumstances, and is expressed according to contemporary linguistic customs.

This foundational principle has implications for the reading of the Hebrew Scriptures and for Jewish-Christian relations. In Church history, the Hebrew Scriptures were thought to be fully grasped only by perceiving their Christological meaning, a conviction that involved a certain devaluation of Israel's experience. On the other hand, *Dei Verbum's* critical approach claims that the sacred texts must first be comprehended on their *own* literary, cultural, and theological terms, which might be devoid of Christological concern. Israel's prophets, for example, should first be heard as speakers of God's messages in particular historical situations, and not primarily as foretellers of the coming of Christ.

Such consequences of a critical reading of the Hebrew Scriptures were not developed in the Council's declaration. Indeed, *Dei Verbum,* while praising the revelatory value of the Hebrew Scriptures, held that "the Old Testament was deliberately so orientated that it should prepare for and declare in prophecy the coming of Christ,"[95] and that its books "attain and show forth their full meaning in the New Testament."[96]

This tension between what might be loosely called the critical and Christological approaches to the Hebrew Scriptures reflects both the committee-composed nature of the Vatican II documents and the ancient Christian habit of accepting only a Christological biblical hermeneutic. Although the critical methodologies upheld by Vatican II characterize current Catholic biblical scholarship, the habituation to Christological approaches persists, with the result that today "we are as yet nowhere close to knowing how to write an Old Testament theology."[97] Nevertheless, with *Dei Verbum* the critical reading of the Bible became normative in the Catholic tradition, and its principles continued to be developed in other documents.

2. "INSTRUCTION ON THE HISTORICAL TRUTH OF THE GOSPELS" (1964)

The critical outlook was evident in the Pontifical Biblical Commission's 1964 "Instruction on the Historical Truth of the Gospels." The instruction emphasized that "to judge properly concerning the reliability of what is transmitted in the Gospels, the interpreter should pay diligent attention to the three stages of tradition by which the doctrine and the life of Jesus have come down to us."[98] These stages were identified as: (1) Jesus' life and teaching, (2) the preaching of the Apostles, and (3) the Work of the Evangelists.[99]

This schema promoted a sensitivity to the distinction between events in the ministry of Jesus and their subsequent presentation by the evangelists. Certain aspects of the Gospels, such as their portrayal of the Pharisees, their attitudes toward Judaism and the Torah, and their accounts of Jesus' execution, could be seen as determinatively influenced by the Gospel writers' interests and social setting. Such an awareness of the originating contexts of the Gospel texts was subsequently applied in documents relating to Jews and Judaism, as was seen above.[100]

3. "INSTRUCTION ON THE BIBLE AND CHRISTOLOGY" (1984)

A later instruction from the Pontifical Biblical Commission entitled "The Bible and Christology" also had consequences for Jewish-Christian issues. The document recognized that "studies of Judaism with all its variety at the time of Jesus are clearly a preliminary and necessary condition for the full understanding of [him]," and that such studies could be the basis for "a fruitful dialogue between Jews and Christians."[101] It also preferred to use the expression "Prior Testament" instead of the conventional "Old Testament."[102]

The instruction carefully distinguished between the way in which Jesus was understood before and after "the manifestations of him as one raised from the dead."[103] This difference was seen not as an "interruption," but as an "advance . . . [that] is to be regarded as a constitutive element of Christology itself."[104] The perception that the "[Christian] faith has its origin and progressive growth in Jesus' resurrection"[105] means that certain Gospel passages of significance for the Jewish-Christian encounter may contain post-resurrectional theological insights not reflective of the historical setting of Jesus' ministry. For example, the high priest's demand to know whether Jesus was "the Son of the Blessed One," and his cry of "blasphemy!" to Jesus' reply that he would see "the Son of Man seated at the right hand of the Power" (Mark 14:61-64), display so many post-resurrectional Christological ideas that one must wonder whether the high priest could conceive of such a line of inquiry prior to Jesus' death. Likewise, the editorial remark in John 5:18 that "the Jews were seeking all the more to kill him . . . [because Jesus called] God his own Father, thereby making himself equal to God," seems more appropriately situated in a post-resurrectional debate between the Johannine Church and the local synagogue rather than in the historical ministry of Jesus.

It should also be noted that the 1984 instruction insisted upon the normativity of the New Testament as opposed to patristic and medieval definitions. "The 'auxiliary' languages employed in the Church in the course of the centuries do not enjoy the same authority, as far as faith is concerned, as the 'referential language' of the inspired authors."[106] It, therefore, warned against defending classic doctrinal formulations by appealing to the New Testament in ways which ignored critical exegetical questions. "For instance, it can happen that the historicity of all the details in certain Gospel episodes is too easily admitted. These might rather have had a theological purpose according to a literary convention of that time."[107]

This insistence on the normative authority of critically-interpreted biblical texts has consequences for the classic doctrinal tradition. It suggests a possible direction for future developments in the modern Church's renunciation of anti-Judaism. Those who developed patristic Christological formulations understandably did not read the Bible according to the modern norms advocated in the instruction. The Church Fathers presupposed the historicity of New Testament texts, including those containing anti-Jewish polemic. This reading, of course, conformed with the patristic "de-Judaizing process . . . which tended to undervalue the Jewish origins of the Church."[108] It follows that patristic Christological formulations are subject to modern reassessment for two reasons: (1) they are subject to the normative authority of the scriptures as *critically* understood; and (2) as historically-conditioned creedal statements,[109] they were devised in a Church that was hostile toward Judaism. Thus, for example, the failure of the Nicene Creed to consider either the Jewishness of Jesus or the Jewish tradition is understandable given its authors' hermeneutical practices and socio-political context. But such an omission needs revaluation given the modern Church's exegetical norms and its developing positive theological stance toward Judaism.[110] This sort of revaluation has not yet occurred in ecclesial documents, although the foundational principles for such a process have now been articulated.

4. "THE CHURCH AND RACISM" (1988);
   "UPROOTING ANTI-SEMITISM" (1990)

In addition to these biblical statements, instructions on racism and anti-Semitism have also been promulgated. A prominent feature of these documents is the explicit admission of Christian culpability for acts of prejudice and violence against Jews. In an instruction issued in 1988 by the Pontifical Justice and Peace Commission, entitled "The Church and Racism," the authors rejected any attempt to "to gloss over the weakness and even, at times, the complicity of certain church leaders, as well as other members of the church, in this phenomenon [of racism]."[111] They went on to observe that

> The Christian Middle Ages also made distinctions among peoples on the basis of religious criteria: Christians, Jews, and "infidels." It is for this reason that, within "Christendom," the Jews, considered the tenacious witnesses of a refusal to believe in Christ, were often the object of serious humiliation, accusations and proscriptions.[112]

Similarly, a statement issued in 1990 by the International Catholic-Jewish Liaison Committee, co-sponsored by the Vatican Commission for Religious Relations with the Jews and the International Jewish Committee on Interreligious Consultations, indicated that their

> . . . discussion led to the recognition that certain traditions of Catholic thought, teaching, preaching and practice in the patristic period and

in the Middle Ages contributed to the creation of anti-Semitism in Western society. In modern times many Catholics were not vigilant enough to react against manifestations of anti-Semitism. The Catholic delegates condemned anti-Semitism as well as all forms of racism as a sin against God and humanity, and affirmed that one cannot be authentically Christian and engage in anti-Semitism. . . . [This requires] repentance as [was] expressed by Archbishop Edward Idris Cassidy, president of the Holy See's Commission for Religious Relations With the Jews, when he said in his opening statement: "That anti-Semitism has found a place in Christian thought and practice calls for an act of *teshuvah* (repentance) and of reconciliation on our part as we gather here in this city [of Prague], which is a testimony to our failure to be authentic witnesses to our faith at times in the past."[113]

These comments represent a significant development from *Nostra Aetate*. Although that Vatican II declaration had condemned anti-Semitism, it demonstrated little awareness of the Christian anti-Jewish tradition. These two documents, on the other hand, explicitly recognize, and reject, that heritage.

"The Church and Racism" noted that the Church's anti-Jewish tradition was not the only cause of the *Shoah*. It explored the role of eighteenth and nineteenth century "scientific" theories on race:

It is well known that the National-Socialist totalitarian party made a racist ideology the basis of its insane program aimed at the physical elimination of those it deemed belonging to "inferior races." This party became responsible for one of the greatest genocides in history. This murderous folly struck first and foremost the Jewish people in unheard-of proportions, as well as other peoples, such as the Gypsies and the Tziganes, and also categories of persons such as the handicapped and the mentally ill.[114]

Thus, while not denying the impact of the Christian anti-Jewish tradition, the commission saw it as only one of the factors which contributed to the *Shoah*. The document went on to condemn contemporary varieties of anti-Semitism, and observed that anti-Zionism, can serve "at times as a screen for anti-Semitism, feeding on it and leading to it."[115]

In a unique passage, the "Church and Racism" explored the meaning of the Election of the People Israel and denied that it resulted from or caused any sort of elitism:

The choice of the Jewish people does not contradict this universalism [of salvation]. It was a divine pedagogy which wanted to assure the preservation and development of faith in the Eternal, who is unique, thus giving a basis to the ensuing responsibilities. If the people of Israel were aware of a special bond with God, they also affirmed that there was a covenant of the entire human race with him, and that even in the covenant made with them, all peoples are called to salvation: "All the tribes of the earth shall bless themselves by you," God told Abraham.[116]

The Election of Israel, therefore, is understood not as an election to privilege but as a summons to responsibility with the purpose to benefit all humanity.

F. The National Conference of Catholic Bishops

Situated in a nation with an extraordinary amount of religious freedom, and living alongside the largest Jewish community in the world, the Church in the United States has been in a unique position to enter into dialogue with Judaism and to advance the process inaugurated by *Nostra Aetate*.[117] Through a series of statements issued by both the entire body of American bishops and by its various sub-committees, the National Conference of Catholic Bishops has been an influential voice in the developing Jewish-Christian rapprochement. Its words have been cited by Vatican documents on the subject, an unusual honor for a local episcopal conference.[118]

1. "GUIDELINES FOR CATHOLIC-JEWISH RELATIONS" (1967)

In their 1967 "Guidelines," the United States bishops called for diocesan agencies to promote Jewish-Christian relations; advocated extensive education on Jewish-Christian issues throughout the Church, including parish pulpits, seminaries, and colleges; encouraged prayer in common with Jews; and insisted upon dialogue and joint social action at all levels.[119]

Educationally, the bishops declared that "school texts, prayerbooks, and other media should, under competent auspices, be examined in order to remove not only those materials which do not accord with the content and spirit of [*Nostra Aetate*], but also those which fail to show Judaism's role in salvation-history in any positive light."[120] They also called for "a frank and honest treatment of the history of Christian anti-Semitism in our history books, courses, and curricula."[121]

The 1967 "Guidelines" was possibly the first ecclesial document to address specifically the Christian portrayal of the Pharisees. "[There must be] an explicit rejection of the historically inaccurate notion that Judaism of [Jesus'] time, especially Pharisaism, was a decadent formalism and hypocrisy, well exemplified by Jesus' enemies."[122] On a related matter, they also called for "a full and precise explanation of the use of the expression 'the Jews' by St. John and other New Testament references which appear to place all Jews in negative light."[123]

2. "STATEMENT ON CATHOLIC-JEWISH RELATIONS" (1975)

In 1975 the United States bishops released a "Statement on Catholic-Jewish Relations," which presented a historical overview of the Jewish-Christian relationship and the significance of *Nostra Aetate*. The statement recognized that a new era in Jewish-Christian relations had begun:

> Much of the alienation between Christian and Jew found its origins in a certain anti-Judaic theology which over the centuries has led not only to social friction with Jews but often to their oppression. One of the most hopeful developments in our time, powerfully assisted by *Nostra Aetate*, has been the decline of the old anti-Judaism and the reformation of Christian theological expositions of Judaism along more constructive lines.[124]

And so, the bishops noted that theologians had the task "to explore the continuing relationship of the Jewish people with God and their spiritual bonds with the New Covenant and the fulfillment of God's plan for both Church and Synagogue."[125] They insisted that "homilists and liturgists pay special attention to the presentation and interpretation of scripture so as to promote among the Catholic people a genuine appreciation of the special place of the Jewish people as God's first-chosen in the history of salvation and in no way slight the honor and dignity that is theirs."[126]

The statement also offered a key paragraph concerning Jewish self-definition and Jewish reverence for the Holy Land:

> In dialogue with Christians, Jews have explained that they do not consider themselves as a church, a sect, or a denomination, as is the case among Christian communities, but rather as a peoplehood that is not solely racial, ethnic, or religious, but in a sense a composite of all these. It is for such reasons that an overwhelming majority of Jews see themselves bound in one way or another to the land of Israel. Most Jews see this tie to the land as essential to their Jewishness. Whatever difficulties Christians may experience in sharing this view they should strive to understand this link between land and people which Jews have expressed in their writings and worship throughout two millennia as a longing for the homeland, holy Zion.[127]

These thoughts were to prove influential in later Church documents and contributed to part of the 1985 Vatican "Notes."[128]

3. "GUIDELINES FOR CATHOLIC-JEWISH RELATIONS" (1985)

In 1985 the United States bishops revised the earlier 1967 "Guidelines." While most of the previous document was reiterated, there were a number of significant additions. For one thing, there was an expanded discussion of the inappropriateness of Christian proselytizing of Jews engaged in dialogue:

> Proselytism, which does not respect human freedom, is carefully to be avoided. While the Christians, through the faith life of word and deed, will always witness to Jesus as the risen Christ, the dialogue is concerned with the permanent vocation of the Jews as God's people, the enduring values that Judaism shares with Christianity and that, together, the Church and the Jewish people are called upon to witness to the whole world.[129]

In addition, the 1985 "Guidelines" emphasized the "Hebrew Scriptures as a source of faith with their own perpetual value" and also "a recognition of Judaism as a living tradition that has had a strong and creative religious life throughout the centuries since the birth of Christianity from a common root."[130]

The bishops also added a section which highlighted "the closeness on many central doctrines between Jesus' teaching and that of the Pharisees. Many Jewish teachers adopted positions similar to those of Jesus on the critical religious and social issues of the time."[131]

5. CRITERIA FOR THE EVALUATION OF DRAMATIZATIONS OF THE PASSION

In 1988 the Bishops' Committee for Ecumenical and Inter-religious Affairs issued *Criteria for the Evaluation of Dramatizations of the Passion*. This document synthesized the principles articulated in previous Vatican and National Conference of Catholic Bishops instructions in order to "provide practical applications regarding . . . depictions and presentations of the events surrounding the passion and death of Jesus."[132] Importantly, the Committee declared that "the principles herein invoked are applicable . . . to all levels of Christian instruction and education, whether written (textbooks, teachers manuals, etc.) or oral (preaching, the mass media)."[133] Thus, their norms are relevant not just for dramas, but also for textbook analyses.

The statement begins by acknowledging the central place of Holy Week in the Church's liturgy. Therefore, any presentations of the "sacred mysteries" observed in that Week must "conform to the highest possible standards of biblical interpretation and theological sensitivity. . . . Any presentations that explicitly or implicitly seek to shift responsibility from human sin onto this or that historical group, such as the Jews, . . . obscure a core gospel truth."[134]

Following from this foundational axiom, the document mentions the rich diversity of first-century Judaism and notes that the Gospels only convey some of this diversity. Presentations of the passion, "should strive to present the diversity of Jewish communities at the time of Jesus, enabling viewers to understand that many of Jesus' major concerns (e.g., critique of Temple policies) would have been shared by other Jews of his time. . . . (perhaps especially certain Pharisees).''[135] In addition, ''Jesus must not be depicted as opposed to the Law (Torah),''[136] ''Jesus and the disciples must not be set dramatically in opposition to his people, the Jews,''[137] and ''Jesus and his teachings should not be portrayed as opposed to or by 'the Pharisees' as a group . . . [who should not] be depicted as party to the proceedings against Jesus.''[138]

Regarding depictions of the period following Jesus' arrest, the instruction has this to say:

> Jews should not be depicted as avaricious (e.g., in Temple money-changer scenes); blood thirsty (e.g., in certain depictions of Jesus' appearances before the Temple priesthood or Pilate); or implacable enemies of Christ (e.g., by changing the small ''crowd'' at the governor's palace into a teeming mob). . . . The secrecy surrounding Jesus' ''trial'' was motivated by the large following he had in Jerusalem and the Jewish populace, far from wishing his death, would have opposed it had they known and, in fact, mourned his death by Roman execution (cf. Luke 23:27). Any crowd or questioning scene, therefore, should reflect the fact that some in the crowd and among the Jewish leaders (e.g., Nicodemus, Joseph) supported Jesus and that the rest were manipulated by his opponents, as is made clear in the gospels.[139]

The committee observed that in presenting the life of Jesus the Gospels can reflect the debates that occurred between the early Church and the Jewish Synagogue. To ignore this exegetical principle and ''to generalize from such specific and often later conflicts to an either/or opposition between Jesus and Judaism is to anachronize and, more basically, to vitiate the spirit and intent of the gospel texts.''[140]

On a related biblical note, the document observes that the Gospels are not primarily historical, but rather theological works. Therefore,

> . . . to attempt to utilize the four passion narratives literally by picking one passage from one gospel, and the next from another gospel, and so forth, is to risk violating the integrity of the texts themselves. . . . It is not sufficient for the producers of passion dramatizations to respond to responsible criticism by appealing to the notion that ''it's in the Bible.'' One must account for one's selections.[141]

The committee also called for care in the lighting and staging of characters and groups. Costuming, makeup, and lighting could be used to isolate Jesus and the disciples from ''the Jews.'' But it is crucial that Jesus and his followers be clearly shown as ''Jews among Jews'' by means of common dress and common actions, such as prayer.[142] In other words, portraying the distinctions between groups should be historically correct. The Romans, for instance, should be clearly depicted as a foreign military presence occupying Jewish lands.[143] Likewise, the known historical character of Pontius Pilate should be accurately dramatized.[144]

Lastly, the committee instructed that any potentially offensive or negative Gospel element, such as the "blood-curse" in Matthew 27:25, "cannot, in good conscience, be used."[145]

6. GOD'S MERCY ENDURES FOREVER (1988)

In 1988 the Bishops' Committee on the Liturgy released "Guidelines on the Presentation of Jews and Judaism in Catholic Preaching" under the main title *God's Mercy Endures Forever*. After acknowledging that "the Holocaust drew its fiery breath from the ancient, sometimes latent, but always persistent anti-Semitism which, over the centuries, found too large a place within the hearts of too many Christian men and women," the document stated its intention "to see to it that our liturgical celebrations never again become occasions for that anti-Semitic or anti-Judaic sentiment that sometimes marred the liturgy in the past."[146] To achieve this, the committee offered "assistance to Catholic preachers so that Jews and Judaism are rightly presented in homilies and other forms of preaching."[147] As with the previous document, these guidelines are also applicable to the presentation of similar materials in religion textbooks.

The document emphasized the Jewish origins of Christian worship forms,[148] and rejected the earlier Christian tendency "to dichotomize the Bible into two mutually contradictory parts."[149] It insisted that *Nostra Aetate* had "established as an overriding hermeneutical principle for homilists" that Jews should never be presented as rejected or accursed by God.[150]

Perhaps the committee's most important work is to be found in the section dealing with preaching during Advent. In it one finds the most detailed discussion of the question of prophecy-fulfillment to appear in any ecclesial document to the present time:

> The [Advent] lectionary readings from the prophets are selected to bring out the ancient Christian theme that Jesus is the "fulfillment" of the biblical message of hope and promise, the inauguration of the "days to come". . . . This truth needs to be framed very carefully. Christians believe that Jesus is the promised Messiah who has come, but also know that his messianic kingdom is not yet fully realized. The ancient messianic prophecies are not merely temporal predictions but profound expressions of eschatological hope. Since this dimension can be misunderstood or even missed altogether, the homilist needs to raise clearly the hope found in the prophets and heightened

in the proclamation of Christ. This hope includes trust in what is promised but not yet seen. While the biblical prophecies of an age of universal *shalom* are "fulfilled" (i.e., irreversibly inaugurated) in Christ's coming, that fulfillment is not yet completely worked out in each person's life or perfected in the world at large. It is the mission of the Church, as also that of the Jewish people, to proclaim and to work to prepare the world for the full flowering of God's Reign, which is, but is "not yet."[151]

This expansion of the principles mentioned in the 1985 Vatican "Notes"[152] is marked by an emphasis on a futurist eschatology. Such a future orientation results in a redefinition of the term "fulfillment." Typically understood as the accomplishment of something foreseen in the past, it is now seen as the "irreversible inauguration" of things not yet realized. This approach promotes collaboration in preparing for the Reign of God, a dynamic that was also evident in the "Notes."

In addition, *God's Mercy Endures Forever* indicates that in some Gospel accounts of disputes between Jesus and Pharisees, "Jesus appears to have been participating in internal Pharisaic debates on various points of interpretation of God's law. . . . Jesus' interpretation of biblical law is similar to that found in some of the prophets and ultimately adopted by rabbinic tradition as can be seen in the *Talmud.*"[153]

The text also encouraged joint prayer between Catholics and Jews. Such prayers could include passover seders (although these should retain their Jewish identity and not be Christianized),[154] "services of reconciliation" and *shoah* observances.[155]

Finally, the committee recommended that homilists feel "free to draw on Jewish sources (rabbinic, medieval, and modern) in expounding the meaning of the Hebrew scriptures and the apostolic writings."[156] Among many other suggestions, this represented an explicit recognition of the ongoing spiritual value of Judaism, perhaps to an unprecedented degree.

7. "TOWARD PEACE IN THE MIDDLE EAST" (1989)

In 1989 the United States bishops issued their third statement on the situation in the Middle East.[157] While largely diplomatic and political in content, the statement has implications for the ongoing Jewish-Christian encounter.

The statement stressed the intricacies of the situation and avoided any simplistic treatment of the region's difficulties. Since "political, religious, cultural, and moral issues" are involved, "reducing the reality of the Middle East to one dimension . . . inevitably distorts the nature of the problems people and nations face there."[158]

The bishops demonstrated considerable sensitivity to the motivations and needs of the peoples in the area. Israelis were seen to "live with a sense of political and psychological vulnerability which outside observers (especially in a country as large and physically protected as the United States) often fail to understand."[159] Noting that Israel was geographically vulnerable, at peace with only one of its Arab neighbors, and the persistent target of terrorist actions, the bishops perceived that "in the minds of Israelis, both the objectives they seek—security and territory—and their means are morally justified, because what is at stake is their survival as a people."[160]

The Palestinians, on the other hand, were recognized as in need of the status conferred upon sovereign states. "Both territory and sovereignty are needed if Palestinians, living inside and outside the Israeli occupied territories, are to realize their political identity."[161]

These considerations led the bishops to outline specific proposals for furthering peace in the region:

> The assertion that each party, Israel and the Palestinian people, has a fundamental right to a homeland establishes the framework in moral terms for political negotiations. . . . The result of recognizing the same right in both parties, then limiting its extent to allow for fulfillment of both rights, should work toward a settlement which achieves three objectives. First, it should formalize Israel's existence as a sovereign state in the eyes of the Arab states and the Palestinians; second, it should establish an independent Palestinian homeland with its sovereign status recognized by Israel; third, there must be negotiated limits to the exercise of Palestinian sovereignty so that it is clear that Israel's security is protected.[162]

"Toward Peace in the Middle East" provides three principles for discussing the Arab-Israeli conflict: (1) the issues are not to be treated simplistically; (2) a sensitivity to the needs of all parties must be present; and (3) the fundamental rights of all parties must be realized within the limits needed for those parties to achieve their rights to a significant degree.

To conclude this subsection, all of the statements published under the auspices of the National Conference of Catholic Bishops have sought to implement and further *Nostra Aetate*. As the result of a socio-political situation which promotes inter-religious dialogue and amity, the Church in the United States has developed an impressive and innovative legacy of documentary reflections on the Jewish-Christian relationship. Furthermore, these documents provide the specific and immediate framework for evaluating the presentation of Jews and Judaism in current American Catholic religion textbooks.

G. Summary

This chapter has described the modern Church's renunciation of its anti-Judaic tradition as a process begun by *Nostra Aetate* and furthered in subsequent ecclesial documents. Due to this study's focus on American religion texts, statements by Vatican agencies, by John Paul II, and by the United States bishops were considered. However, it must be noted that significant instructions were issued by other bishops' conferences,[163] by local dioceses,[164] by dialogue or collaborative groups,[165] and by other Christian traditions.[166] In addition, a massive body of scholarly, theological literature on the subject has emerged.[167]

The net effect of this extensive activity has been the contradiction of each element of the Church's long tradition of anti-Judaic sentiment. Beginning with *Nostra Aetate's* implicit rejection of the foundational supersessionist idea that the Church had replaced a delegitimated Judaism, the entire anti-Jewish theological superstructure has come under scrutiny. A process of revision in such areas as biblical hermeneutics, Christology, ecclesiology, education, eschatology, liturgy, soteriology, and systematic theology has begun.

The Roman Catholic documents discussed in this chapter provide a convenient window on this unfolding process. They also provide authoritative guidelines for use in assessing the quality of Catholic religious education materials. This leads to two comments about the developing Catholic documentary tradition.

First, these documents have emerged from within an ongoing process of reflection. Later instructions have amplified and expanded the ideas articulated in earlier ones. For example, *Nostra Aetate* was criticized for discussing anti-Semitism as if it were a phenomenon alien to the Church's history. More recent statements, as we have seen, have become explicit in their confession of the Church's anti-Judaic history. Similarly, earlier documents appeared not to recognize the hermeneutical implications of their assertion that the Jewish community continues as a living faith tradition. The "Old Testament" was still described primarily as the harbinger of the "New." Later instructions have emphasized the sacred character of the "Hebrew Scriptures" on their own, non-Christological terms.

This ongoing developmental dynamism means that the authority of these documents has to be understood holistically. While in the Roman tradition the greatest weight is placed upon the declarations of ecumenical councils, with *Nostra Aetate* we are dealing with something radically new. In the words of Cardinal Johannes Willebrands, president of the Vatican Commission for Religious Relations with the Jews, "Never before has a systematic, positive, comprehensive, careful and daring presentation of Jews and Judaism been made in the Church."[168] This means that *Nostra Aetate* must be interpreted in the light of the ongoing process of refinement and development which it has initiated. The ideas which it advanced in preliminary form have evolved in succeeding documents, thereby bringing them to more mature expression. In some ways *Nostra Aetate* can be understood as the infant beginnings of a new Christian stance toward Judaism, which later instructions have fostered into a vigorous adolescence. How the vistas of *Nostra Aetate* will appear when they grow into full "adulthood" remains to be seen.

In any case, the trajectories of thought which *Nostra Aetate* has sparked are just as important as its own unprecedented, but still preliminary, formulations. Thus, for example, although the conciliar document itself is comfortable with the language of the "Old Testament," the fact that its own principles have contributed to the appearance of new phrases such as "Hebrew Scriptures" and "Prior Testament" must not be overlooked.

Later Vatican, papal, and local documents provide the lenses through which the authoritative ideas of *Nostra Aetate* must be seen. To paraphrase Eugene Fisher, "They are, taken together, the definitive utterance of the Catholic tradition, the *magisterium* on the subject universally binding on the presentation of the Catholic faith by catechists and homilists alike."[169]

Second, in addition to understanding the authority of these Roman Catholic documents in an organic or holistic manner, cognizance must be taken of the existence of other Catholic ecclesial statements. In some cases, these other instructions display a certain lack of awareness of the concerns enunciated in the Jewish-Christian texts. For example, a recent Vatican document called for increased study of the patristic writers in seminary curricula. The text seemed oblivious to the anti-Jewish social climate in which the Church Fathers lived or to modern difficulties with patristic supersessionist hermeneutics.[170]

Likewise, the first draft of the *Catechism for the Catholic Church* has been criticized for reducing prophecy to prediction, for treating the Hebrew Scriptures as most valuable as a preparation for the New Testament, for referring to Pharisaism as "hypocritical casuistry," for caricaturing the complexities of Jewish messianic traditions, and for conveying numerous supersessionist attitudes.[171] Since each of these practices is in violation of the documents surveyed in this chapter, the question of the authority of the "Jewish-Christian" texts relative to that of other instructions arises.

The problem illustrates the radical newness of the process begun by *Nostra Aetate.* Although the development of subsequent literature has been rapid, it presumably will take longer than twenty-five years to alter centuries-old habits of thought. The inconsistency of ecclesial documents probably owes much to the sheer inertia of the previous anti-Judaic mindset.

In this transitional period, therefore, it would seem reasonable to observe the following axiom: those documents which directly address topics relevant to the Church's understanding of Judaism are to be given greater authority than instructions which impinge on them only indirectly in the process of discussing other topics.

By taking these two points into account—namely, the need for a holistic understanding of the modern Church's documentary rejection of anti-Judaism and the priority to be assigned to such documents when dealing with pertinent topics—a solid and authoritative basis for assessing Catholic religion textbooks has been established.

Notes

[1] Vatican II, *Lumen Gentium* (1964) 16.

[2] Flannery, *Anguish of the Jews,* 51; Ruether, *Faith and Patricide,* 179.

[3] This writer prefers the term *Shoah,* the "Destruction," (or the "destroying wind") to the more popular "Holocaust." The latter in the biblical tradition refers to immolated sacrifices offered to God for the remission of sins, an awful image for the events of Nazi Germany. An alternative, "the Abomination" has suggestive biblical resonances. [See A. Roy Eckardt, *Jews and Christians: The Contemporary Meeting* (Bloomington: Indiana University Press, 1986) 29ff.].

[4] John M. Oesterreicher, *The New Encounter Between Christians and Jews* (New York: Philosophical Library, 1986) 104–114. Note also the observation of the Vatican "Guidelines" (1974) that the Council was situated in "circumstances deeply affected by the memory of the persecution and massacre of Jews which took place in Europe just before and during the Second World War" [Preamble].

[5] See the two collections edited by Helga Croner, *Stepping Stones to Further Jewish-Christian Relations* (New York: Stimulus, 1977) and *More Stepping Stones to Jewish-Christian Relations* (New York: Stimulus, 1985). See also The World Council of Churches, *The Theology of the Churches and the Jewish People: Statements by the World Council of Churches and Its Member Churches* (Geneva: WCC Publications, 1988).

[6] "Biblical criticism" will be employed herein in a broad sense, incorporating all types of critical analysis of the Scriptures, including form, source, redaction, historical, literary, and sociological criticism.

[7] Vatican II, *Nostra Aetate* (1965) 4.

[8] See Oesterreicher, *The New Encounter,* 103–295.

[9] Vatican II, *Nostra Aetate* (1965), 4. Emphasis added.

[10] Eugene J. Fisher, "Official Roman Catholic Teaching on Jews and Judaism: Commentary and Context," in *In Our Time: The Flowering of Jewish-Catholic Dialogue,* eds. Eugene J. Fisher and Leon Klenicki (New York/Mahwah: Paulist, 1990) 6.

[11] Vatican II, *Nostra Aetate* (1965) 4.

[12] Ibid.

[13] Ibid.

[14]Fisher, "Roman Catholic Teaching," 7. This principle has immense implications for the study of patristic exegesis. See also ch. 2, n. 57, and nn. 106–109 in this chapter.

[15]For instance, the olive tree metaphor from Romans 11 is immediately followed by a reference to Ephesians 2:14-16, which discusses how Christ has unified Jew and Greek in his person. This approach is more supersessionist than Paul's image of grafting branches, and may represent more conventional Christian views on the status of Judaism.

[16]For example, the condemnation of antisemitism fails to admit that Christians were guilty of this sin over the centuries [see Marc H. Tanenbaum, "A Jewish Viewpoint on Nostra Aetate," in *Twenty Years of Jewish-Catholic Relations,* eds. Eugene J. Fisher, A. James Rudin, and Marc H. Tanenbaum (New York/Mahwah: Paulist, 1986) 52]. Moreover, in addressing the historical question of the "Christ-killer" charge, the declaration could be accused of failing to treat the accusation's influence as a "theological categorization" [Jeremy Cohen, "Robert Chazan's 'Medieval Anti-Semitism'," in *History and Hate: The Dimensions of Anti-Semitism,* ed. David Berger (Philadelphia: Jewish Publication Society, 1986) 69–70]. It also left murky the scriptural relationship between the Hebrew Scriptures and the New Testament [Leon Klenicki, "From Argument to Dialogue: *Nostra Aetate* Twenty-Five Years Later," in Fisher and Klenicki, *In Our Time,* 82–83].

[17]As noted in A. James Rudin, "The Dramatic Impact of *Nostra Aetate*," in Fisher, Rudin, and Tanenbaum, *Twenty Years of Jewish-Catholic Relations,* 15–18.

[18]Vatican "Guidelines" (1974) Preamble.

[19]Ibid. See Fisher, "Roman Catholic Teaching," 7.

[20]Vatican "Guidelines" (1974) Preamble.

[21]Ibid.

[22]Ibid. Emphasis added.

[23]Ibid., I.

[24]Ibid.

[25]Ibid.

[26]Ibid., III.

[27]Klenicki, "From Argument to Dialogue," 84.

[28]Vatican "Guidelines" (1974) II. Note the use of the present tense.

[29]Ibid., II.

[30]Ibid.

[31]Vatican II, *Dei Verbum* (1965) 12.

[32]Vatican "Guidelines" (1974) III.

[33]Ibid., II.

[34]Ibid.

[35]Ibid., III. This axiom would also apply to the new *Catechism of the Catholic Church.*

[36]Ibid., IV.

[37]Ibid., Conclusion. Note also the expression "earlier Covenant," which again suggests the perpetual validity of Judaism.

[38]Fisher, "Roman Catholic Teaching," 12.

[39]Vatican, "Notes" (1985) Conclusion, 27.

[40]Ibid., I, 8.

41Ibid., I, 2.

42Ibid., n. 1.

43Ibid., II, 5.

44Ibid., II, 3.

45Ibid., II, 6–7. Emphasis added.

46As explained by Bishop Jorge Mejia of the commission. See his "A Note for the Presentation of the Document of the Commission for Religious Relations with the Jews" in Fisher and Klenicki, *In Our Time,* 55.

47Vatican, "Notes" (1985) II, 8.

48Ibid., II, 9.

49Fisher, "Roman Catholic Teaching," 14. See also Mejia, "A Note," 55.

50Vatican, "Notes" (1985) II, 10–11.

51Ibid., III, 12.

52Ibid., III, 13–14.

53Ibid., III, 16.

54Ibid., III, 19.

55Ibid., III, 17–18.

56Ibid., III, 19.

57Ibid.

58Ibid., IV, 21, A.

59Ibid., IV, 22.

60Ibid., V.

61Ibid., VI, 25.

62Fisher, "Roman Catholic Teaching," 17. Emphasis in original.

63Idem, "Implementing the Vatican Document, 'Notes on Jews and Judaism in Preaching and Catechesis,' " *The Living Light* 22/2 (January 1986) 107.

64Vatican, "Notes" (1985), VI, 25. It might be parenthetically noted that the instruction did not advocate by this historical sensitivity an understanding of the Jewish-Christian relationship according to a simple "two covenant model." The commission's stress on the mysterious bond between Judaism and the Church seemed to preclude viewing them "as two parallel ways of salvation" [I, 7].

65Ibid., VI, 25.

66Ibid.

67See the observations of the International Jewish Committee on Interreligious Consultations, cited marginally in *Origins* 15/7 (July 4, 1985) 102–104. See also the comments in Klenicki, "From Argument to Dialogue," 87–90.

68For a convenient collection of his remarks until 1986, see *Pope John Paul II On Jews and Judaism: 1979–1986,* eds. Eugene J. Fisher and Leon Klenicki (Washington, U.S.C.C., 1987).

69John Paul II, "To a Delegation of the American Jewish Committee" (March 16, 1990).

70Vatican, "Notes" (1985) Preamble; I, 2,3,6; V, 23; VI, 25.

71John Paul II, "To the West German Jewish Community" (November 17, 1980).

72Ibid.

73Idem, "To American Jewish Leaders" (September 11, 1987).

74Idem, "To the West German Jewish Community" (November 17, 1980).

75Ibid.

[76]Idem, "To the Jewish Community in Rome" (April 13, 1986).

[77]Idem, "To the Jewish Community in Australia" (November 26, 1986).

[78]See Eugene J. Fisher, "Pope John Paul II's Pilgrimage of Reconciliation: A Commentary on the Texts," in *John Paul II On Jews and Judaism,* 10.

[79]John Paul II, "To Representatives of Jewish Organizations" (March 12, 1979).

[80]Idem, "To the Jewish Community in Rome" (April 13, 1986).

[81]Idem, "To Christian Experts in Jewish-Christian Relations" (March 6, 1982).

[82]Idem, "To the West German Jewish Community" (November 17, 1980).

[83]Idem, "To Representatives of the Anti-Defamation League of B'nai B'rith" (March 22, 1984).

[84]Idem, "To the Jewish Community in Australia" (November 26, 1986). Note also: "You are our dearly beloved brothers and, in a certain way, it could be said that you are our elder brothers" ["To the Jewish Community in Rome" (April 13, 1986)]; and "I have constantly sought to deepen and develop our relationships with the Jews, 'our elder brothers in the faith of Abraham' " ["To Archbishop John May" (August 8, 1987)].

[85]Fisher, "John Paul II's Pilgrimage," 9.

[86]John Paul II, "To Christian Experts in Jewish-Christian Relations" (March 6, 1982).

[87]John Paul II, "Apostolic Letter on the 50th Anniversary of the Beginning of World War II" (August 27, 1989).

[88]John Paul II, "To American Jewish Leaders" (September 11, 1987).

[89]John Paul II, "To the Jews in Warsaw" (June 14, 1987).

[90]Idem, "To Archbishop John May" (August 8, 1987).

[91]Idem, "Apostolic Letter on Jerusalem" (April 20, 1984) and "To American Jewish Leaders" (September 11, 1987).

[92]John Paul II, "To European Bishops preparing for the 1991 European Synod of Bishops" (June 5, 1990) 7.

[93]Ibid., 8.

[94]Vatican II, *Dei Verbum* (1965) 12.

[95]Ibid., 15.

[96]Ibid., 16.

[97]Joseph Blenkinsopp, "Tanakh and the New Testament: A Christian Perspective," in *Biblical Studies: Meeting Ground of Jews and Christians,* eds. Lawrence Boadt, Helga Croner, and Leon Klenicki (New York/Ramsey: Paulist/Stimulus, 1980) 113. The echoes of this tension in the liturgical field are apparent in Joseph Jensen, "Prediction-Fulfillment in Bible and Liturgy" *Catholic Biblical Quarterly* 50/4 (October 1988) 646–662.

[98]Pontifical Biblical Commission, "Instruction on the Historical Truth of the Gospels" (1964) VI, 2.

[99]Ibid., VII–IX.

[100]E.g., Vatican, "Notes" (1985) IV, 21, A: "Certain controversies reflect Jewish-Christian relations long after the time of Christ."

[101]Pontifical Biblical Commission, "The Bible and Christology" (1984) 1.1.5.4.

[102]E.g., Ibid., 1.1.6 (c).

[103]Ibid., 1.1.11.2 (a).

[104]Ibid.

[105]Ibid., 1.2.3.1.

[106]Ibid., 1.2.2.1.

[107]Ibid., 1.2.1.2. The French rather than the Latin version of this sentence has been followed for clarity of expression.

[108]NCCB, "Statement" (1975).

[109]See Pontifical Biblical Commission, "The Bible and Christology" (1984) 1.1.2.1 and 1.2.2 which acknowledges that doctrinal formulations are as culturally and historically conditioned as the scriptures.

[110]See Gabriel Fackre, *Authority: Scripture in the Church for the World,* vol. 2, *The Christian Story: A Pastoral Systematics* (Grand Rapids: Eerdmans, 1987) 182.

[111]Pontifical Justice and Peace Commission, "The Church and Racism" (1988) I, fn.

[112]Ibid., I, 2.

[113]Int. Cath.-Jew. Liaison Com., "Uprooting Anti-Semitism" (1990) 235.

[114]Pontifical Justice and Peace Commission, "The Church and Racism" (1988) I, 7.

[115]Ibid., II, 15.

[116]Ibid., III, 20.

[117]This favorable environment has been recognized by John Paul II ["To American Jewish Leaders (September 11, 1987)] and by the United States bishops themselves [NCCB, "Guidelines" (1967)].

[118]Fisher, "Roman Catholic Teaching," 17.

[119]NCCB, "Guidelines" (1967). Recommended Programs 1–4, 6–7.

[120]Ibid., Recommended Programs, 5.

[121]Ibid., Recommended Programs, 10c.

[122]Ibid., Recommended Programs, 10e.

[123]Ibid., Recommended Programs, 10g, referring to *Nostra Aetate,* 4.

[124]NCCB, "Statement" (1975).

[125]Ibid.

[126]Ibid.

[127]Ibid.

[128]Vatican, "Notes" (1985) VI, 25.

[129]NCCB, "Guidelines" (1985) General Principles, 6.

[130]Ibid., Recommended Programs, 10a.

[131]Ibid., Recommended Programs, 10e.

[132]NCCB, *Dramatizations of the Passion* (1988) Preliminary Considerations.

[133]Ibid.

[134]Ibid., Preamble, A, 1.

[135]Ibid., B, 2.

[136]Ibid., B, 3a.

[137]Ibid., B, 3c.

[138]Ibid., B, 3f.

[139]Ibid., B, 3d,e.

[140]Ibid., B, 3g.

[141]Ibid., C, 1b-c.

[142]Ibid., B, 3h.

[143]Ibid., B, 3i.

[144]Ibid., C, 2b.

[145]Ibid., C, 1d.

[146]NCCB, *God's Mercy Endures Forever* (1988) Preface.

[147]Ibid.

[148]Ibid., 1-4.

[149]Ibid., 5-6.

[150]Ibid., 7.

[151]Ibid., 11.

[152]Vatican, "Notes" (1985) II.

[153]NCCB, *God's Mercy Endures Forever* (1985) 19.

[154]Ibid., 28.

[155]Ibid., 27, 29.

[156]Ibid., 31i.

[157]Earlier statements were released in 1973 and 1978.

[158]NCCB, "Toward Peace in the Middle East" (1989) Preamble.

[159]Ibid., I.

[160]Ibid.

[161]Ibid., I.

[162]Ibid., IV, A, 1.

[163]Such as: French Bishops, "Pastoral Orientations" (1973); West German Bishops, "The Church and the Jews" (1980); Bishops of West Germany, Austria, and Berlin, "Accepting the Burden of History" (1988); and Polish Bishops, "Jewish-Catholic Relations" (1990).

[164]See, for example, Dioceses of New York, Rockville Center, and Brooklyn, "Catholic-Jewish Relations" (1969); and Archdiocese of Galveston-Houston, "Guidelines" (1975).

[165]E.g., NCCB-ADL, *Within Context* (1987) and Archdiocese of Los Angeles-AJC, "The Holocaust: At the Edge of Comprehension" (1990).

[166]See WCC, *The Theology of the Churches and the Jewish People* (1988).

[167]See Michael Shermis, *Jewish-Christian Relations: An Annotated Bibliography and Guide* (Bloomington/Indianapolis: Indiana University Press, 1988). See also Eugene J. Fisher, "A New Maturity in Christian-Jewish Dialogue: An Annotated Bibliography 1975-1989," in Fisher and Klenicki, *In Our Time,* 107-161.

[168]Cited in Fisher, "Roman Catholic Teaching," 4.

[169]Ibid.

[170]Congregation for Catholic Education, "Study of the Fathers of the Church" (1990).

[171]Mary C. Boys, "Scripture in the Catechism" in *The Universal Catechism Reader: Reflections and Responses,* ed. Thomas J. Reese (San Francisco: Harper and Row, 1990) 43-54. It should be noted that this first draft of the proposed universal catechism is not "a definitive text." In response to various criticisms it has been stated that the text would be revised in several areas, including its "use of sacred Scripture" and its presentation of "non-Christian religions." See Cardinal Joseph Ratzinger, "Update on the Universal Catechism," *Origins* 20/22 (November 8, 1990) 356-359, esp. 358.

PART TWO

THE PORTRAYAL OF JEWS
IN MODERN RELIGION TEXTBOOKS

4

Previous Studies of Christian Religion Textbooks

A. The Thering Study

The first major study of how American Catholic religion textbooks portrayed Jews and Judaism was undertaken by Rose Thering in 1961. Her investigation was part of a wider series of studies sponsored by the American Jewish Committee. This broad-based project was concerned with intergroup relations among the diverse racial, ethnic, and religious groups which compose American society. It explored whether contemporary secondary textbooks issued by Catholic, Jewish, and Protestant publishing houses in the fields of literature, social studies, and religion promoted or hindered intergroup amity.[1]

Thering's part in this undertaking was to assess how Catholic religion textbooks treated a number of outgroups, including Jews. Her study measured the positivity and negativity of outgroup references according to these sociological criteria:

1. PORTRAIT OR DESCRIPTIVE CHARACTERISTICS
Are positive or negative descriptive terms used of the outgroup or of individual outgroup members?

2. FACTUAL MATERIALS: DISTORTION/CORRECTION
Is historical data accurate? Are efforts made to correct stereotype? Are varying interpretations provided?

3. CREEDS—CODES—PRESTIGE FIGURES
Do statements of Catholic authorities or teachings promote or hinder intergroup amity?

4. REJECTION/ACCEPTANCE
Do references encourage rejection, hostility, avoidance or acceptance, respect, support?

5. BLAMES OTHERS/CRITICIZES SELF
Is the author's own group involved or separated from responsibility for harm to an outgroup?[2]

Thering's sociological analysis found that with regard to Jews and Judaism there were both positive and negative references in Catholic religion textbooks. However, all of the statements rated as positive by these criteria essentially praised Judaism for being the harbinger of Christianity. For example:

> Christ first revealed his presence on earth to the Jews, the chosen people of the Old Testament, and indeed, to the humblest and poorest and most believing among the Jews, the shepherds.[3]

More disturbing was Thering's discovery of widespread negative assertions about Jews in Catholic textbooks. Most of these comments fell into three categories, as in these quotes:[4]

1. THE JEWS REJECTED JESUS
Christ, by his miracles and preaching, tried to conquer the obstinacy of the Jews and to bring them to repentance. The Jews, on the contrary, by the bad influence of their hypocrisy and pride, hindered the spread of the knowledge of God among the nations.

The Jews . . . have refused to accept Christ, and since his time they have been wanderers on the earth without a temple, or a sacrifice, and without the Messiah.

2. THE JEWS KILLED JESUS
Since Pilate could not find anything wrong with Christ, he decided to disfigure his pure and beautiful body, so that even the bloodthirsty Jews would back down and say that Christ had had enough. . . . when the mob saw this, the chief priests took up a cry that put a curse on themselves and on the Jews for all time: "his blood be upon us and on our children."

Why did the Jews commit the great sin of putting God himself to death? It was because the Lord told them the truth, because he preached a divine doctrine that displeased them, and because he told them to give up their wicked ways.

3. THE PHARISEES WERE BLIND HYPOCRITES
No man is less pitied than one who has deliberately gouged out his own eyes. Hence, no one has sympathy for the Pharisees because they deliberately made themselves blind to the inspiring miracles and teachings of Christ.

The presence of such statements shows how entrenched parts of the ancient anti-Jewish tradition had become. It should be noted that Thering's study predated *Nostra Aetate,* which definitively rejected these inimical assertions.

B. The Olson Study

The parallel study of American Protestant texts was done by Bernhard E. Olson at Yale University and was published in 1963.[5] He examined samples of four different varieties of Protestant texts representing fundamentalism (Scripture Press), conservatism (Lutheran Church), liberalism (Unitarian-Univeralist Church), and neo-orthodoxy (Presbyterian Church).[6]

Olson found that Jews were mentioned extremely often. Jews were mentioned in 43.8 percent of the neo-orthodox units, 56.4 percent of the conservative units, 60.6 percent of the liberal units, and 66.3 percent of the fundamentalist units.[7] Olson observed that this preoccupation with Jews was unavoidable because of Christian origins within Judaism. However, because of its minority status such prominence and visibility could easily result in the Jewish community becoming a "vulnerable target."[8]

Using statistical methods to measure the degree of ethnocentrism vs. anti-ethnocentrism in the Protestant materials, Olson was able to determine the overall degree of positivity or negativity in the presentation of various groups. The findings for references to Judaism were as follows:[9]

Liberal	Neo-orthodox	Fundamentalist	Conservative
+48.6	+44.3	+7.9	−15.4

Like Thering, Olson also found that certain themes generated greater negativity. These included:

1. The crucifixion
2. The conflict between Jesus and the Pharisees
3. The conflict between Church and Synagogue
4. The problem of Gentile inclusion
5. The themes of rejection and unbelief[10]

While many of these biblically-related topics tended to be the occasions of greatest negativity against Jews, Olson was persuaded that the scriptures themselves were not the sole causative factor. He found numerous instances when the same biblical passage was interpreted quite differently by the different Protestant groups.[11]

Repeated instances of this interpretational variance confirmed that the overall attitude toward Jews remained constant within each tradition whether or not a biblical passage was being treated. "The publisher would communicate his ethnocentrism or anti-ethnocentrism in his comments *regardless of the nature of the scripture as a whole.*"[12] Although anti-Jewish sentiment increased when certain scriptural topics were under consideration, they only intensified an independently-existing bias. Other, non-biblical factors were plainly at work.[13]

Finally, Olson had an important insight regarding the positive materials. It seemed that the most favorable references to Jews and Judaism occurred in those texts which were most cognizant of the Jews as an abiding people, living among Christians today, and to whom Christianity owes a spiritual debt.[14]

C. The Pro Deo and Louvain Studies

Under the auspices of the Sperry Center for Intergroup Learning, two studies of European Catholic materials were undertaken beginning in 1967. Research into Italian and Spanish Catholic textbooks published between 1940 and 1964 was conducted by the International University of Social Studies "Pro Deo" in Rome. The Catholic University of Louvain in Belgium examined French-language materials used between 1949 and 1964. The Louvain study also conducted an opinion survey to discern the attitudes toward Jews and Judaism held by Catholics who had been educated with those texts.[15]

Both of these studies examined materials that for the most part preceded Vatican II. The few textbooks studied which were published after the Council did show some improvements, but the sample was too small to provide conclusive results.[16]

As in the American studies, the Pro Deo team found that Jews were the most frequently named non-Catholic group, named twice as often as Protestants in Italian texts and in excess of six times more often than Protestants in Spanish materials. The ratio of negative to positive references to Jews in Italian texts was found to be about 5 to 1, and about 3 to 2 in the Spanish books, but the Spanish negative comments were generally much more vituperative than the Italian.[17] The Louvain study found that references to Judaism were more balanced in French textbooks, but positive comments tended to refer to Jews before Christ.

The Louvain scholars held that, despite improvements, Jews were still being described in a "mythical and inaccurate" manner as a foil for Christianity.[18] The two studies categorized several types of negative remarks, as these sample quotations illustrate:

1. INVECTIVE
These people seemed like a pack of starving dogs who wanted to bite him [the Savior] and tear him to pieces with their teeth.

2. SLEIGHT OF HAND
The first eleven [of the apostles] were born in Galilee; the last, Judas, was a Jew.

3. MISREPRESENTATION
They [the Pharisees] persist in deliberately rejecting God.

4. TAMPERING WITH JESUS' SAYINGS
The withered fig tree represents the Jewish people . . . they deserved their curse and the condemnation of Christ.

5. LOADED THEOLOGICAL ARGUMENTS
The city of Jerusalem and the Jewish people grew irreversibly closer to the catastrophe predicted by Jesus in punishment for their obstinate blindness and the deicide perpetuated on Calvary.

6. LIBEL
They [the Jews] were also accused, on better grounds, of mocking the Christian religion and sacrilegiously profaning the consecrated host, of murdering a Christian child instead of the paschal lamb on Holy Thursday and perhaps crucifying him on Good Friday to make sport of and sneer at the death of Christ.

7. APPEALS TO FEAR
. . . the worst modern aberrations, from Masonry to Bolshevism, find many adherents among Jews.[19]

In sum, these studies concluded that many young European Catholics had recently been taught that:

1. The Jews are collectively responsible for the Crucifixion and that they are a "deicide people."

2. The Diaspora is the Jews' punishment for the Crucifixion.

3. Jesus predicted this punishment and that the Jews remain cursed by him and by God.

4. The Jewish people rejected Jesus because of their materialism.

5. The Jewish people have put themselves beyond hope of saving.

6. The Jews are unfaithful and guilty of apostasy.

7. Judaism once was the best religion, but became ossified, and finally ceased to have meaning with the coming of Jesus.

8. The Jews are no longer the Chosen People, but have been superseded as such by Christians.[20]

It must once more be recalled that with Vatican II many of these ideas were explicitly rejected. There was some evidence of improvement in postconciliar texts, especially in French books which had removed all talk of Jews as an accursed people.[21] Nonetheless, it seems that the overall picture of 1950s European Catholic textbooks in terms of Jews and Judaism was rather bleak.

Three final points from the Pro Deo and Louvain studies bear mentioning. First, the Pro Deo team shared Olson's view that although much hostility to Jews appeared in connection with certain New Testament topics, the anti-Jewish bias originated in the authors' interpretation of the biblical texts and not in the Bible itself.[22]

Second, the Louvain survey of opinion made the interesting discovery that anti-Semitic sentiments were more often expressed by those who had lapsed in their Catholic practice than by steady churchgoers. This was seen to suggest that some of the Church's renewed appreciation of Judaism was being conveyed to Church congregations, but was being missed by disaffected Catholics.[23]

Finally, both studies indicated a disturbing and total absence of any mention of the *Shoah*, and hardly any references to the State of Israel. The fact that "we do not yet have a satisfactory theology of Israel" was thought to relate to this deficiency.[24]

D. The Strober Study

In 1972 the American Jewish Committee sponsored a research project by Gerald S. Strober, which sought to determine if the 1963 Olson study had had any salutary effects on American Protestant textbooks. It also explored the extent of anti-Jewish components in teaching materials aimed at black Protestants, the amount of material dealing with recent historical events relevant to Judaism, and whether or not publishers had a conscious intergroup relations policy. Strober examined twelve different educational publications promulgated by either conservative or mainstream Protestant groups.[25]

He summarized his findings with these conclusions:

> 1. The problems unearthed in the Olson study generally remained, with the exception of the materials prepared by the Missouri Lutheran Synod which had hired consultants to address the issue. Certain topics engendered the greatest negativity: (A) the nature of Judaism; (B) Jesus' relation to his Jewish contemporaries; (C) the Pharisees; (D) the Jews' rejection of Jesus as Messiah; and (E) the crucifixion. The conservative literature remained predominantly negative (again, except for the Missouri Lutheran Synod), and while the mainstream materials were more favorable, the tendency toward negativity was still present.
>
> 2. When treated at all, recent Jewish-Christian developments received only superficial attention.
>
> 3. Black Protestant texts displayed no special hostility toward Jews and Judaism when compared with other Protestant materials.
>
> 4. Few policies or procedures relating to intergroup relations had been developed.[26]

5. Few texts mentioned the *Shoah* or the State of Israel, and some of those that did were most problematic.[27] Strober concluded that this was because of "the widespread failure of Christians to come to grips with the facts of the holocaust."[28]

E. The Fisher Study

In 1976 Eugene J. Fisher investigated Catholic religious educational series, combining some of the techniques of the Thering and Olson studies. By replicating Thering's analysis on contemporary texts and then comparing his results with hers, Fisher discovered that "American Catholic religion materials are significantly more positive toward Judaism than they were before the Vatican Council."[29] All the sixteen series analyzed received a positive score according to the "General Imbalance" statistic (i.e., the ratio of positive to negative remarks). Whereas Thering's work yielded an overall positive imbalance of + .435, Fisher's application of her criteria in 1976 disclosed a + .674 figure, a considerable improvement.[30] As in previous studies, Jews were more frequently mentioned than any other religious group.[31] Very importantly, all references to Jews as a people cursed because of the crucifixion were either completely absent or explicitly condemned.[32]

However, Fisher realized that time had revealed a problem with Thering's analytic tool. Since 1961 authoritative Catholic statements had been issued, notably *Nostra Aetate* and the 1974 Vatican "Guidelines," which had established specific *theological* principles regarding Catholic teaching about Jews and Judaism. Such axioms altered the assessments that would be made using purely sociological criteria. For example, comments rated positively by Thering that praised Judaism as Christianity's predecessor would be judged negatively by the subsequent theological norms.

Therefore, in order to measure the impact of Church documents on religion textbooks, Fisher devised a second set of criteria with which to gauge the directionality (positive, negative, ambiguous, or neutral) of references to Jews and Judaism. These "modified criteria" were based on the theological principles highlighted in ecclesial statements.[33] He also classified references in thematic and historical period categories so as to isolate particularly troublesome topics:[34]

Theme Categories	*Period Categories*
1. Jesus as a Jew	1. Hebrew Scriptures
2. Jesus and the Jews	2. New Testament
3. The Pharisees	3. Rabbinic Judaism
4. The Crucifixion	4. Middle Ages
5. Divine Retribution	5. Reformation—
6. The Holocaust	Twentieth century

Theme Categories	Period Categories
7. Modern Israel	6. Twentieth Century
8. Relationship of Covenants	7. General or Today
9. Crusades	

Using his modified theological criteria, Fisher obtained somewhat less positive results on high school texts than by using Thering's sociological criteria, + .606 versus + .674 respectively, but still far more positive than Thering's 1961 figure of + .435.[35] But Fisher found a marked difference when applying the new criteria to elementary-level textbooks. Fisher's application of Thering's sociological criteria to current elementary series yielded a general imbalance score of + .367, whereas his modified theological criteria produced a score of + .167, a loss of some 54 percent.[36] These general averages indicated that there were more negative references to be found in primary texts than secondary ones, and that the post-*Nostra Aetate* theological norms produced less positive results, especially in elementary textbook series.

As he had hoped, Fisher's classification of his results into period and theme categories isolated problematic topics. Negative or low positive scores were found in both primary and secondary texts in these areas:[37]

Theme Categories	Period Categories
Jesus and the Jews	New Testament
The Pharisees	
The Crucifixion	
Relationship of Covenants*	
[*in elementary series]	

In addition, Fisher observed that there were "almost no references to Jews and Judaism between the close of the New Testament period and the twentieth century, . . . [perhaps reinforcing] the idea that Judaism ceased to be religiously vital after the coming of Christ."[38]

F. Summary

All the earlier textbook studies highlighted above revealed the enduring presence of traditional anti-Judaic themes. While great progress was visible between the earlier and later researches, especially in American Catholic texts, certain troublesome topics continued to promote negativity toward Jews and Judaism. Table 4 lists the recurrent problematic areas revealed by these previous textbook analyses.

Table 4				
Recurrent Problematic Topics in Previous Textbook Studies				
Thering 1961 [American Catholic]	Olson 1963 [American Protestant]	European 1967 [French Italian, & Spanish Catholic]	Strober 1972 [American Protestant]	Fisher 1976 [American Catholic]
crucifixion	crucifixion	crucifixion	crucifixion	crucifixion
divine punishment	church— synagogue conflict	divine punishment	Jesus and the Jews	Jesus and the Jews
Pharisees	Pharisees	Pharisees	Pharisees	Pharisees
	Gentiles in the church	Judaism as ossified religion	nature of Judaism	relation of OT/NT
Jewish rejection of Christ	Jewish rejection of Christ		Jewish rejection of Christ	

A comparison of this table with those of the New Testament and patristic anti-Jewish formulations given above (Tables 1 and 2) shows that the topics which produced the most negativity in twentieth-century textbooks involve precisely the same ideas which have characterized the Christian anti-Jewish tradition from its inception. It is not surprising that attitudes which had prevailed for more than a millennium-and-a-half would not suddenly vanish, despite the fact that remarkable progress had been made in modern texts.

Furthermore, although more blatant anti-Jewish polemic had been reduced, such as the virtual elimination of the ''Jews as an accursed people'' theme from later American and French textbooks, more subtle expressions of anti-Jewish motifs persisted.

Some years after conducting his textbook analysis, Eugene Fisher warned against the following practices which less obviously perpetuate hostility toward Jews and Judaism:

1. a "latent Marcionite approach" to the Hebrew Scriptures which relegates them to mere background to the New Testament, such as by the use of promise/fulfillment language.

2. the tacit perpetuation of the deicide charge by failing to adequately treat New Testament polemics.

3. a facile use of simplistic dichotomies to contrast Judaism and Christianity, such as depicting Judaism as a religion of justice and Christianity as a religion of love. Such pairings often arise when discussing the Pharisees or Judaism in general.

4. an overemphasis on some practice or feature in order to distinguish Jesus or the first-century Church from Jewish contemporaries; for example, overstating such things as Jesus' "abba experience," the sexism of 1st-century Judaism, or the purported *birkat ha-minim*.[39]

These cautions deserve to be kept in mind in the ongoing evaluations of any Catholic teaching materials.

Notes

[1] The results of this A.J.C. project were not issued in their entirety in a single publication. The studies of Catholic texts were eventually summarized in print by John T. Pawlikowski, *Catechetics and Prejudice* (New York: Paulist, 1973). See also the March-April issue of *Religious Education* (Vol. 55, No. 2) in which the following preliminary synopses appeared: Trafford P. Maher, "The Catholic School Curriculum and Intergroup Relations," 117–122; Bernhard Olson, "Intergroup Relations in Protestant Teaching Materials," 123–138; and Bernard D. Weinryb, "Intergroup Content in Jewish Religious Textbooks," 109–116. Full details of the Protestant study are found in Bernhard Olson, *Faith and Prejudice: Intergroup Problems in Protestant Curricula* (New Haven: Yale University, 1963).

[2] Adapted from Thering, "Religious Textbooks," 89–96; and Fisher, "Content Analysis," 51–53.

[3] Pawlikowski, *Catechetics and Prejudice,* 81.

[4] Ibid., 81–86.

[5] Olson, *Faith and Prejudice.*

[6] Idem, "Intergroup Relations," 123.

[7] Idem, *Faith and Prejudice,* 351.

[8] Ibid., 23–24.

[9] Idem, "Intergroup Relations," 127.

[10] Ibid., 130.

[11] E.g., idem, *Faith and Prejudice,* 39.

[12] Idem, "Intergroup Relations," 35. Italics in original.

[13] A related finding were instances in which Jews apparently served as vehicles for expressing the author's bias against other groups. For example, when commenting

about alleged Pharisaic legalism, one writer was moved to remark, "Romanism teems with this Pharisaic spirit as a filthy kitchen does with vermin." Ibid., 42.

[14] Ibid., 42.

[15] The results of both studies were summarized in English by Claire Hutchet Bishop, *How Catholics Look at Jews: Inquiries into Italian, Spanish, and French Teaching Materials* (New York: Paulist, 1974).

[16] Ibid., 14, 31.

[17] Ibid., 86–88.

[18] Ibid., 90–91. Again, there was inconclusive evidence of a decrease in the number of negative comments after Vatican II. [Ibid., 31.]

[19] Ibid., 33–45.

[20] Ibid., 31.

[21] Ibid., 19.

[22] Ibid., 86–87.

[23] Ibid., 61.

[24] Ibid., 92, 98–100.

[25] Gerald S. Strober, *Portrait of the Elder Brother: Jews and Judaism in Protestant Teaching Materials* (New York: American Jewish Committee, 1972) 10-11.

[26] Ibid., 12–13.

[27] Ibid., 37–42.

[28] Ibid., 42.

[29] Eugene J. Fisher, *Faith Without Prejudice: Rebuilding Christian Attitudes Toward Judaism* (New York: Paulist, 1977) 125.

[30] Idem, "A Content Analysis of the Treatment of Jews and Judaism in Current Roman Catholic Textbooks and Manuals on the Primary and Secondary Levels" (Ph.D. diss., New York University, 1976) 79.

[31] Idem, *Faith Without Prejudice,* 128.

[32] Ibid., 133.

[33] These theological criteria are examined in detail in chapter 5.

[34] Fisher, "Content Analysis," 124–127. Definitions of these categories are found in Appendix 1.

[35] Ibid., 81.

[36] Ibid., 83. Note that a direct comparison with Thering's 1961 study was impossible because she had analyzed only secondary textbooks.

[37] Ibid., 131–132.

[38] Idem, *Faith Without Prejudice,* 131.

[39] Eugene J. Fisher, "Research on Christian Teaching Concerning Jews and Judaism: Past Research and Present Needs" *Journal of Ecumenical Studies* 21/3 (Summer 1984) 425–430.

5

Methods and Criteria
for Assessing Texts

A. General Procedure

The procedures used in this textbook analysis were based on those used by Eugene Fisher in 1976. They are outlined here both to explain the mechanics of this study and in the hopes that readers will use the same methods to evaluate other materials in terms of their treatments of Jews and Judaism.

In this study, each lesson of student texts and teacher's manuals was examined.[1] It was decided whether the lesson made reference to Jews or Judaism ("J/J").[2] If the lesson had such references, these were then classified in various theme and period categories. (For definitions of these categories see Appendix 1.) Several classifications were possible, but at least one period category must have been indicated.[3] Next, the overall lesson was rated as either positive (+), negative (−), ambiguous (+/−), or neutral (0) in its J/J references.[4] This rating was done according to the criteria listed in section D below. All of this information was recorded in a computer database according to the file layout presented in Table 5, one such file per lesson.[5]

B. Statistical Operations

The principal statistical measures obtained in this study were the coefficient of preoccupation and the general imbalance score. The coefficient of preoccupation specifies the fraction of textbook lessons that make reference to Jews and Judaism. The imbalance score indicates the positivity or negativity of those references.

The coefficient of preoccupation was obtained by tallying the number of units that referred to Jews and Judaism and then calculating the ratio of this sum to the total number of units examined. Thus, where "r"

Table 5
Sample Data-Gathering Layout

Publisher:_____ Series Title: _____
Primary_____ Secondary_____ Lesson #_____ J/J? Yes__ No __
Grade Level:_____ Pages: Text _____ Manual_____

Directional Score: *Positive* *Negative* *Ambiguous* *Neutral*
_____ _____ _____ _____

Period Categories: *Theme Categories:*

1. Hebrew Scriptures ____ 1. Jesus as a Jew ____
2. New Testament ____ 2. Jesus and the Jews ____
3. Rabbinic Judaism ____ 3. The Pharisees ____
4. Middle Ages ____ 4. The Crucifixion ____
5. Reformation to 5. Divine Retribution ____
   Twentieth Century ____ 6. The *Shoah* ____
6. Twentieth Century ____ 7. Modern Israel ____
7. General or Today ____ 8. Relationship of
   Covenants ____
9. Crusades/
   Inquisition ____

Notes:

---

is the relevant content and "t" is the total content, $C_{pr} = r/t$. If thirty out of fifty units had material related to Jews and Judaism, the coefficient of preoccupation would be 30/50 or 60 percent. In evaluating the data classified in the period and theme categories, the same formula was applied, except that "r" equaled the total of all units which referred to a particular theme or period category and "t" equaled the total number of units dealing with Jews and Judaism.[6] In addition to showing how often Jews and Judaism appear in Catholic texts, the coefficient of preoccupation is also important for measuring the absence of Jewish references in specific period categories. For example, scant treatment of Jews and Judaism after the New Testament period could indicate that a textbook series gave the impression "that Judaism ceased to be religiously vital after the coming of Christ."[7]

In 1976 Fisher gauged the direction of references to Jews and Judaism in his period and theme categories using the formula for general score of imbalance. When "p" is the number of positive references, "n" is the number of negative references, and "G_{imb}" is the general score of imbalance, $G_{imb} = p - n/p + n$. For example, Fisher discovered that 157 secondary units referred to Jews and Judaism in a New Testament period setting. Of those units eighty-three were positive, forty-one were negative, and thirty-three were ambiguous or neutral. The general imbalance would thus equal $83 - 41/83 + 41 = 42/124 = +.339$.[8] This formula can be employed to calculate general imbalances within specific categories, to calculate imbalances by series or grade level, or to make comparisons with the total imbalance.

General imbalance scores of $+1.0$ and -1.0 represent the respective extremes of positivity and negativity. An imbalance score of 0.0 would mean either that all the J/J references in the lessons were neutral or that the positive and negative comments canceled each other out. The latter alternative would indicate that the total effect of the lessons in question was an ambiguous or mixed message about Jews and Judaism.[9]

C. Evaluated Texts

It was a goal of this study to examine all current Catholic religion series in use in the United States. Publishers were sent an invitation to participate in this study, and several were kind enough to forward copies of their publications for review.

Several of the publishers indicated that current series were either being updated or discontinued. Some revisions were not yet available. This study, therefore, has examined the most recently printed texts, excluding those soon to be replaced. It should also be noted that only multi-grade level series were evaluated. Sacramental, lectionary-based, or family-centered catechetical materials were not considered. The following is a list of those series which this study analyzed:

Publisher	Series Title (P = Primary; S = Secondary)
Ave Maria Press	Friendship in the Lord (S)
Benziger Publishing Company	Come, Follow Me (P)
Brown Publishing/Roa Media	Focus Books (P)
	Fullness of Life (S)
	To Live is Christ (S)
The Center for Learning	Centering Faith(S)
Hi-Time Publishers	Hi-Time Program (S)
Ignatius Press	Faith and Life (P)
Loyola University Press	Christ Our Life (P)
William H. Sadlier, Inc.	Coming to Faith (P)
St. Mary's Press	The Sharing Program (S)

Publisher	Series Title
St. Paul's Books and Media	Alive in Jesus (P)
Silver Burdett & Ginn	This Is Our Faith (P)
Winston Press	The Joy Program (P)
[Total Primary Series: 8	Total Secondary Series: 6]

D. The Directional Criteria

This section provides the criteria used to determine the "directionality" of J/J references; i.e., were they positive or negative? Based upon Fisher's 1976 criteria, they have been rephrased into a choice between positive or negative alternatives for ease of use. The listing is accompanied by endnotes which cite relevant ecclesial statements from 1964 to the present. Due to the varying degrees of detail with which certain topics have been treated in ecclesial statements, individual criteria are footnoted in some categories, especially biblical ones, while in others the documentary references are given for the category as a whole. These citations serve to ground the present use of these directional criteria in the ongoing tradition of Catholic thought.

It should be noted that bracketed negative alternatives in the following list denote the lack of treatment of a subject. Such absences cannot be scored negatively since an absence means there are no references to Jews or Judaism to which to assign direction. Failures to treat topics are disclosed by the preoccupation scores.

THE HEBREW SCRIPTURES

1. Is the Hebrew covenant seen:
   [+] as remaining the root, source, foundation, and promise of the new covenant?
   [−] or as rendered void by the New Testament?[10]

2. Is the inspiration or validity of the Hebrew Bible:
   [+] recognized in its own right?
   [−] or is it read only as a precursor to the New Testament?[11]

3. Do lessons picture the Hebrew Bible as a:
   [+] source of inspiration for Jesus, the New Testament authors, and later Christian writers? as *the* Scripture of the New Testament Church?
   [−] or as simply a list of predictions seen to have been realized?[12]

4. Is the Hebrew Bible and the Jewish tradition founded upon it compared with the New Testament:
   [+] in such a way that both traditions are seen to be founded on both love and justice?

[−]   or in a false way that sees the Hebrew Bible as forming a religion of justice, fear, and legalism in contrast to a New Testament stress on God's love?[13]

5. Is the fact noted that the phrase "Old Testament":
    [+]   is seen by some Jews as insulting to the continuing validity of the Hebrew Bible?
    [−]   [No negative rating is to be assigned for use of "Old Testament," unless it is stated that the "Old" has been abrogated by the "New."][14]

6. Is the religion of the Hebrew Bible presented as:
    [+]   dynamic and valid currently?
    [−]   or as a fossilized preparation for Christianity?[15]

7. Are characters in the Hebrew Bible treated as:
    [+]   Israelites/Jews?
    [−]   or as "hidden" Christians?[16]

8. Are the biblical people presented in a such a way that:
    [+]   they can be identified with as fallible models of faith?
    [−]   or is their infidelity stressed?[17]

9. Are the prophets seen as:
    [+]   God's spokespersons who seek fidelity to the Torah covenant?
    [−]   or only as predictors of the future whose importance surpasses the Torah?

10. Are the prophetic writings:
    [+]   understood as part of a tradition of self-criticism that should guide Christian self-appraisal?
    [−]   or are they used to show the failure of Jewish faith in contrast to Christian fidelity?[18]

JUDAISM IN THE NEW TESTAMENT PERIOD

1. Does the text indicate that the Judaism out of which Christianity was born was:
    [+]   dynamic and vital?
    [−]   or degenerate, legalistic, corrupt, or materialistic?[19]

2. Is the Judaism of Jesus' time shown to be:
    [+]   composed of many groups and movements whose main features are fully described?
    [−]   or as very monolithic or made up of groups only described in negative stereotypes?[20]

3. Are Jewish ideas about the Messiah:
    [+]   shown to be many and varied?
    [−]   or are they reduced to the awaiting of a political king?[21]

4. Is New Testament Judaism described in terms:
   [+] of its accomplishments such as the rise of the synagogue, the literature of the times, and early rabbinic works?
   [−] or in terms of stagnation and lifelessness?²²

THE PHARISEES²³

1. Are the Pharisees portrayed:
   [+] in an objective way according to the best information available?
   [−] or in hostile stereotypes as legalists, hypocrites, etc.?

2. Are the Pharisees portrayed as:
   [+] composed of various "schools," such as those of Hillel and Shammai?
   [−] or as all the same? Are comments about Pharisees applied to "the Jews" at large?

3. Are the Pharisees portrayed as:
   [+] leaders in the period of revolutionary social and religious creativity after the demise of the Temple?
   [−] or always in negative contrast to Jesus and the Church?

4. Is the interaction between Jesus and the Pharisees:
   [+] shown to be both positive and negative?
   [−] or as always negative?

JESUS AND THE JEWS

1. Does the portrayal of Jesus:
   [+] clearly establish his Jewishness? that he considered himself to be a faithful, Torah-abiding Jew? explain his actions in terms of his Jewishness?
   [−] or does it present him as opposed to the Jewish tradition or as intending to begin a religion in opposition to Judaism? are his acts explained without reference to his Jewishness?²⁴

2. Do the lessons:
   [+] note the Jewishness of the disciples and the early Church?
   [−] or do they state or imply that "the Jews" rejected Jesus?²⁵

3. When phrases like "some Jews" or "some leaders of the Jews" are used:
   [+] is adequate background given in the teachers' manual so that it will be clear *why* such terms are used?
   [−] or is inadequate data given so that pupils will be unprepared to deal with anti-Jewish New Testament passages at Sunday Mass?²⁶

4. Is Jesus pictured:
   [+] in context as a Jew who thought and debated within the Jewish milieu?
   [−] or as opposing or condemning Judaism?[27]

5. In the presentation of the ministry of Jesus:
   [+] is it explained in the teachers' manuals and embodied in the texts that Gospel passages are rooted in the experiences of Jesus' followers both before *and* after the resurrection, and that they are colored by the circumstances which prevailed at the time of their composition?
   [−] or are Gospel verses simply cited and conflated with little or no regard for the complex origins of the Gospels' textual tradition?[28]

6. In explaining the significance of the life, death, and raising of Jesus:
   [+] is reference made to the future end of his work of bringing about God's Reign when Jesus returns in glory?
   [−] or is the impression given that the Reign of God has appeared in all its fullness?[29]

THE CRUCIFIXION

1. Is it made clear that:
   [+] "what happened at his passion cannot be blamed upon all Jews then living, without distinction, nor upon the Jews of today" (*Nostra Aetate,* 4)?
   [−] or is there explicit or implied assigning of blame to 'before and Jews" for the death of Jesus?[30]

2. Are the historical and exegetical complexities of the passion narratives:
   [+] evident, especially in the teachers' manuals?
   [−] or are biblical texts employed in a facile, uncritical manner so that polemic is perpetuated?[31]

3. Is the Roman role in the crucifixion:
   [+] made clear by noting that crucifixion was a Roman practice? that the chief priest was appointed by Pilate? that Pilate was not known as indecisive?
   [−] or is it minimized by failing to note these items? by portraying Pilate as determined to rescue Jesus?[32]

4. Is it shown:
   [+] that the New Testament does not mention the Pharisees as being involved in Jesus' arrest, trial, or death?
   [−] or is it stated or implied that they were involved?[33]

5. Is guilt for the crucifixion:
   [+] placed where it belongs theologically: on all humanity?
   [−] or are "the Jewish leaders" actually blamed in concrete descriptions of the passion?[34]

DIVINE RETRIBUTION

1. Is the notion that Jewish suffering is the result of divine retribution for their alleged rejection of Jesus:
   [+] explicitly condemned?
   [−] or is the notion explicitly or implicitly conveyed?[35]

RABBINIC AND MEDIEVAL JUDAISM[36]

1. Does mention of Jews cease with the New Testament period:
   [+] no?
   [−] [yes?]

2. How are Jews presented in the texts:
   [+] are major Jewish contributions to Western "Christian" history treated and fairly developed?
   [−] or are Jews cited in Church history only as victims of persecution?

3. Does the account of Judaism in these periods:
   [+] mention the great religious importance of the Mishnah and the Talmud, or the role of Spanish Jewry in developing Scholastic philosophy, or their role in giving access to Arabic scholarship?
   [−] or does Judaism, when mentioned, seem stagnant and lifeless?

4. Does the story of European history:
   [+] include reference to the influence of Jewish intellectual and theological thought (e.g., Maimonides on Aquinas, Spinoza on Pascal, Jewish mysticism, etc.)?
   [−] [or is it only the story of Western "Christendom"?]

5. In short, is Jewish history:
   [+] seen in all its vitality and creativity? Is it treated positively, if at all?
   [−] or is it treated only as a passive backwater of Christian history? If not treated, so that there is a long silence between the New Testament and the *Shoah* in the twentieth century, except perhaps as victims of persecution, is there a link between the last appearance of Jews as "Christ killers" and their next appearance as suffering victims?

THE CRUSADES AND THE INQUISITION[37]

1. Do texts treating Church history:
    [+]   honestly admit to Christian mistreatment of Jews in various periods of history? Is repentance urged?
    [−]   or is persecution of Jews, when mentioned at all, described in ways in which seem to remove Christians from involvement?

2. Are "excesses" of the Crusades and the Inquisition:
    [+]   treated with candor?
    [−]   or is an attempt made to cover over or even justify these events?

3. Is the history of Christian anti-Judaism:
    [+]   clearly traced, along with its consequences in pogroms, ghettos, etc.?
    [−]   [or is this history part of an excluded "null curriculum"'?]

4. On the other hand:
    [+]   are the efforts of some popes to stop the practice of forced conversions and protect Jews noted as models of a more Christian practice?
    [−]   [or is the proper Christian response to oppression not discussed?]

THE REFORMATION TO THE TWENTIETH CENTURY[38]

1. Is the story of the contributions of Jews to:
    [+]   the Reformation and the Enlightenment presented?
    [−]   [or is this passed over in silence?]

2. Is the Jewish role in European and American economic growth:
    [+]   portrayed accurately? Is their involvement in the growth of trade and labor unions discussed?
    [−]   or are Jews seen in terms of false stereotype regarding finances and business?

3. Is there any presentation of:
    [+]   such profound Jewish movements as Hasidism and Zionism? Are important figures like Buber, Rosenzweig, Freud, and Einstein depicted as Jews?
    [−]   or are major Jewish figures or movements not identified as such?

4. Is there evident an appreciation of
    [+]   the development of and differences between Reform, Orthodox, and Conservative Jewry, especially in the United States?
    [−]   or are modern Jews treated in a monolithic fashion?

5. Are there references to:
   [+] Hebraic and Biblical origins of much of the thought of early American colonists and United States charter documents?
   [−] [or are such debts to the Hebraic tradition not cited?]

THE *SHOAH*[39]

1. Are the implications of the *Shoah* for typical Christian beliefs:
   [+] addressed, at least in the upper grade levels?
   [−] [or are they not mentioned?]

2. Are relevant facts about the *Shoah* noted:
   [+] such as its happening in "Christian" nations or the heroism of Christian "rescuers"?
   [−] [or is Christian involvement in the *Shoah* absent?]

3. Is the Church's silence about the death camps:
   [+] handled in a fair and balanced manner?
   [−] [or is it not even acknowledged?]

4. Are there explicit condemnations of:
   [+] anti-Semitism, including new forms like anti-Zionism?
   [−] [or is there an absence of such denunciations?]

5. Are writings of survivors:
   [+] used where suitable in liturgies, etc.?
   [−] [or are they not mentioned?]

THE MODERN STATE OF ISRAEL[40]

1. Is there adequate explanation of the Jewish concept of peoplehood:
   [+] "a peoplehood that is not solely racial, ethnic, or religious but in a sense a composite of all three" (NCCB, 1975)?
   [−] or are references to Jews as a "race" or a "religion" to be found?

2. Do texts help students to understand:
   [+] "the link between the Land and People which Jews have expressed in their writings and worship throughout two millennia as a longing for the homeland, holy Zion" (NCCB, 1975)?
   [−] or is the importance of the Land in Jewish thought discounted [or left untreated]?

3. Do texts help students to gain understanding of:
   [+] the view of American Jews with regard to the State of Israel?
   [−] [or are the feelings of American Jews in this regard not treated?]

4. Is the right of national self-determination:
    [+] explicitly recognized of both Israel and of the Palestinians?
    [−] or is one group or the other not fairly treated?

5. If mention is made of the Arab–Israeli conflict:
    [+] is an adequate background for both sides of the issue presented?
    [−] or is the complex disagreement treated simplistically?

6. Is Zionism seen as:
    [+] movement for liberation in response to both European and Moslem oppression?
    [−] or along racial lines?

THE RELATIONSHIP BETWEEN THE COVENANTS

1. Is it made clear that the Jewish covenant with God:
    [+] was not abrogated with the establishment of the Christian covenant in Christ?
    [−] or is its continuing validity denied or ambiguous?[41]

2. Is the point clearly made that:
    [+] "God holds the Jews most dear" (*Nostra Aetate*) and that the continuing Election of the Jewish people is basic for a valid Christian understanding of Judaism?
    [−] or is this denied or treated ambiguously?[42]

3. Is an attempt made to see this ongoing salvific role of Judaism:
    [+] on Jewish as well as Christian terms; e.g., as the "sanctification of the Name"?
    [−] or is the Jewish salvific role seen in exclusively Christian terms?[43]

4. Even if not fully developed:
    [+] is an effort made to frame a positive approach to Jewish-Christian relations based on biblical and official sources while avoiding indifferentism?
    [−] [or is there no effort to express a theology of the Christian-Jewish relationship?][44]

5. Are there enough activities, data, and attitudinal exercises for varying age levels by which Christians can:
    [+] "learn by what essential traits the Jews define themselves in the light of their own religious experience" [Vatican "Guidelines" (1974)]?
    [−] [or is there little or no concern for an awareness of Jewish self-definition and religious observances?][45]

GENERAL AND TECHNICAL ASPECTS

1. Does the overall scope and sequence of the series:
   [+] integrate Jews and Judaism throughout the lessons, where suitable?
   [−] or are all positive references to Jewish history, beliefs, and customs restricted to a single chapter in a single text?[46]

2. Do pictures having clearly identifiable Jewish figures:
   [+] show them as "good guys" or both "good and bad guys"?
   [−] or are the figures clearly "bad guys?"[47]

3. Are Jesus, Mary, and the apostles:
   [+] pictured as Jewish? any forelocks, prayer shawls, phylacteries?
   [−] or do they appear as northern Europeans or modern Americans?[48]

4. Does the series on whatever level:
   [+] try to replace negative myths with a positive approach to Jews and Judaism?
   [−] [or does it merely avoid negatives?][49]

5. Is data given to teachers and pupils:
   [+] to understand how misconceptions can arise from biblical passages used in the liturgy?
   [−] or is this critical awareness lacking, thereby encouraging misunderstanding?[50]

6. Are the Judaic origins of the sacraments:
   [+] made clear throughout the series and fully explained in the teacher manuals?
   [−] [or is no treatment of the Jewish origins of the sacraments given?][51]

7. Are Jewish feasts and customs:
   [+] explained or used as examples of prayers and celebrations?
   [−] [or are there no references to Jewish feasts and customs?][52]

8. Are Church documents on Jews and Judaism:
   [+] cited and explained in the teachers' manuals and embodied in the texts?
   [−] [or are they not cited?] if cited in manuals, are they not embodied in the texts?[53]

9. Are Jewish tales and sayings:
   [+] used in suitable places and correctly identified?
   [−] [or are such resources not used?][54]

10. Do the teachers' manuals:
    [+] encourage activities with local Jewish communities: visits to

each other's houses of worship, dialogues, joint service projects?

[–]   [or is there no promotion of "cross-cutting relations" to promote inter-group amity?][55]

Notes

[1] Fisher, "Content Analysis," 40–41.

[2] Ibid., 38. See definition in Appendix 1.

[3] Ibid., 125–126.

[4] Ibid., 43.

[5] The layout is based on Fisher's data sheet [Ibid., 350].

[6] Ibid., 55–56.

[7] Idem, *Faith Without Prejudice,* 131.

[8] Idem, "Content Analysis," 130, 133.

[9] For further information on the validity and reliability of this statistical instrument see Philip A. Cunningham, "A Content Analysis of the Presentation of Jews and Judaism in Current Roman Catholic Religion Textbooks." (Ph.D. diss., Boston College, 1992) 165–171.

[10] Vatican II, *Nostra Aetate* (1965), 4; Vatican, "Guidelines" (1974) II; West German Bishops, "The Church and the Jews" (1980) II; John Paul II, "To the Jewish Community in Rome" (April 13, 1986); NCCB, *God's Mercy Endures Forever* (1988) 8–9.

[11] Vatican, "Notes" (1985) 6; NCCB, *God's Mercy Endures Forever* (1988) 31, a,b,c.

[12] Vatican, "Notes" (1985) III; Pontifical Biblical Commission, "The Bible and Christology" (1984) 1.1.5.1.

[13] French Bishops, "Pastoral Orientations" (1973) IV,c; Vatican, "Guidelines" (1974) III.

[14] French Bishops, "Pastoral Orientations" (1973) V, a; West German Bishops, "The Church and the Jews" (1980) II, 1; Vatican, "Notes" (1985) n. 1; NCCB, *God's Mercy Endures Forever* (1988) 14–15.

[15] Vatican, "Guidelines" (1974) III; John Paul II, "To the West German Jewish Community" (November 17, 1980); Idem, "To Christian Experts in Jewish-Christian Relations" (March 6, 1982); Vatican, "Notes" (1985) I, 3; II, 10; VI, 25; NCCB, *God's Mercy Endures Forever* (1988) 11.

[16] This criterion is partially the consequence of the critical biblical principles in Vatican II, *Dei Verbum* (1965) 12. Note also the words of John Paul II, "To the Jewish Community in Rome" (April 13, 1986): ". . . the *shalom* hoped for by the lawmakers, prophets, and wise men of Israel," which categorizes the patriarchs and prophets as belonging to Israel.

[17] Vatican, "Guidelines" (1974) II; NCCB, *God's Mercy Endures Forever* (1988) 13.

[18] For the last two criteria, see: Vatican II, *Dei Verbum* (1965) 12; West German Bishops, "The Church and the Jews" (1980) VI,2; Vatican, "Notes" (1985) II, 6–7;

John Paul II, "To the West German Jewish Community" (November 17, 1980); Idem, "To the Jewish Community in Rome" (April 13, 1986); NCCB, *God's Mercy Endures Forever* (1988) 15; NCCB–ADL, *Within Context* (1987) 4–5.

[19] NCCB, "Guidelines" (1985) 10, d–e; NCCB, *Dramatizations of the Passion* (1988) B, 2.

[20] Vatican, "Guidelines" (1974) III; NCCB, *Dramatizations of the Passion* (1988) B, 2; NCCB-ADL, *Within Context* (1987) 2–3.

[21] This is a consequence of the preceding criterion, but see also the related discussions of Messianism in West German Bishops, "The Church and the Jews" (1980) 7; and NCCB, *God's Mercy Endures Forever* (1988) 11–12.

[22] Vatican, "Notes" (1985) VI; NCCB, "Guidelines" (1985) 10, a,d,f; NCCB, *God's Mercy Endures Forever* (1988) 31, i.

[23] This category enunciates the principles contained in: French Bishops, "Pastoral Orientations" (1973) IV, d; Vatican, "Guidelines" (1974) II; Vatican, "Notes" (1985) III, 16–19; NCCB, "Guidelines" (1985) 10, e–f; Idem, *God's Mercy Endures Forever* (1988) 19; Idem, *Dramatizations of the Passion* (1988) B,1,3f; NCCB–ADL, *Within Context* (1987) 3–4.

[24] West German Bishops, "The Church and the Jews" (1980) I; Pontifical Biblical Commission, "The Bible and Christology" (1984) 1.1.5; Vatican, "Notes" (1985) III; NCCB, *Dramatizations of the Passion* (1988) B,3,c.

[25] Vatican II, *Nostra Aetate,* 4; NCCB, *Dramatizations of the Passion* (1988) B,3,b,d,e.

[26] Vatican, "Guidelines" (1974) II; NCCB, "Guidelines" (1985), Recommended Programs, 4; Idem, *God's Mercy Endures Forever* (1988) 21–24; Idem, *Dramatizations of the Passion* (1988) C.

[27] Vatican, "Notes" (1985) III, 12, 13, 17; NCCB, *Dramatizations of the Passion* (1988) B,3.

[28] Pontifical Biblical Commission, "Instruction on the Historical Truth of the Gospels" (1964) VI–IX; Idem, "The Bible and Christology" (1984) 1.1.11.2 (a); Vatican "Notes" (1985), IV, a; NCCB, *God's Mercy Endures Forever* (1988) 20; Idem, *Dramatizations of the Passion* (1988) C.

[29] Vatican, "Guidelines" (1974) II; West German Bishops, "The Church and the Jews" (1980) IV, 1; Vatican, "Notes" (1985) II, 8–11; NCCB, *God's Mercy Endures Forever,* 11.

[30] Vatican, "Guidelines" (1974) III; Vatican, "Notes" (1985) IV, 2.

[31] NCCB, *Dramatizations of the Passion* (1988) C; Idem, *God's Mercy Endures Forever* (1988) 23; NCCB-ADL, *Within Context* (1987) 7.

[32] NCCB, *Dramatizations of the Passion* (1988) B,3,i, C,2,b.

[33] Ibid., B,3,f; Vatican, "Notes" (1985) III, 19.

[34] Ibid., III, 22; NCCB, *Dramatizations of the Passion* (1988) A.

[35] Vatican II, *Nostra Aetate,* 4: ". . . the Jews should not be presented as repudiated or cursed by God, as if such views followed from the holy scriptures." See also John Paul II, "To the West German Jewish Community" (November 17, 1980), who referred to Jews as "the People of God of the Old Covenant, never revoked by God."

[36] This category enunciates the principles contained in: Vatican, "Guidelines" (1974) III; Idem, "Notes" (1985) VI; NCCB, "Guidelines" (1985) Recommended Programs, 5; Idem, *God's Mercy Endures Forever* (1988) 31, i.

[37] This category enunciates the principles contained in: NCCB, "Statement" (1975); Idem, "Guidelines" (1985) Recommended Programs, 10, c; Pontifical Justice and Peace Commission, "The Church and Racism" (1988) I, n, 2; Bishops of West Germany, Austria, and Berlin, "Accepting the Burden of History" (1988) 2; Int. Cath.-Jew. Liaison Com., "Uprooting Anti-Semitism" (1990) 235.

[38] This category enunciates the principles contained in: French Bishops, "Pastoral Orientations" (1973) IV, a; Vatican, "Guidelines" (1974) III; Idem, "Notes" (1985) VI; NCCB, "Guidelines" (1985) Recommended Programs, 5; Idem, *God's Mercy Endures Forever* (1988) 31, i.

[39] This category enunciates the principles contained in: NCCB, "Statement" (1975); West German Bishops, "The Church and the Jews" (1980) V, 7; Vatican, "Notes" (1985) VI, 6; NCCB, "Guidelines" (1985) Recommended Programs, 10, c; John Paul II, "To the Jews in Warsaw" (June 14, 1987); Idem, "To American Jewish Leaders" (September 11, 1987); Pontifical Justice and Peace Commission, "The Church and Racism" (1988) I,n,2,7, II,15; Bishops of West Germany, Austria, and Berlin, "Accepting the Burden of History" (1988); NCCB, *God's Mercy Endures Forever* (1988) Preface, 29; Int. Cath.-Jew. Liaison Com., "Uprooting Anti-Semitism" (1990) 235; Polish Bishops, "Jewish-Catholic Relations" (1990).

[40] This category enunciates the principles contained in: French Bishops, "Pastoral Orientations" (1973) V,e; Vatican, "Guidelines" (1974) Preamble; NCCB, "Statement" (1975); Vatican, "Notes" (1985) VI, 25; NCCB, "Guidelines (1985) General Principles, 9; John Paul II, "Apostolic Letter on Jerusalem" (April 20, 1984); Idem, "To the Jews in Warsaw" (June 14, 1987); Idem, "To American Jewish Leaders" (September 11, 1987); Pontifical Justice and Peace Commission, "The Church and Racism" (1988) II,15; NCCB, "Toward Peace in the Middle East" (1989).

[41] French Bishops, "Pastoral Orientations" (1973) III; NCCB, "Statement" (1975); John Paul II, "To the West German Jewish Community" (November 17, 1980); Vatican "Notes" (1985) I, 3; John Paul II, "To American Jewish Leaders" (September 11, 1987).

[42] See n. 32.

[43] French Bishops, "Pastoral Orientations" (1973) V, b; Vatican, "Guidelines" (1974) Preamble; NCCB, "Statement" (1975); Idem, "Guidelines" (1985) General Principles, 9.

[44] NCCB, "Guidelines" (1967) Recommended Programs, 5; Idem, "Statement" (1975); Vatican, "Notes" (1985) I.

[45] See nn. 32, 35.

[46] Vatican, "Notes" (1985) I, 2: "Because of the unique relations that exist between Christianity and Judaism . . . the Jews and Judaism should not occupy an occasional and marginal place in catechesis: Their presence there is essential and should be organically integrated."

[47] NCCB, *Dramatizations of the Passion* (1988) 3, h.

[48] Ibid., 3, a,h,i.

[49] See n. 35.

[50] Vatican II, *Nostra Aetate* (1965) 4; Vatican, "Guidelines" (1974) II, III; Idem, "Notes" (1985) IV; NCCB, "Guidelines" (1985) Recommended Programs, 4, 5; Idem, *Dramatizations of the Passion* (1988), C.

⁵¹ Vatican, "Guidelines" (1974) II; Idem, "Notes" (1985) V; NCCB, *God's Mercy Endures Forever* (1988) 1-4.

⁵² Vatican, "Guidelines" (1974) Preamble; John Paul II, "To Christian Experts in Jewish-Christian Relations" (March 6, 1982): "To assess [our Jewish roots] carefully in itself and with due awareness of the faith and religious life of the Jewish people as they are professed and practiced still today can greatly help us to understand better certain aspects of the life of the Church. Such is the case of liturgy whose Jewish roots remain still to be examined in depth, and in any case, should be better known and appreciated by our faithful."

⁵³ Vatican II, *Nostra Aetate* (1965) 4; Vatican, "Guidelines" (1974) III; Idem, "Notes" (1985) I, 1-8, Conclusion, 27; NCCB, "Guidelines" (1985) Recommended Programs, 5; Idem, *Dramatizations of the Passion* (1988) Preliminary Considerations.

⁵⁴ Vatican, "Guidelines" (1974) Preamble; NCCB, *God's Mercy Endures Forever* (1988) 31, i.

⁵⁵ Vatican, "Guidelines" (1974) I, IV; NCCB, "Guidelines" (1985) Recommended Programs, 1-6; Idem, *God's Mercy Endures Forever* (1988) 27-29.

6

Jews and Judaism
in Current Catholic Textbooks

A. Primary Series

In this study 1,867 primary grade lessons were examined. Table 6 lists the results of the analysis according to the period and theme categories.

Just under half of all primary lessons alluded to Jews and Judaism. Most J/J references occurred in connection with the Bible, as was the case in earlier textbook studies. Allusions to Jews in historical periods from rabbinic times to the twentieth century were absent or minimal.

The overall general imbalance of all primary J/J references was comfortably positive at + .495. However, certain categories scored negatively. These were the thematic categories of Jesus and the Jews, the Pharisees, the Crucifixion, and the Relationship Between the Covenants. As Table 4 showed, these same topics were found to be troublesome in previous textbook studies. The present analysis found that there were patterns to the negativity in these categories which are discussed in section C below.

Graph 1 compares these findings with the 1976 Fisher study according to period and theme categories with preoccupation scores greater than 5 percent.[1] As this graph makes clear, there was improvement, on the primary level, in every significant period and theme category. The greatest improvements occurred in the treatments of Jesus and the Jews and of the Pharisees, although both of these remained negative in 1992.

It should be noted that one of the most positive features of the Fisher study was the discovery that the idea of a divine retribution against Jews for their supposed rejection of Jesus had been expunged from American Catholic textbooks. "The only references to the idea . . . clearly condemn the notion."[2] Sadly, the same cannot be claimed today. One primary series twice declared that Jerusalem was destroyed because its people

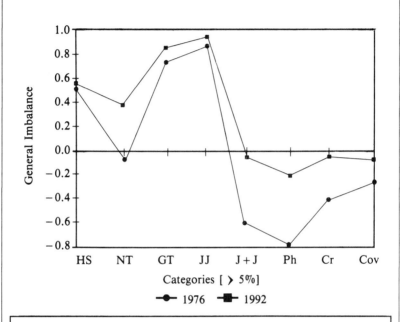

Graph 1
Comparison with Fisher Study [Primary]

Period Categories	Theme Categories

HS = Hebrew Scriptures
NT = New Testament
GT = General or Today

JJ   = Jesus as a Jew
J + J = Jesus and the Jews
Ph   = the Pharisees
Cr   = the Crucifixion
Cov = the Relationship
between the
Covenants

Note: Only categories with J/J preoccupations
greater than 5 percent appear on this chart.

"did not believe in the Savior."[3] Fortunately, these were the only two lessons in the 932 J/J primary lessons to do this.

Moreover, these two references to a divine punishment of Jerusalem did not occur in one of the more frequently used series, which leads to a final cautionary point about the results of this content analysis of primary religion textbooks. Table 6 does not necessarily provide a picture of current primary catechesis in the United States. One of the limits of this study is that all textbook series are treated equally, whereas, in reality, all series are not evenly distributed around the country. Some are used much more widely than others. It so happens that those primary series that received the most negative ratings in this study are also the least utilized in the various dioceses. Therefore, the present state of affairs is certainly somewhat better than indicated by Table 6. To garner a more

	Table 6		
	Analysis by Period and Theme		
	Primary Series		
Period Categories Theme Categories	Relevant Units	Preoccupation	Imbalance
1. Hebrew Scriptures	550	59%	+ .56
2. New Testament	485	52%	+ .37
3. Rabbinic Judaism	–	–	–
4. Middle Ages	4	0.4%	+ 1.00
5. Reformation to Twentieth Century	4	0.4%	+ 1.00
6. Twentieth Century	19	2%	+ 1.00
7. General or Today	145	15%	+ .88
1. Jesus as a Jew	194	20%	+ .92
2. Jesus and the Jews	153	16%	– .04
3. The Pharisees	58	6%	– .23
4. The Crucifixion	70	7%	– .03
5. Divine Retribution	2	0.2%	– 1.00
6. The *Shoah*	14	1%	+ 1.00
7. Modern Israel	6	0.6%	+ 1.00
8. Covenant (OT/NT)	77	8%	– .06
9. Crusades/ Inquisition	4	0.4%	+ 1.00

Total Number of Primary Units: 1867   Total Number of J/J Units: 932
Percentage of Preoccupation: 49%   General Imbalance: + .496

precise statistical picture one would need to include the relative distributions of the eight primary series into the calculations. That data is available only from publishers, who, because of the competitive nature of their business, were unwilling to disclose their sales figures when asked to do so.

B. Secondary Series

Nine hundred and thirty-six secondary lessons, comprising six secondary series, were evaluated in this study. Thus, in some ways, this analysis is the obverse of the Fisher study. In 1976 he evaluated ten secondary series and five primary ones, whereas the present research examined six secondary series and eight primary ones. Table 7 provides the details of the current secondary analysis.

Table 7 Analysis by Period and Theme Secondary Series			
Period Categories Theme Categories	Relevant Units	Preoccupation	Imbalance
1. Hebrew Scriptures	801	44%	+ .87
2. New Testament	197	48%	+ .08
3. Rabbinic Judaism	4	0.9%	+ .33
4. Middle Ages	6	1%	+ 1.00
5. Reformation to Twentieth Century	–	–	–
6. Twentieth Century	37	9%	+ 1.00
7. General or Today	128	31%	+ .96
1. Jesus as a Jew	65	16%	+ .96
2. Jesus and the Jews	70	17%	– .16
3. The Pharisees	62	15%	– .38
4. The Crucifixion	31	7%	– .49
5. Divine Retribution	–	–	–
6. The *Shoah*	31	7%	+ 1.00
7. Modern Israel	10	2%	+ 1.00
8. Covenant (OT/NT)	30	7%	+ .52
9. Crusades/ Inquisition	2	0.5%	+ 1.00
Total Number of Secondary Units: 936 Total Number of J/J Units: 413			
Percentage of Preoccupation: 44% General Imbalance: + .601			

On the whole, 44% of the secondary lessons contained J/J references. And, as in the primary series and in earlier studies, the vast majority of these occurred in connection with Biblical themes.

The secondary series presented a positive picture of Jews and Judaism, receiving an overall imbalance score of + .601. However, there were specific theme categories in which J/J comments were predominantly negative: Jesus and the Jews, the Pharisees, and the Crucifixion. Here, too, there were certain patterns to the defects pertinent to each of these categories, as explained below in section E.

In comparing these results with the 1976 Fisher analysis, there were roughly equal preoccupation scores, with the exception of the Hebrew Scriptures, which grew from 24 percent to 44 percent. This might be explained by the significant number of 1992 secondary texts which focused on social justice issues. These books often cited the Hebrew ethical tradition. Such an emphasis does not appear to have been so prevalent in the 1976 textbooks, judging from the titles in the list of texts which Fisher examined.[4]

There was also a decrease in J/J references in the Relationship Between the Covenants category from 26 percent to 7 percent. A similar decline was seen in the primary series (36 percent to 8 percent). The simplest explanation for this phenomenon is that supersessionist remarks about the Hebrew Bible were rarer in 1992.

Graph 2 compares the 1976 and 1992 studies on the basis of their general imbalance scores in categories with preoccupations greater than 5 percent.

Although in the primary series there was general improvement across the board, the curves for the two studies on the secondary level almost overlap, indicating relatively little change. But in the crucifixion category there is an obvious decline. In 1976 that subject was barely positive (+ .03). In 1991 it was quite negative (− .49). Given the history of the deicide charge against Jews, this deterioration is particularly disturbing.

These points should be noted. In the six secondary series rated in this study, there were few crucifixion J/J references. Two series contained only one such reference, a third made three allusions, two others had eight J/J references, and the sixth series contained ten. The majority of these thirty-one references were either short, careless comments (such as, "It was the Jewish leaders, especially the Pharisees, who were responsible for the opposition that eventually led to Jesus' crucifixion."[5]), or were uncritical quotations of New Testament polemical or accusatory speech, frequently Acts 2:23 ("This man . . . you [Israelites] killed, using lawless men to crucify him"[6]). The fewer, lengthier treatments tended to be more carefully considered:

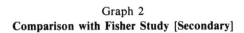

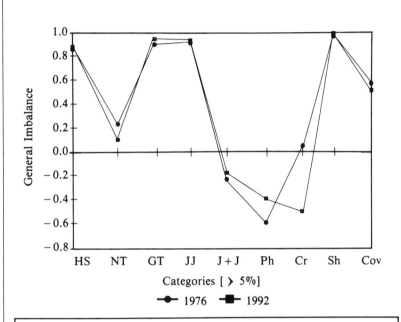

Graph 2
Comparison with Fisher Study [Secondary]

Period Categories	Theme Categories

HS = Hebrew Scriptures	JJ = Jesus as a Jew
NT = New Testament	J + J = Jesus and the Jews
GT = General or Today	Ph = the Pharisees
	Cr = the Crucifixion
	Sh = the *Shoah*
	Cov = the Relationship between the Covenants

Note: Only categories with J/J preoccupations
greater than 5 percent appear on this chart.

> The question of Jewish guilt for Jesus' death has been an intense issue in our century. At the Second Vatican Council, the bishops issued a strong statement removing any basis for anti-Semitism, hatred against the Jews. . . . Pontius Pilate, a Roman governor, pronounced the death sentence on Jesus. Some of the religious leaders saw Jesus as a threat and wished to remove him from the scene. So they brought Jesus to trial. But Jesus' own people were no more guilty of his death than we are. Christians know that sin brought about Jesus' death— the sin of all people from all times.[7]

In other words, the poor handling of Jesus' death in the secondary series is the result of the thoughtless repetition of caricature and/or of New Testament polemic in most of a small number of references. While this does not represent a regression back to the libelous language found in the earliest textbook studies,[8] this sort of carelessness must be faulted nonetheless. More will be said on this subject in section C below.

Finally, it might be observed that the two graphs presented in this chapter have somewhat similar shapes. On both the primary and secondary levels, and in both the 1976 study and the present one, certain subjects concerning Jews were typically handled well according to the directional criteria, but others were consistently dealt with poorly.

C. Discussion of the Results by Period and Theme

As noted above, certain categories were consistently troublesome, while others were usually handled well. There were also recurrent patterns of positivity or negativity in particular categories from one series to the next. This section discusses period and theme categories whose J/J preoccupations were greater than 5 percent, examining details of these "patterns" of thought.

Some preliminary comments are needed concerning those categories with lesser preoccupation scores. One of the conclusions of Fisher's 1976 study was that there were "almost no references to Jews and Judaism between the close of the New Testament period and the twentieth century . . . [perhaps reinforcing] the idea that Judaism ceased to be religiously vital after the coming of Christ."[9] The same distribution of J/J references was found in this analysis as well. There were only a handful of remarks about rabbinic Judaism or about the violence done against Jews during the Crusades and the Inquisition. A student would only guess that a rich religious tradition was continuing to develop and grow among medieval and renaissance Jews. Modern Jewish religious movements were scarcely mentioned.

This observation should be put into an overall context, though. There were actually very few lessons which portrayed *Christian* history with any sort of thoroughness. Some of those series which did treat Church history did so in a fairly romantic fashion which idealized ecclesial virtues while minimizing serious failings. Thus, the lack of treatment of the ongoing Jewish tradition relates to a certain deficiency in presenting history in general.

Still, Fisher's concern that Judaism would implicitly be viewed as religiously lifeless must be taken seriously. One other factor needs to be considered. There were a number of series that had many J/J references in the General or Today category. Some of these regularly alluded to modern Jewish practice when discussing the Hebrew Scriptures or the Jewishness of Jesus. For example:

> Like the Jewish community, the Christian community calls itself "the people of the book." The Hebrew Bible is a sacred book for Christians and Jews. The Hebrew Bible was written long before the coming of Jesus. The Jewish people have a special love for God's Word in the Hebrew Bible. They give the Hebrew Bible a special place of honor in their worship houses. From the time they are very young, Jewish boys and girls study God's Word and its meaning for today. Because He was a Jew, Jesus grew up with a great love for God's Word, the Hebrew Bible.[10]

> In the Jewish tradition the Exodus is regarded as *the* great saving act whereby God rescued the Israelites from slavery and established them as a people. . . . To this day, Jews recite the story of the Exodus as part of the Passover celebration.[11]

> This is the prayer which our Jewish brothers and sisters recite after reading the Torah: Holy One of Blessing, your presence fills creation. You gave us the Torah of truth and planted within us eternal life. Holy One of Blessing, you give us the Torah.[12]

To the extent that a series contains frequent similar allusions to contemporary Jewish practice, it would seem that to that extent Judaism is conveyed as being religiously vital *today*. The potentially negative effects of a lack of a full treatment of post-New Testament Jewish history, then, might be considerably corrected by giving students a healthy respect for the spiritual depth and dynamism of Judaism in the present. If it is clear that modern Jews have a profound religious life, it would probably be less likely that one would imagine that Judaism ceased to have religious value after the coming of Christ.

Unfortunately, few series took advantage of all the chances to discuss modern Judaism, for example when treating the sacraments or Jesus. Nevertheless, if a thorough presentation of Christian history is not a high priority in curricular design, and if therefore an adequate treatment of Jewish history becomes unlikely, then publishers can work to avoid the danger to which Fisher rightly refers by multiplying the number of positive allusions to Jewish faith and practice today.

The patterns found within each of the major period and theme categories will now be considered. Suggestions to overcome negative patterns in each category are found in chapter 7.

THE HEBREW SCRIPTURES

This category was handled fairly well in most of the textbooks evaluated in this study. Of the fourteen series examined, only one scored negatively concerning the Hebrew Scriptures. Indeed, twelve of the series had imbalance scores greater than + .50. By and large, the Hebrew Scriptures were respected on their own terms, were alluded to as the inspired writings of a faith-filled people, and were presented as important for the Christian (and often, the Jewish) communities of today. The following two examples are typical of the tone with which the Hebrew Scriptures were treated:

> The Israelites tried to put God first in their lives in many ways. They worshiped God in the Temple of Jerusalem. They studied the commandments in their synagogues. They prayed to God before and after every meal. What is most important, they put God first in their lives by trying to do God's will. Sometimes the Israelites found it hard to put God first in their lives. But they discovered that only when they put God first did they live in freedom.[13]

> God revealed himself in much the same way as people do. He chose a group of people, the people of Israel. We call them the Chosen People. In words and deeds, God made himself known to them. Although God is not a human person, Israel came to know him as a living, loving being. Therefore they talked about God's feelings. More than anything, God wanted a personal relationship with these people. He showed them that he was willing to trust them and to travel with them, to live with them and to love them as a Father and friend. And so Israel came to know God as the one God, the only God they could love and trust.[14]

There were, however, three recurrent problems in this category involving (1) the prophets; (2) Jewish Messianic expectations; and (3) the nature of the Torah. Regarding the first, many series stated explicitly that:

> Your students may associate the term prophet with someone who predicts the future. In the biblical tradition, the role of the prophet is more complex. The prophet was the conscience of Israel. Rather than calling for a new plan, the prophet reminded God's People of the old plan that God had revealed to Israel at Mount Sinai. The prophet attempted to keep the People faithful to covenant in the midst of the surrounding pagan cultures of Israel's neighbors.[15]

Yet not infrequently, sometimes in the very same series, the prophets were functionally presented as future forecasters when Jesus was discussed.

> The final Song of the Servant (Isa 52:13–53:12) describes in great detail the sinless servant who gives up his life for the sins of his people and saves them from punishment at the hands of God. Ask the students to . . . note specific similarities between the Suffering Servant and Jesus. Point out that only in Jesus is this prophecy perfectly fulfilled.[16]

While there was no separate theme category on the prophets in this study, and hence no accurate statistics about this deficiency, it was a rare series which did not succumb to the tendency to revert to a simplistic portrayal of prophetic speech in regard to Jesus. Indeed in a few series such a predictive understanding of the prophets was the norm and not the exception:

> The prophets enlightened the people by telling things about the Messiah, the Redeemer to come: where He would be born; who His mother would be; how He would live and work; how He would die and rise.[17]

> The various prophets had told the Jewish people that the Messiah would indeed come to them, but they never said exactly *who* he would be. Most of the people expected a great and powerful military leader who would free them from political oppression. That this Savior would be God himself, come down to liberate them from their spiritual slavery to sin and the devil was not what they expected. But the prophets did give the people some clues about the Messiah, ways to recognize him once he came. They said he would be a member of the tribe of Judah (Gen 49:8-10); he would be born of a virgin (Isa 7:14) in the town of Bethlehem (Mic 5:2-4). A great star would shine in the sky to announce the Messiah's birth (Num 24:17), and he would live for a time in Egypt (Hos 11:1-4). This Redeemer would preach God's good news to the poor and the lowly (Isa 61:1-3), but he would be rejected by the people who would cause him much suffering (Isa 53:1-12). You probably recognize the life of the Lord Jesus in the above prophecies; many of the Jews did, and they accepted him as the Messiah sent from God. But many others did not.[18]

While all the series were not as extreme as these, the tendency to refer to the prophets in this way was present in most. In particular, sometimes more accurate descriptions of the prophets were forgotten when the lesson concerned the season of Advent. For instance, "In this lesson you can broaden your students' appreciation for the birth of the Lord in Bethlehem by showing them how this was foretold in scripture."[19]

The second recurrent difficulty concerned Jewish Messianic expectations. A few series were outstanding in this regard, portraying the complexity of the issue, at least in the teacher's manuals, with considerable sophistication:

> It is important that the students recognize that the Christian understanding of the messiah was a change from that of Judaism. The messianic hope of the Jewish people grew over a long period of time. By the time of Jesus it has come to include certain elements . . . 1) Although they did idealize the messianic figure to the point of the superhuman, their hope was never for a divine messiah, like Jesus, who is truly God and truly human. 2) The Jewish expectation always contained an element of nationalism, unlike the messiahship of Jesus . . . in Jesus the whole notion of messiahship was recast and not simply restored in a purer form.[20]

This sort of presentation was rare. Much more common were simplistic, one-dimensional references to messianic expectations. Some of these were found in the Jesus and the Jews category as well as in the Hebrew Scriptures one. Some examples follow:

> Long ago, however, people began to think that God was far away from them. They even thought God might be angry with them for not leading good lives. They waited and hoped and prayed for God to send them a *Messiah*. This Savior would show them the way to be with God forever.[21]

> [From a fictitious interview with a student of the law:] "I mean all the guys at school kept speaking about this Messiah that was due to be born. . . . As you know we had been waiting for a Messiah for centuries."[22]

> God promised [David] that someday a very special person would be born in David's family. This person would be very important to the world. This person would be God's gift to the world. David was happy to hear God's promise. He wondered who this special person would be.[23]

Finally, there occasionally appeared references which cast the Hebrew tradition in an unfavorable and distorted light. These instances were not as frequent as the flawed allusions to the prophets or Messianic thought, but they occurred often enough to be of concern. Many of these comments were intended to provide a foil against which Jesus could be favorably contrasted:

> After many years, some of the Israelites no longer understood the full beauty or real power of God's commandments. They did not understand them as part of a covenant of love. Instead, they followed the rules but did not open their hearts to God. On the outside, their actions seemed correct. But in their hearts they were not really loving

God and others. . . . Again and again Jesus spoke against this empty kind of living.[24]

[From a fictitious conversation between God and angels about the Israelites:] "They're still scared stiff of me. If they keep burning those goats and oxen, that sacrificial smoke is going to pollute the whole place."[25]

The people of Old Testament times never do find full and complete peace with God. Only the coming of Jesus Christ in the New Testament brings the possibility of peace to all creation.[26]

Again, these three areas of difficulty did not outnumber the far more numerous positive references to the Hebrew Scriptures. They do, however, present a pattern of distortion which needs correction.

NEW TESTAMENT

Themes concerning New Testament topics posed serious problems in the textbooks. Six of the fourteen series were rated negatively in this category, and three others, although positive, scored less than + .25.

While specific difficulties will be treated in relation to the theme categories, one overarching defect can conveniently be discussed here. This is the regular practice of quoting or citing polemical New Testament passages without providing sufficient, if any, explanation about such verses. For instance, "John 5:39-40: Christ tells the Jews that they claim to study Scripture in order to find eternal life, yet fail to come to Him Who is eternal life and to Whom the Scriptures testify."[27] One of the most popular passages employed in this way was Acts 2:23, in which Peter prophetically accuses the Israelites of killing Jesus through the agency of the Romans. This verse was often simply repeated without any instruction about the historical or theological responsibility for the crucifixion.

While it might be unwise to confront primary grade students with the intricacies of critical exegesis, surely their teachers should receive instruction about the sensitivity of New Testament polemic in regard to Jews. Most of the series did not attempt to do this.

The series which scored most positively in this study were those which avoided the mindless repetition of New Testament polemic and/or explained the social and cultural background of such passages.

GENERAL OR TODAY

J/J references in this category were extremely positive. Eight series scored + 1.00 and all others but one had imbalance scores greater than + .75. It was clear that the religious life of modern Jews was held in high esteem. Sabbath observances, the Passover Seder, and the Ten Commandments were the most frequently discussed subjects. Several series suggested that visits to local synagogues be undertaken or that local rabbis or other Jewish leaders be guest speakers for religion classes. As noted above, some series established an edifying continuity between modern Judaism and the biblical Hebrew tradition which tended to multiply the tone of positivity toward Jews.

JESUS AS A JEW

This subject, also, tended to be handled well. Eleven series had imbalance scores of + 1.00 in this category, and all were above + .79. It was made clear to both students and teachers that Jesus and his disciples and relatives were all Jews.

While all the series taught that Jesus was a Jew, however, only about half of them pointed out that Jesus of Nazareth was dependent on his Jewish heritage for his understanding of God, the Covenant, and the life of faith. Certainly, these kinds of comments increase the esteem in which Judaism would be held by readers. For example:

> Jesus was proud of the fact that He was a Jew. He knew that His people had a special relationship with God. They were the chosen people. God had formed a covenant with them and promised to be with them forever. Jesus saw this as so important that everything He did reflected His Jewish faith and culture. His dress, His style of teaching and His theology were based on Judaism. He believed that some of this background needed to be changed. But He didn't want to throw it away. He wanted to make it better. . . . As a Jewish man of His times, Jesus also wore over His shoulders a shawl with four huge tassels. It was to remind Jesus of the 613 laws that made up the Torah. This was not merely a collection of rules. It was the will of God. Through obedience to the Torah, Jesus and the people of Israel grew closer to God. The prayer shawl reminded them of this fact.[28]

> Mary and Joseph raised Jesus in their Jewish tradition. From them, Jesus learned how to pray and to care for the poor and needy.[29]

JESUS AND THE JEWS

This was one of the three most negative categories revealed by this analysis. In the calculation of the overall general imbalance scores, this category scored negatively on both the primary and secondary levels.

There were a number of reasons for this assessment. Two of them have been mentioned earlier; namely, the practice of utilizing New Testament polemical language without exegetical guidance and the tendency to depict the complex development and variance of Jewish Messianic expectation in a simplistic and monolithic fashion.

Related to the former difficulty was the propensity to discuss first-century Judaism as a legalistic religion, oppressed by a burdensome weight of numerous statutes. For example:

As Jesus lived and observed life around Him, He recognized that the teachers of the law and the religious leaders preached an attitude that was narrow, rigid, legalistic, and unbending. It was missing a *heart,* the meeting-ground of His own relationship with the Father.

Overemphasis had been put on many laws, and they had come to be like prison bars. Some Pharisees and Sadducees were creating idols out of religious laws. They were no longer seen as helping people to worship the Lord God.

Jesus tried to change these rigid interpretations and teach people the true LAW OF LOVE.[30]

For some of the religious leaders of Jesus' day, however, observance of their interpretation of the Law became more important than the Law itself. They put almost insurmountable burdens on the people (telling them, for example, that they could walk thirty-nine steps on the Sabbath, but not forty, and so forth). People were judged by some of their Jewish leaders on whether their every action conformed exactly to their own strict interpretation of the original Law of Moses. In other words, conformity to their own strict interpretation of the Law became the law! (See Mark 7:7 and Matt 23:23).

Jesus recognized this. He saw that observance of the Law as interpreted by those leaders of the Jews and imposed on the people was too heavy a burden. For that reason, he opposed those leaders of the Jews and the way they interpreted the Law. He talked over and over again about the importance of love. He insisted that people should act out of love of God and love of neighbor, not out of fear of breaking the law. So insistent was he about this, that love became known as "his law."[31]

To the Jews at the time of Jesus, the Sabbath was a day of prayer and strict rest to honor the Lord of creation. Many types of work were forbidden. A faithful Jew could not tie or untie a rope, put out a lamp, light a fire, sew two stitches, or write two letters of the alphabet. A Jew also could not take medicine, walk more than three thousand feet, or wear hair ornaments.[32]

In Jesus' time, some of the religious leaders of the Jews seemed to forget the loving forgiveness that God had shown their ancestors. Instead, they kept reminding people only about God's justice, especially that he punishes every sin that we commit. They spoke of God as if he were a merciless judge who found joy in condemning everyone— except the most learned and religious of people![33]

The last example brings up another point. Many of the texts qualified negative statements about Jewish leaders with the adjective "some." While in an individual sentence this practice might be of some benefit, in terms of an entire series it becomes irrelevant. If students consistently and exclusively read about "some" religious leaders who were legalistic or opposed Jesus without ever encountering the "other" Jewish leaders who emphasized a loving heart and supported him, then the picture presented of first-century Judaism is functionally negative. This was also a problem in the Pharisees and the crucifixion categories. Students were regularly confronted with "some" Pharisees who criticized Jesus, but hardly ever met the "other" Pharisees who admired or agreed with him. Likewise, continual statements that "some" Jewish leaders were instrumental in orchestrating the crucifixion, without ever mentioning the "other" leaders who defended Jesus, result in a sweeping portrayal of the Jewish leadership as responsible for his execution. In other words, use of differentiating words like "some" becomes meaningless when not accompanied by references to the "others."

Another troublesome feature was a tendency to highlight the uniqueness of Jesus or his message by inaccurately portraying first-century Judaism. In some series, for instance, there was a pronounced tendency to claim that Jesus said things about God never before imagined, especially referring to God as Abba:

> Jesus said we should call our God not just a father, but "Abba, Father." The Aramaic word *abba* is best translated into English as *daddy, papa,* or even the more childlike name given father by infants, *dada.* It is the name used by little Hebrew children as they sit on their father's knee, playfully tugging at his beard. That is the attitude we are to have toward our God—that of a child who is secure in the arms of a father who loves him or her without reservation, unconditionally. No one had ever before suggested such an image of God. No longer could people view God as apart from them, removed, unreachable.[34]

> [After a discussion of the Lord's Prayer:] The word Jesus used for Father comes from the Aramaic, *Abba.* At the time of Jesus, *Abba* was the common, familiar name used by Jewish children to address their fathers. We can literally translate it as "Papa" or "Daddy." The word must have shocked the followers of Jesus who would never dare to address God in so intimate a manner.[35]

> No Jew before or after Jesus is known to speak to God as *Abba.*[36]

Each of these assertions is debatable. They surely produce a distorted and stereotypical view of Judaism. Indeed, that result aptly summarizes the overriding problem of the negative J/J references in this category. By uncritically using New Testament polemic, by purveying inaccurate data about first-century Judaism, and by not recognizing the complex variety of first- century Jewish thought, little is done to remedy the situation decried in recent ecclesial documents: "There is evident in particular a painful ignorance of the history and traditions of Judaism, of which only negative aspects and often caricature seem to form part of the stock ideas of many Christians."[37]

THE PHARISEES

This was also one of the most negative categories revealed by this analysis. Only a handful of series tried to provide an objective description of the goals, variety, and practices of the Pharisaic tradition. Some offered more balanced presentations when treating the origins or purposes of the Pharisees, but regressed to cliche in more numerous, casual allusions. A number of series simply engaged in the mindless repetition of conventional stereotypes and polemics:

> [Pharisees] were devout laypersons. A layperson is one who is not ordained for religious work. However, they were powerful religious leaders. They believed that Judaism was a religion based on the strict observance of the law. They looked down on the poor and uneducated because they felt that these people were not strict enough about the law and compromised with the Romans.[38]

> I am Zechariah the Pharisee. I have studied the law of Moses since I was a child. I go to the Temple every day to teach and study the law. I fast and keep all the rules. I am better than anybody else. Others respect me. They bow when I pass.[39]

> Wherever Jesus, the new king of Israel went, he was followed about by angry men who argued with him because they did not like what he was saying or doing. Some of these men were Pharisees. Some of the Pharisees were so concerned with the special laws that God had given them through Moses that they often forgot about loving God and others. Instead, they thought only of themselves. They thought they were perfect, and they wanted to look perfect by following every law without making one little mistake. But their hearts were cold, proud, and unloving.[40]

> [A secondary series provided this litany of polemical references in order to stress the point that "Jesus was at odds with the Pharisees":]
> a. The Pharisees watch Jesus closely to find some fault in Him. John 4:1-3.
> b. The Pharisees propose questions about the interpretation of the law. Matthew 22:34-40.
> c. The Pharisees try to trap Jesus in a wrong answer. Matthew 22:15-22; Mark 12:13-17; Luke 20:20-26.
> d. The Pharisees are scandalized at the conduct of Jesus—His association with publicans and sinners. Matthew 9:9-13; Luke 5:30-32; Mark 2:13-17.
> e. The Pharisees are scandalized by Jesus' laxness in the sabbath observance. Matthew 12:2-8; Mark 2:24-28; Luke 6:2-5.
> f. The Pharisees are upset with His healing on the Sabbath. Luke 14:1-6.

  g. The Pharisees object to His claim of the power to forgive sin. Luke
     5:17-26.
  h. The Pharisees claim he is in league with the devil. Matthew 12:24-
     28.[41]

Such typical presentations of the Pharisees directly violate several
Catholic ecclesial instructions on the Bible and on the presentation of Jews
and Judaism, perhaps most notably:

> An exclusively negative picture of the Pharisees is likely to be inac-
> curate and unjust.[42]

> [There must be] an explicit rejection of the historically inaccurate no-
> tion that Judaism of [Jesus'] time, especially Pharisaism, was a deca-
> dent formalism and hypocrisy, well exemplified by Jesus' enemies.[43]

> Jesus and his teachings should not be portrayed as opposed to or by
> "the Pharisees" as a group.[44]

THE CRUCIFIXION

This, too, was one of the most negative categories, although there
was a significant difference between primary and secondary texts in comparison with the Fisher study. On the primary level there appears to have
been substantial improvement since 1976. The general imbalance score
rose from − .42 to the barely negative − .04. Almost precisely the reverse
occurred on the secondary level. In those textbooks, treatment of the
crucifixion was rated as + .03 in 1976, but dropped to − .49 in 1992.

As noted above, the problems of the secondary texts seemed to stem
from carelessness. In lengthy discussions about Jesus' death, the secondary books tended to be more positive. But this positivity was offset by
far more numerous casual allusions that tended to implicate Jews or Jewish leaders in a sweeping manner.

The primary series generally seemed to be more careful in this regard. In particular, one publisher which had been the most negative in
the Fisher study in regards to the crucifixion, demonstrated great awareness and conscientiousness in this study and scored a + 1.00 in this category.[45]

Many series on both levels cited *Nostra Aetate's* denial of widespread
Jewish responsibility. However, they did not consistently work to avoid
implying that very thing. The most common problem was the simplistic
quoting of polemical passion narrative passages. Although no series ad-
duced the blood-curse in Matthew 27:25, most did claim that Pilate was
manipulated by Jewish leaders and tried earnestly to free Jesus. Very few
series provided any extra-biblical information about Pilate. Nor was the
nature of the relationship between Pilate and the high priest explored with
any regularity. There were also careless allusions to crowds. Such refer-

ences tended to implicate the Jewish people at large. For example, "Pilate wanted to release Jesus at this point, but the people demanded his death."[46]

Some series tried to establish reasons for the opposition to Jesus that resulted in his death. Few included any political motivations on the part of Pilate. Most stressed religious opposition to Jesus as the prime factor in his death, an emphasis which by its very nature would tend to enlarge Jewish involvement. Sometimes this religious opposition was typified as Jewish reaction to the "blasphemy" that Jesus claimed to be equal to God or the Son of God, thereby injecting post-resurrectional and polemical dimensions into the presentation. The following quotation illustrates several of the difficulties evident in this category:

> [Jesus' death] is prepared for in the accounts of the confrontations he had with Jewish religious authorities. The trial and condemnation of Jesus were the final steps in a series of confrontations that Jesus experienced throughout his ministry. . . . [Jesus] was a "dangerous man," "upsetting the people," as the Jewish leaders said, and claiming to be equal to God. (See John 5:18 and 10:33). Hence, in the final confrontation, Jesus was condemned for blasphemy. Under Jewish Law, he deserved death. (See Matt 26:65,66.)[47]

The problem with such uncritical expositions is that they are far too simple. While concrete recommendations for dealing with the complexities of the crucifixion are offered in chapter 7, at this point it must be stated that the precise degree of High Priestly/Roman involvement in Jesus' death is very difficult to assess. Definitive assertions in this regard, especially when they tend to perpetuate the ancient Christian tendency to condemn "the Jews" in sweeping fasion, must be avoided.

THE RELATIONSHIP BETWEEN THE COVENANTS

This category was handled better in the secondary series than in the primary ones. Four of the six secondary series stated or strongly implied that Jews remain in covenantal relationship with God and that the "Old" Testament was not nullified by the "New." Only three of the eight primary series did the same.

A few series were blatantly supersessionist in this category. Others were ambiguous. On this subject, it should be noted, ambiguity was stated by the directional critieria to be negative. There had to be unambiguous declarations about the ongoing covenantal status of Jews. Occasionally, ambiguity was the result of the way the Church was described. Use of the definite article, as in "the Church is the new People of God,"[48] could be read in a supersessionist manner. Regular use of the past tense when discussing the chosen status of Israel was similarly questionable.[49]

This theme, with the possible exception of the crucifixion, is probably the most definitively treated topic in modern ecclesial documents. Therefore, the abiding covenant between God and Israel ought to be a *sine qua non* in Catholic religious education. On the other hand, this realization has enormous, not fully realized, implications for Christian self-understanding. This fact may contribute to a hesitancy to discuss the subject in any depth in religion textbooks.

CONCLUSION

The 1985 Vatican "Notes" advised that "Jews and Judaism should not occupy an occasional and marginal place in catechesis: Their presence there is essential and should be organically integrated."[50] It could be argued that the overall preoccupation scores produced in this study indicate that this centrality of Judaism for the Church is evident in current textbooks. Roughly half of the twenty-eight hundred lessons evaluated made some reference to Jews and Judaism. However, this does not mean that Judaism is "organically integrated" into the texts since many references were fairly peripheral.

On the other hand, the absence of significant J/J references in non-biblical categories, except for General or Today, is cause for concern. Of course, the relative scarcity of non-biblical lessons helps to explain this lack. Nonetheless, more frequent discussion of the religiously vital Jewish tradition should occur in lessons on Church history.

In terms of the imbalance scores, the words of the Vatican "Notes" regarding the pervasive influence of caricature and stereotype in Christian attitudes toward Jews and Judaism remain important. Such distortions widely prevailed when treating Jesus and the Jews, the Pharisees, and the Crucifixion. While improvements have occurred, and while the defamatory language revealed in earlier textbook studies has been eliminated, there is still much work to be done.[51]

Notes

[1] The figures for the 1976 study are found in Fisher, "Content Analysis," 131–132. A notable feature in comparing the two studies is the rough equivalence of the preoccupation scores. Those categories which were present in fewer than 5 percent of the J/J references in 1976 were similarly distributed in 1992. With the exception of the Covenant category, which occurred about 1/5 as often in the present study, the same is true of the more frequently occurring categories.

[2] Fisher, *Faith Without Prejudice,* 133.

[3] *Christ Our Life,* 3:146. See also 4:137. The number before the colon refers to the grade level, the number following it to the page.

⁴ See Fisher, "Content Analysis," 357–362.

⁵ *To Live is Christ,* Bible (T):266. T refers to the teacher's manual.

⁶ *Centering Faith,* Church History:11.

⁷ *Friendship in the Lord,* Jesus: 178–179.

⁸ See pp. 74–77.

⁹ Fisher, *Faith Without Prejudice,* 131.

¹⁰ *Focus Books,* 3:194.

¹¹ *Come, Follow Me,* 6T:46a. Italics in the original.

¹² *Alive in Jesus,* 6T:245.

¹³ *Coming to Faith,* 4:93.

¹⁴ *Alive in Jesus,* 6:12.

¹⁵ *Come, Follow Me,* 6T:109.

¹⁶ Ibid., 6T:151.

¹⁷ *Christ Our Life,* 6T:293.

¹⁸ *Faith and Life,* 7:41. Italics in the original.

¹⁹ *This Is Our Faith,* 4:143b.

²⁰ *Alive in Jesus,* 6T:121–122.

²¹ *Come, Follow Me,* 4:10.

²² *Centering Faith,* Christian Scriptures:57.

²³ *Joy,* 1:H3.

²⁴ *Christ Our Life,* 6:83.

²⁵ *Centering Faith,* Jesus:14.

²⁶ *Hi-Time,* Peace (T):2–3.

²⁷ *Christ Our Life,* 4T:21. See also 6T:13.

²⁸ *Hi-Time,* Jesus:3/6.

²⁹ *Coming to Faith,* 3:222.

³⁰ *Centering Faith,* Jesus:45. Emphasis in the original.

³¹ *To Live Is Christ,* Church History:62.

³² *Come, Follow Me,* 4T:30.

³³ *Faith and Life,* 7:121.

³⁴ *The Sharing Program,* II:149. Italics in the original.

³⁵ *Come, Follow Me,* 4T:55.

³⁶ *This Is Our Faith,* 7:41. For further discussion of the Abba issue see Geza Vermes, *Jesus the Jew: A Historian's Reading of the Gospels* (Philadelphia: Fortress, 1967) 69–82; Paula Fredriksen, *From Jesus to Christ: The Origins of the New Testament Images of Jesus* (New Haven: Yale University Press) 91; James H. Charlesworth, *Jesus Within Judaism: New Light From Exciting Archaeological Discoveries* (New York: Doubleday, 1988) 132–135; and Clark Williamson, "Jesus of Nazareth," Paper presented at the Christian Study Group on Jews and Judaism, Baltimore, March 25, 1990, 11–15.

³⁷ Vatican, "Notes" (1985) 27.

³⁸ *This Is Our Faith,* 7:23. For a discussion and rejection of the idea that Pharisees "looked down on the uneducated" see Sanders, *Jesus and Judaism,* 190–191.

³⁹ *Joy:* 4:L7. This quote seems to be a re-phrasing of the Parable of the Pharisee and the Tax-Collector in Luke 18:9-14.

⁴⁰ *Faith and Life,* 4:81. This quotation is a good illustration of the way the word "some" is used. In this series there was not a single positive reference to the Pharisees.

All that students would ever learn about the Pharisees is negative, even if the text purports to be discussing only "some" of them.

    [41] *Centering Faith,* Jesus (T):65–66.

    [42] Vatican, "Notes" (1985) III, 19.

    [43] NCCB, "Guidelines" (1967) Recommended Programs, 10e.

    [44] NCCB, "Dramatizations of the Passion" (1988) B, 3f.

    [45] *Alive in Jesus* released by St. Paul Books and Media. See Fisher, "Content Analysis," 307–317.

    [46] *This Is Our Faith,* 7:100.

    [47] *To Live Is Christ,* New Testament:102.

    [48] *Christ Our Life,* 4:18.

    [49] For instance, "Who were God's chosen people? [Ans:] Jews." Ibid., 1T:143.

    [50] Vatican, "Notes" (1985) I,2.

    [51] Those interested in the details of how each publisher and series scored in the statistical analysis should consult Philip A. Cunningham, "A Content Analysis of the Presentation of Jews and Judaism in Current Roman Catholic Religion Textbooks" (Ph.D. diss., Boston College, 1992). This is available from University Microfilms International, 300 N. Zeeb Road, Ann Arbor, MI 48106 (800-521-0600); Order Number 9217440.

7

Reflections and Recommendations

A. The Content Analysis and Ancient Anti-Judaic Themes

The results garnered by this analysis of current Catholic religion text-books can be usefully compared with the conclusions reached in the first two chapters of the study. It will be recalled that certain anti-Jewish concepts emerged from the polemical social circumstances of New Testament times, but that these ideas were disjointed and unstructured (see Table 1). In the patristic period, however, these originally disparate notions were assembled, as a result of the social forces of the time, into an overarching framework of theological anti-Judaism (see Table 2). This system was to dominate Christian religious thought about Jews and Judaism until the twentieth century.

Current religion textbooks would seem to share the qualities of New Testament materials since their negative elements were not organized into any anti-Judaic system. Indeed, the aspects of the patristic anti-Judaic superstructure were discernible in the textbooks only in an attenuated form, if at all.

However, several polemical New Testament themes were evident in many of the series. Naturally, this was most commonly seen in textbooks which simply quoted polemical Gospel passages without providing any commentary on their origins or interpretation. In order of frequency of appearance, New Testament anti-Judaic motifs which appeared in current religion books were: (1) the Pharisees as hypocrites who hated Jesus, (2) the prophets as foretellers of Jesus, (3) Jewish responsibility for the crucifixion, (4) Judaism as legalistic, (5) the Old Covenant as obsolete, [and, in one series, (6) the destruction of Jerusalem as a result of Jewish rejection of Jesus]. The only New Testament rhetorical argument which was totally absent in the textbooks was the linkage of Jews with the demonic.

This observation leads to several conclusions. First, the most important single deficiency in present textbooks is the minimal application or complete lack of critical biblical insights when dealing with New Testament polemic. This is a particularly glaring flaw in regard to teacher's manuals. Very few manuals provided religion teachers with any information on this subject. When treating such sensitive and historically complex issues as the events which led to Jesus' execution, for example, it is absolutely imperative that teachers be acquainted with the relevant factors. Religion teachers, especially volunteers, need such background if their lessons on matters pertaining to Jews and Judaism are not to perpetuate stereotype.

Second, current textbooks do little to equip either students or their teachers with the ability to cope with the New Testament polemical texts that they will encounter as liturgical readings. This is a problem even if a particular series avoided repeating rhetorical attacks in its own pages. Some series which scored positively in this analysis did so by simply eschewing negative biblical passages. While this is useful in its own way, it does not contribute to an understanding of the human, contentious aspects of the Bible. Without adequate education on the social contexts of the New Testament books, anti-Judaic ideas will be purveyed at Christian worship regardless of how benign instructional textbooks are in and of themselves.

Third, if the anti-Judaic theological system that prevailed until this century is envisioned as an onion, then recent textbook studies indicate that most of the layers of that onion have by now been peeled away. The 1961 Thering research revealed frequent recourse to the patristic anti-Jewish framework, including references to the wandering and accursed Jews, to Jews as bloodthirsty deicides, and to Jews as the inveterate foes of the Gospel. The 1976 Fisher analysis, and this present study as well, show that these features of the Christian anti-Jewish tradition have vanished from the textbooks. All that remains are the central leaves of the onion, the originating New Testament polemic which lies at the center of Christian anti-Judaism, but which is also capable, through biblical criticism, of being peeled away in its turn and shown to be theologically insubstantial. That is the work which remains to be done.

B. Ecclesial Documents and Textbook Publishers

It is difficult to assess the impact of ecclesial documents on Christian instructional materials pertaining to Jews and Judaism. Clearly, *Nostra Aetate* played a pivotal, reorienting role and has had enormous influence. It is the effect of subsequent documents that is elusive.

For instance, numerous ecclesial instructions, as noted in chapter 3, have warned against portraying first-century Judaism as heartless legalism or the Pharisees as uniformly and unalterably opposed to Jesus. Yet, these two errors were regularly encountered in this content analysis.

It may be that the guidelines issued by local episcopal conferences and their various sub-committees are treated with less deference that those released by Vatican offices. The former have tended to be more detailed in their applications of biblical criticism to Jewish-Christian issues, whereas the latter have been more general and sweeping.[1] Local documents often intend to spell out the implications of Vatican assertions.

This would suggest either that Vatican declarations must become more precise or that local directives be given greater weight by textbook authors and publishers.

On the other hand, textbook publishers are confronted with several major challenges. First, they must prepare instructional materials on a subject that is evolving very rapidly. The issue of the relationship between the covenants, for instance, has not yet fully realized implications for the Church's own self-definition and therefore touches on every aspect of Christian faith. How much of the novelty of this unprecedented situation to convey in textbooks is a significant issue.

Similarly, the question of the interpretation of the Hebrew Scriptures is intricate and complex. Critically speaking, these texts should be read with a view to discerning their authors' intentions and immediate purposes. These usually have little intrinsic connection with Jesus of Nazareth. This modern approach is radically different from the Christological reading of the Old Testament that has prevailed throughout Church history. How this difference in hermeneutical perspective is to be handled, particularly in liturgical contexts, is a matter of ongoing dispute. It presents a puzzle for textbook authors who, after all, are trying to highlight the significance of Jesus Christ for their readers.

Second, as noted earlier, ecclesial documents themselves are not consistent in their pronouncements on religious education and the Jewish-Christian relationship. For example, the Vatican "Notes" declare that "Jews and Judaism should not occupy an occasional and marginal place in catechesis: Their presence there is essential and should be organically integrated."[2] Yet the United States Bishops recently issued "Guidelines for Doctrinally Sound Catechetical Materials" that enumerated eighty-seven doctrinal guidelines, only one of which referred to Jews and Judaism. Ironically, that one comment urged that "Judaism . . . not appear marginal and unimportant. . . ."[3] Faced with inconsistent and sometimes almost contradictory statements, publishers could reasonably choose simply to avoid treating these topics.

Nevertheless, many authoritative Catholic statements have insisted on the need for thorough and precise religious education on the subject of Jews and Judaism. Although there might exist some confusion during this transitional period from an ancient inimical stance to a friendly, and even symbiotic, orientation toward Judaism, such confusion does not preclude the urgent need for accurate teaching materials. To this end here are suggestions on how to improve textbook, and indeed all manner of written and verbal, presentations of Jews and Judaism.

C. Recommendations by Period and Theme Category

HEBREW SCRIPTURES

This category was handled fairly well according to this analysis, but there were problematic topics: the prophets, Jewish Messianic expectations, and the nature of the Torah.

The prophets should not be presented as though they uttered predictions about the birth, death, and raising of Jesus. Rather, their inspired utterances about the presence of God in the lives and history of the Hebrew people and about appropriate covenantal behavior should be described as *resonating* with the disciples' experience of Jesus. In reflecting back after the resurrection on the meaning of Jesus' life, his Jewish followers found in the Hebrew Scriptures words which helped to explain what it was they had experienced. In particular, the Hebrew Bible helped them come to grips with why the one they considered to be God's Anointed One had been crucified.

It is a matter of direction. The prophets were not gazing forward with precognitive vision into the future ministry of Jesus. Rather, by looking backward into their Hebraic tradition, Jesus and his Jewish friends found meaning and purpose for their activities. Thus, when treating the suffering servant songs of Second Isaiah, it is inappropriate to say that the prophet predicted what would happen to Jesus, as several series stated. Simply put, the prophet wanted to assure the Jewish exiles in Babylon that their suffering would ultimately lead to blessing for themselves and others. After discussing the prophet's message in context, the textbook could say, "When we Christians read these words, we are reminded of Jesus. He, too, suffered and out of his suffering came blessing for all." Such an approach is essentially transferring to a modern context the same dynamic which was operative in the minds of Jesus' followers. They read the words of Second Isaiah and gained insight into their horrible experience of Jesus' execution. For them, the resurrection "fulfilled," brought to fullest expression, the principle articulated by the prophet that God can bring good out of the suffering of the faithful.

Understanding the prophets in this way preserves the integrity of the original prophetic inspiration. It allows that inspiration to resonate endlessly through the centuries of human history, generating new inspired moments as both Jews and Christians seek to relate their own lives to their faith tradition. It also treasures the multiple applications of prophetic insight that are possible for Jews and Christians. Jews naturally find meaning and understanding in grappling with the prophets' words in their own day. Christians legitimately see in Christ the ultimate expression of the insights articulated by the prophets, and can use both the prophets and Christ to provide meaning in their lives.

Perceiving the post-resurrectional application of the prophets to Jesus as essentially a creative reinterpretation of the biblical tradition also has implications for how Jesus' first-century contemporaries are viewed. They had no predictive blueprint detailing who and what "the Messiah" would be. Those Jews who did not think of Jesus as God's Anointed were not stupid or malicious because they failed to perceive what the prophets had supposedly made obvious. It is only when one reads the prophets *through* the person of Jesus that resonances with his life are detected.

Thus, textbook treatments of the prophets must convey that their words have revelatory value even if not comprehended through Jesus. A Christological perspective represents only one possible "lens" through which to read prophetic words. It should rightfully be noted as an important Christian approach to the prophets, from the present era to the past tradition through Christ, but the rightful modern Jewish encounter with their own ancestral tradition independently of Christ must be respected.

Of course, this issue also relates to the subject of Jewish messianic expectations. Ideas about a coming "Messiah" are only tenuously present in the Hebrew Bible, and usually refer not to some figure in the far distant future but to an individual in the writers' present or imminent future. The diversity of Messianic thought later in the Second Temple Period was immense. It is thus not correct to describe Jews waiting and praying for "*the* Messiah" which God had promised. This is especially true during the time the Hebrew Bible was written, but is also true immediately before and during the life of Jesus.

This subject is best dealt with in a very general fashion. Jews probably prayed for God to come to Israel's aid, but the precise form that aid might take was envisioned in a wide variety of ways. Therefore, Jesus cannot be made to "fit" any particular expectation derived from the Hebrew Scriptures. What should be emphasized is that in Jesus new categories of thought had to appear. "Messiah" or "Christ" was quickly reduced from a titular status to simply part of Jesus' name because previous messianic ideas were simply not adequate to convey the disciples' experience of the Raised One. "Lord" and "Son of God" were far more important descriptions of Jesus for the apostles.

Finally, the Torah must never be alluded to as burdensome. It would be well to eliminate references to the "Law" altogether because of the negative associations that word has acquired in the Christian mind over the centuries. The Teaching of Moses or the Books of Teaching would be more accurate translations when the word Torah itself is not used, and would avoid conventional caricatures. Jewish concern to observe the Torah, whether in the past or the present, should be characterized as a laudable effort to try to understand and to do what God expects of a covenanted People. It should be stressed that Jews try to be faithful to Torah in gratitude and praise of the God who has favored them. They are not trying to draw close to a distant God or trying to earn that God's favor. Similarly, Catholics try to be faithful to the teaching of Christ in gratitude and praise of the God who has favored them through the life and death of that God's Son. They are not trying to earn God's favor.

NEW TESTAMENT

While detailed recommendations are presented in the theme categories below, the single most important action to improve New Testament topics is to provide critically sound information in the teacher's manuals and to embody critical exegetical principles in the student texts.[4]

GENERAL OR TODAY

This category was generally rated very positively in the content analysis. One suggestion is for future textbooks to use the present tense whenever possible and appropriate when discussing the Hebrew or Jewish traditions. A few series did this to great effect in the present study and multiplied the number of positive J/J references accordingly. For example, the following came from a lesson dealing with the Ten Commandments, "By observing God's laws, the Jewish people show all other peoples who they are and what they believe to be important. First and foremost, they believe in one God who is the only God, more important than anything or anyone else in life."[5]

JESUS AS A JEW

References to the Jewishness of Jesus were overwhelmingly positive. However, the impact that his heritage would have had upon Jesus was seldom explored. Indeed, to a certain extent there was a tendency to abstract Jesus from his Jewish environment by trying to stress unique aspects of his teaching. Therefore, this category could be made even more effective in promoting a favorable attitude toward Jews and Judaism by highlighting all of those aspects of the Jewish tradition that inspired Jesus and his ministry. These could include the love of God and neighbor, the covenantal responsibility for social justice, the practice of prayer with a loving Father, reverence for the Torah, and the anticipation of God's glory being revealed in human history.

JESUS AND THE JEWS

The content analysis showed this category to be troublesome. Future educational materials must avoid the perennial temptation to reduce first-century Judaism to a myopic preoccupation with legal minutiae. Current research is revealing a diverse complexity in Second Temple Judaism. Similarly, Jewish Messianic expectations, as previously noted in reference to the Hebrew Scriptures, were above all multiform and variegated. It is incorrect to describe Jewish ideas about the Messiah in a uniform or monolithic fashion or to claim that Jesus obviously met such expectations. The dynamic richness of first-century Jewish thought should be conveyed in textbooks.

Many series emphasized the disputes between Jesus and Jewish contemporaries. While such arguments undoubtedly occurred and need to be treated, it is misleading to present only areas of disagreement. Although Jesus differed with "some" Jews, the "other" Jews with whom he agreed should be discussed. If the commonalities between Jesus and various Jewish groups are not mentioned, Jesus is portrayed as outside the ambit of Second Temple Judaism, and, effectively, as non-Jewish.

Such disputes should also be depicted as part of the social milieu of the time. Jesus was one participant in an ongoing and multifaceted debate within Second Temple Judaism, sometimes echoing the thoughts of one group, and at other times criticizing the views of other groups. He was fully immersed in the tumultuous intricacies of first-century Jewish thought. It should not be implied that he stood outside or above the situation. Jesus' ministry is accurately understood only from *within* its Jewish matrix.

Care should also be taken when trying to present the novel aspects of Jesus' message. The richness of Jewish thinking should not be minimized in order to provide a more striking contrast with Jesus. For instance, while Jesus certainly stressed that love should motivate a believer's actions, this fact should not be presented in a way which suggests that other Jews had never thought of this. Claims to the effect that "no other Jew before Jesus ever imagined that . . ." should be avoided. This was the case regarding Jesus' "Abba experience," which was overstated in several series. The scanty evidence available shows that some other Jews did indeed refer to God as "Abba." Sweeping assertions to the contrary are unwarranted.

In several of the texts, the phrase "the Jewish leaders" often appeared. This is, perhaps, too ambiguous a term, especially in reference to opponents of Jesus. It tends to blur the distinctions between such divergent groups as the Pharisees and the chief priests, thereby promoting the impression that all Jewish authorities of whatever stripe and persuasion were unanimously hostile to Jesus.

It might also be recalled that in Jesus' day modern distinctions between religion, politics, and economics were non-existent. Jesus' activities had political and social implications, as well as "religious" ones. Discussions of Jesus' ministry and the views of other Jews, therefore, should not be restricted to theological issues. The impact of Jesus' message on the social situation of the time, particularly in the light of the Roman domination of the region, should be considered. This factor becomes very important in dealing with the events which led to Jesus' crucifixion.

Finally, teachers at every grade level should be informed about exegetical insights into the origins of New Testament polemic. This is especially true of the Pharisees, but it also applies to Gospel remarks about "the Jews" in general.

It is also pertinent to the presentation of the Acts of the Apostles in which Jews appear as the regular opponents of Paul and other apostles. Some series unthinkingly repeated this scenario, seemingly unaware that the author might have had apologetic or polemical interests in structuring his narrative in this manner. Since little is known about early Jewish antagonism toward the Church, it would be wise not to exaggerate it. In addition, it should be stressed that all of the relevant persons in those early years, including Paul, considered themselves to be Jews. In the first decades of the Church's history, most disputes were intra-Jewish in nature, not battles between "Jews" on the one hand and "Christians" on the other. The Jewishness of both Jesus and the early Church should not be compromised by anachronistically depicting them as outside the boundaries of Judaism.

THE PHARISEES

In most series evaluated in this study, being a Pharisee was synonymous with opposition to Jesus. Stereotypical descriptions of Pharisees as oppressive legalists and hypocrites were common. Such facile use of New Testament polemical language must cease.

To do this, several things might be done. First, it should be noted that just as there was wide diversity of thought among first-century Jews in general, so, too, was there a spectrum of views among the Pharisees. While there is little data about the details of Pharisaic beliefs, it seems from later rabbinic literature that several "schools" of Pharisees were extant in Jesus' time, among them the houses of Shammai and Hillel. The presence of Pharisaic sub-groups means that sentences beginning with words such as "the Pharisees believed that Jesus . . ." are in all probability too sweeping to be accurate. Again, even the use of the qualifying adjective "some" will be inadequate unless the views of the "others" are at some point shown.

As ecclesial documents suggest, commonalities between Jesus and the different factions of the Pharisees should be noted. Both appear to have been interested in the reform of Jewish society and both interpreted the Torah in ways which others contested. It would seem that, in general, Pharisees had ideas about a general resurrection of at least the righteous dead, and they understood God to be intimately involved in human affairs. These concepts are somewhat harmonious with Jesus' thought.

In reality, there is very little historically known about the Pharisees. This precludes both negative and positive absolute declarations about their attitudes toward Jesus, if, indeed, there even was a common "Pharisaic" opinion about him. It is probably fair to suggest that some Pharisees agreed with Jesus' interpretation some of the time (and vice versa), and other Pharisees disagreed with him at other times (and vice versa). The rather monolithic, reflexive opposition to Jesus attributed to "the scribes and the Pharisees" in the Gospels probably stems more from the disputes between post-Second Temple Judaism and the Churches of the evangelists than from encounters between Jesus and Pharisees during his ministry.

In dealing with Gospel references to the Pharisees, care must be taken not to read post-resurrectional debates back into the ministry of Jesus. This is especially true for the echoes of early Church—local synagogue disputes which reverberate throughout the New Testament, as in John 9:22, for example.

On a slightly different subject, the reasons for Paul's initial opposition to the Church are very unclear. While some might be quick to point to his Pharisaism as the cause of his antipathy, it could just as reasonably be suggested that this background aided him in his mission as Apostle to the Gentiles. In any case the events surrounding Paul's initiation into the Church should not be used as another opportunity to identify Pharisees with hostility to Jesus.

THE CRUCIFIXION

This category fared poorly on both the primary and secondary levels. The most effective ways to improve this assessment would be to utilize the insights of critical exegesis regarding the polemical and apologetic nature of the passion narratives and to incorporate what is known historically about the political and social situation at the time of Jesus' execution.

In regard to the latter, the following point cannot be repeated too often: it is impossible to reconstruct historically who initiated and oversaw the series of events which led to the crucifixion of Jesus. Clearly, both the Roman prefect, Pontius Pilate, and the high priest, Caiaphas, played leading roles. But whether the greater part was played by the Roman or priestly establishment cannot be weighed. What is known is that Caiaphas held the high priesthood only at Pilate's pleasure and that he held that position longer than anyone else during Pilate's tenure as prefect. This attests to a high degree of collaboration between the Romans and the Temple leadership.

Thus, to state, as several series did, that Jesus was killed because of the enmity of "Jewish leaders" is simplistic and misleading. First, the pervasive influence of the Roman presence is omitted. Second, the term "Jewish leaders" is imprecise and tends to implicate all Jewish authorities. Third, because of the absence of the Romans, the motives of these "Jewish leaders" were almost always restricted to the modern category of "religious" opposition, most often to the charge of blasphemy.

This leads to recommendations about the use of certain elements from the polemically and apologetically colored, post-resurrectional Gospel passion narratives. Unless the exegetical complexities of these texts are explored, at least in the teacher's manuals, it would seem best to omit any reference to blasphemy, formal trials before the Sanhedrin, crowds, Pilate seeking to obtain Jesus' release, or Barabbas. This is in accord with the general principle of the United States Bishops' Committee for Ecumenical and Relgious Affairs that

> if one cannot show beyond reasonable doubt that the particular gospel element selected or paraphrased will not be offensive or have the potential for negative influence on the audience, . . . that element cannot, in good conscience, be used.[6]

There are significant exegetical and historical reasons for deleting these incidents from textbooks. The blasphemy charge, usually expressed as shock at Jesus' claim to be divine, largely reflects post-resurrectional debates between local synagogues and churches about Jesus' status. While the blasphemy charge might well reflect a historical memory that some of the Temple establishment were offended by the authority which Jesus seemed to relegate to himself, no textbook in this analysis ever offered such a historically nuanced reading of Jesus' conversation with the high priest.

If reasons for priestly opposition to Jesus are to be discussed, there are more historically reliable motives available than the blasphemy charge. First, Jesus clearly relativized the importance of the Temple and its cult. The Gospels somewhat confusedly preserve a saying of Jesus concerning the destruction of the Temple. Such words would not endear him to the priestly aristocracy dependent upon the Temple for their social status. Second, Jesus caused some sort of disturbance in the Temple precincts, an incident which in the synoptic tradition occurred shortly before the feast of the Passover. This disturbance would not only signify a certain disrespect of the Temple in the minds of the priests, it could also portend the imminent outbreak of civil unrest on the Passover, the commemoration of freedom from oppression. Third, John 11:48-50 portrays Caiaphas as concerned about the possibility of Jesus inciting a Roman destruction of the Temple. He declares that it would be better for Jesus to die rather than for the entire people to suffer at Roman hands. This scenario fits well with what is known about Caiaphas' position in the Roman-dominated political and economic power structure, particularly during the potentially unsettled Passover season.

Again, whether the Temple leadership acted at the behest of Pilate or took action on their own initiative, or even some combination of the two, cannot be ascertained. The main point is that in any presentation of the crucifixion the Romans must figure prominently and the motives of high priest must include the political realities of the time. An exclusively "religious" description is likely to be anachronistic and inaccurate.

A formal trial of Jesus before the Jewish Sanhedrin should also not be depicted. The Gospels themselves give contradictory testimony in this regard. The nature of Jesus' encounter with the high priest following his arrest is simply unknown. More likely than not it was an informal "hearing," perhaps to determine whether Jesus' now leaderless followers posed any threat. In any case it is foolish to try to provide details about a clandestine procedure which took place under the cover of darkness. This very setting suggests a certain urgency about the proceedings. Pilate and/or Caiaphas may have felt it was necessary to get Jesus out of the way before his popularity caused problems on the Passover.

Similar reasons preclude any reference to crowds clamoring for Jesus' death, to Pilate's desire to free him, or to the prefect's ploy with Barabbas. All of these elements are so colored by the evangelists' polemical and apologetic interests that historical certitude on these most sensitive issues is simply not possible. On the contrary, Jesus' evident popularity with the people, as evidenced by the haste and secrecy with which his demise was orchestrated, the extra-biblical descriptions of Pilate which cast doubts on the Gospel depictions of him, and the almost inexplicable scene of Pilate being willing to release Barabbas, a man described as an insurrectionist, all argue for great caution in the use of these materials. Plausible reconstructions of the circumstances of Jesus' death can be offered without them.

While the preceding paragraphs explain why certain New Testament passages should be avoided when narrating the demise of Jesus, there still remains a need to provide exegetical knowledge about the passion narratives. The elements treated carefully here, such as the blasphemy charge, the crowds, and the Barabbas incident, are all prominent during Holy Week. Catholics have an annual "refresher course" on New Testament anti-Jewish rhetoric, whether they are aware of it or not.

Thus, at higher grade levels, and in all teacher's manuals, a critical discussion of the apologetic and polemical aspects of the passion narratives is absolutely imperative. Catholics need an "educated ear" so that they will hear these texts without drawing unwarranted historical or theological conclusions, conclusions that will inevitably be unfavorable to Jews.

THE RELATIONSHIP BETWEEN THE COVENANTS

This is probably the most difficult category theologically because it cuts to the heart of the modern Church's rejection of the Christian anti-Jewish tradition. The contemporary Catholic assertion that Jews remain in "a covenant of eternal love which was never revoked,"[7] is the complete reversal of a Christian view which dominated for more than a millennium. By acknowledging the existence of another People of God, a revision of Christian self-definition has been necessitated, but this process of revision is still underway.

Consequently, because of the radical novelty of this situation, the relationship between the covenants is a difficult topic for textbooks to address. Nevertheless, the idea that either Judaism or the Hebrew Scriptures were rendered obsolete by the coming of Christianity can no longer be asserted or even intimated. The intrinsic revelatory worth of the Hebrew Scriptures and the ongoing religious value of the Jewish tradition should be mentioned regularly in educational materials.

One task facing Christian theologians, in dialogue with Jews, is the articulation of the new Christian appreciation of the Jewish vocation in the world and how that divine calling might relate to the Church's vocation. This is an immense undertaking, touching on all aspects of Christian faith. While textbooks are not the proper place to attempt this endeavor, there should be no doubt in students' minds that Jews have a divinely-appointed mission in the world, just as the Church has.

D. Recommendations for Future Research

This study was conducted fifteen years after the 1976 Fisher study, which in its turn was conducted fifteen years after the 1961 Thering analysis. Perhaps another fifteen years should not elapse before this subject is revisited, but hopefully by 2006 similar research will have been undertaken. If a similar methodology is used, it is urged that two new theme categories be included: the prophets and Jewish Messianic expectations. This would provide precise data on two troublesome topics.

This content analysis evaluated standard grade-level textbook series. Lectionary-based programs were not included. Given the difficulties revealed by this study in terms of the facile use of New Testament polemic, one wonders whether such problems might be multiplied in a lectionary series. Since potentially harmful biblical verses would be encountered directly in such programs, the need for critical exegetical background would be that much greater. A content analysis of J/J references in lectionary-based textbooks would be an important venture.

Going beyond the realm of educational materials, research on the actual verbal lessons provided by teachers would be useful. It may be that without substantial teacher education, anti-Jewish stereotypes may be consciously or unconsciously perpetuated regardless of the sophistication of the textbooks that are used.

Indeed, it could be asserted that teacher's manuals alone cannot provide the level of theological knowledge which catechists must have if the modern Church's stated aim to renounce its anti-Judaic past has any hope of realization. The manuals must certainly be accurate, but they themselves are not an educational panacea. Thus, the ongoing educational growth of religion teachers is an absolute necessity. Given the present state of typical parish programs, which rely heavily on minimally-prepared volunteers, the likelihood of having an adequate number of local catechists who are acquainted with the various issues pertaining to Jewish-Christian relations is not great. Continuing research into the preparation of competent local religious educators is very much needed.

The sermons preached at worship are another important consideration. This study has shown that the way in which the New Testament is used has a determinative effect on the positivity or negativity of references to Jews and Judaism. Since polemical texts are included in the lectionary readings, a responsibility to address those texts in an exegetically sound fashion falls upon the homilist. Their words can either foster a positive and accurate knowledge of Jews and Judaism, or they can potentially undo the efforts of textbook publishers in this regard. Research into what is currently being preached from Catholic pulpits about Jews and Judaism is a necessary undertaking. The criteria used herein could be readily adapted for such purposes.

Finally, further work by theologians is necessary if Judaism is indeed to become a central element in Christian education and not continue to be relegated to a marginal or peripheral status. The development of a Christian theology which affirms and is grounded in the dynamic richness of the Hebraic and Jewish traditions of both the past and present is a new task facing the Church in these post-*Nostra Aetate* years. This creative effort is required in all theological disciplines, including Christology and ecclesiology. A theology of Christian *shalom*, denoting wholeness or right-relationship with and for Judaism, is demanded by the Church's new perspective. As such theological work progresses, the possibility of a central place for Judaism in Christian thought and education becomes more possible.

E. Conclusion

This book began by tracing the origins and features of the Christian anti-Jewish tradition. The modern repudiation of that tradition was explored through a survey of recent Catholic documentation. It was seen that all of the negative elements of the anti-Jewish tradition had been rejected in those documents.

It then noted that the same themes which had characterized the anti-Jewish tradition were found in textbooks examined by previous content analyses. Improvements were noted in more recent studies, but certain topics were persistently troublesome.

This content analysis showed that although progress had been made since the 1976 Fisher study, three topics were still being handled poorly in the texts: Jesus and the Jews, the Pharisees, and the crucifixion. It was also observed that the elements of the patristic anti-Judaic theological system had pretty much been eliminated from the textbooks. New Testament polemical themes, however, were still abundant, most often because of a failure to incorporate critical exegetical principles and insights.

This represents the unfinished agenda in the task to have religion textbooks accurately reflect and consciously promote the modern Church's rapprochement with Jews and Judaism. This effort is required not only out of honesty and justice, but also because it is necessary for the Church's own self-understanding as it seeks to be faithful to its Lord. In order for the Church to be more Christian, it must, paradoxically, become more in touch with its Jewish heritage and its Jewish covenantal brothers and sisters. It is my hope that this work will aid Catholic educators in effectively furthering such *shalom*.

Notes

[1] For example, the Vatican "Notes" (1985) repeats *Nostra Aetate's* admonition that Jews cannot be held responsible for the death of Jesus [IV,22], but NCCB, *Dramatizations of the Passion* (1988) elaborates in great detail the precise ramifications of that caveat.

[2] Vatican, "Notes" (1985) I, 2.

[3] NCCB, "Guidelines on Doctrine" (1990) I, 30.

[4] Some recommended literature in this regard, which informs the discussion of New Testament theme categories in the following pages, includes: Richard A. Horsley with John S. Hanson, *Bandits, Prophets, and Messiahs: Popular Movements at the Time of Jesus* (San Francsico: Harper & Row, 1985); Richard S. Horsley, *Jesus and the Spiral of Violence: Popular Jewish Resistance in Roman Palestine* (San Francisco: Harper & Row, 1987); Ben F. Meyer, *The Aims of Jesus* (London: SCM Press, 1979); Jacob Neusner, *Judaisms and Their Messiahs at the Turn of the Christian Era* (New

York: Cambridge Univeristy Press, 1987); Idem, *The Pharisees: Rabbinic Perspectives* (Hoboken: KTAV, 1973); Anthony J. Saldarini, *Pharisees, Scribes, and Sadducees in Palestinian Society* (Wilmington: Michael Glazier, 1988); E. P. Sanders, *Jesus and Judaism* (Philadelphia: Fortress, 1985); and Idem, *Jewish Law from Jesus to the Mishnah* (Philadelphia: Trinity, 1990).

[5] *Focus Books,* 6:57.

[6] NCCB, *Dramatizations of the Passion,* C, 1d.

[7] John Paul II, "To American Jewish Leaders" (September 11, 1987).

Supplement

The Presentation of Jews and Judaism in the *Catechism of the Catholic Church*

A. Introduction: A New Instruction from the Pontifical Biblical Commission

As this volume was in preparation for publication, two ecclesial documents impinging on Jewish-Catholic relations were promulgated. In November 1993, the Pontifical Biblical Commission released a lengthy instruction entitled "The Interpretation of the Bible in the Church."[1] The document argued that "the historical-critical method is the indispensable method for the scientific study of the meaning of ancient texts. . . . Because [the Bible has been composed by human authors], its understanding not only admits the use of this method but actually requires it."[2] It also asserted that the exegetes' task does not end with historical studies; rather, "[t]hey arrive at the true goal of their work only when they have explained the meaning of the biblical text as God's word for today."[3]

In the course of its discussion, the instruction devotes many passages to a much nuanced consideration of the nature of scriptural texts and the relationships among the various parts of the Bible. It explains that for the Church, there exists a "spiritual sense" of the scriptures:

> . . . when read, under the influence of the Holy spirit, in the context of the paschal mystery of Christ and of the new life which flows from it. This context truly exists. In it the New Testament recognizes the fulfillment of the Scriptures. It is therefore quite acceptable to reread the Scriptures in the light of this new context, which is that of life in the Spirit.[4]

Given the validity of this christological and other possible "rereadings" of the Hebrew Bible, the Commission nevertheless acknowledges that:

> The complex relationships that exist between the Jewish and Christian canons of Scripture raise many problems of interpretation. . . . Above all, the church reads the Old Testament in the light of the paschal mystery . . . This new determination of meaning has become an integral element of Christian faith. It ought not, however, mean doing away with all attempt to be consistent with that earlier canonical interpretation which preceded the Christian Passover. One must respect each stage of the history of salvation. To empty out of the Old Testament its own proper meaning would be to deprive the New of its roots in history.[5]

In other words, as suggested by the Vatican "Guidelines" and "Notes" discussed in chapter 3, the Hebrew Scriptures have an independent revelatory value which must be preserved and not simply subsumed by later Christological readings. This need for a variety of interpretative stances is noted by the Commission in its conclusion to a section concerning various usages of biblical material within the Bible itself:

> Granted that the expression of faith, such as it is found in the Scripture acknowledged by all, has had to renew itself continually in order to meet new situations, which explains the "re-readings" of many of the biblical texts, the interpretation of the Bible should likewise involve an aspect of creativity; it also ought to confront new questions so as to respond to them out of the Bible.
>
> Granted that tensions can exist in the relationship between the various texts of sacred Scripture, interpretation must necessarily show a certain pluralism. No single interpretation can exhaust the meaning of the whole, which is a symphony of many voices. Thus the interpretation of one particular text has to avoid seeking to dominate at the expense of others.[6]

It could be argued that the Church today is in the midst of one of these "new situations" with regard to the reversal of its ancient anti-Jewish theology. The instruction, then, would invite us to "reread" biblical texts in ways which affirm, rather than denigrate the Jewish tradition.

Also noted were the interpretative practices of earlier Christians:

> The allegorical interpretation of Scripture so characteristic of patristic exegesis runs the risk of being something of an embarrassment to people today. But the experience of the church expressed in this exegesis makes a contribution that is always useful (Cf. *Divino Afflante Spiritu,* 31–32; *Dei Verbum,* 23). The fathers of the church teach to read the Bible theologically, within the heart of a living tradition, with an authentic Christian spirit.[7]

This significant passage appears related to the statement in the Commission's 1983 instruction, "The Bible and Christology," that "the 'auxiliary' languages employed in the Church in the course of the centuries do not enjoy the same authority . . . as the 'referential language' of the inspired authors. . . ."[8] Thus, the Commission asserts that the value of patristic exegesis is not necessarily in its conclusions, which as was seen in chapter 2 were often formed amidst anti-Jewish debate, but in its reminder that the Bible must be read from within a living community of faith.

Specifically referring to anti-Jewish New Testament passages, the Commission stated that:

> Particular attention is necessary, according to the spirit of the Second Vatican Council (*Nostra Aetate*, 4), to avoid absolutely any actualization of certain texts of the New Testament which could provoke or reinforce unfavorable attitudes to the Jewish people. The tragic events of the past, on the contrary, impel all to keep unceasingly in mind that, according to the New Testament, the Jews remain "beloved" of God, "since the gifts and calling of God are irrevocable" (Rom 11:28-29).[9]

The instruction closes with a crucial warning: "To attempt to bypass [critical exegesis] when seeking to understand the Bible would be to create an illusion and display lack of respect for the inspired Scripture."[10]

B. *The* Catechism of the Catholic Church

Several months after the promulgation of the "Interpretation of the Bible in the Church," the official English translation of the *Catechism of the Catholic Church* became available.[11] Because of its importance as a catechetical text, it seemed appropriate to assess its presentation of Jews and Judaism by means of a content analysis using the same analytic tool, as described above in chapter 5, which had previously been applied to American textbooks. The only changes made in this supplemental analysis were that each numbered paragraph in the *Catechism* was considered a unit (as opposed to the chapter divisions used in the textbook study), and that the theme categories of "Prophets" and "Messiah" were added, as the textbook study recommended.

It will be recalled that the basis of the directional criteria used in the study were the Catholic ecclesial documents examined in chapter 3. How the authority of these materials relates to that of the *Catechism* will be discussed below.

Table 8 presents the results of the content analysis of the *Catechism*. Graph 3 compares these results with those of the U.S. textbook analysis. The latter figures represent the aggregate of the primary and secondary grade-level statistics.

Preoccupation scores between the *Catechism* and the textbooks cannot be directly compared since the two analyses used different "units." However, it is clear that the same periods and themes treated minimally in the textbooks are similarly dealt with in the *Catechism*.

The graph is especially revealing. Both curves have approximately the same shapes, meaning that both the *Catechism* and American religion textbooks were strong and weak in the same areas in their portrayal of Jews and Judaism. Both have difficulties when treating the New Testament topics of Jesus and the Jews, the Pharisees, and the Crucifixion,

Table 8
Analysis by Period and Theme
CATECHISM OF THE CATHOLIC CHURCH

Period Categories Theme Categories	Relevant Units	Preoccupation	Imbalance
1. Hebrew Scriptures	246	74%	+ .22
2. New Testament	108	32%	− .32
3. Rabbinic Judaism	0	−	−
4. Middle Ages	0	−	−
5. Reformation to Twentieth Century	0	−	−
6. Twentieth Century	0	−	−
7. General or Today	59	18%	0
1. Jesus as a Jew	16	5%	+ .69
2. Jesus and the Jews	33	10%	− .65
3. The Pharisees	14	4%	− .45
4. The Crucifixion	13	4%	− .40
5. Divine Retribution	0	−	−
6. The *Shoah*	0	−	−
7. Modern Israel	0	−	−
8. Covenant (OT/NT)	64	19%	− .36
9. Crusades/ Inquisition	0	−	−
10. Prophets	37	11%	− .07
11. Messiah	23	7%	− .75

Total Number of Units: 2865   Total Number of J/J Units: 332
Series Preoccupation: 11.6%   Series Imbalance: + .129

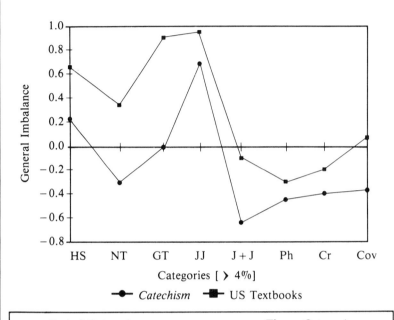

Graph 3
Catechism **Compared with U.S. Textbooks**

Categories [❭ 4%]

●— *Catechism*   ■— US Textbooks

Period Categories	*Theme Categories*

HS = Hebrew Scriptures
NT = New Testament
GT = General or Today

JJ   = Jesus as a Jew
J + J = Jesus and the Jews
Ph   = the Pharisees
Cr   = the Crucifixion
Cov = the Relationship
         between the
         Covenants

Note: Only categories with J/J preoccupations
        greater than 4 percent appear on this chart.

and also with the overall theme of the Relationship between the Covenants. Moreover, in all categories, the American materials consistently score higher than the *Catechism*.

Although the *Catechism* has a number of positive references to Jews and Judaism, most notably explicit statements that the Jewish Covenant with God is perpetual and that Jews as a people cannot be held responsible for the death of Jesus,[12] there were also a number of recurring factors that generated repeated negative assessments. These factors fall into three general areas:

1. AN UNCRITICAL USE OF THE BIBLE

As was found in the textbook study, uncritical citations of scriptural texts can easily generate demeaning remarks about Judaism. The *Catechism* did not employ the nuanced approach of the 1993 Pontifical Biblical Commission instruction, but frequently alluded to the Scriptures in an uncritical manner.

The *Catechism* grasps the "Unity of the Scriptures" and the relationship between Scripture and Tradition[13] in such a way that patristic approaches to the Hebrew Scriptures are all but normative. It will be recalled that chapter two of this book outlined how an entire anti-Jewish theological system was constructed in the patristic period because of rivalries between dynamic rabbinic Judaism and vulnerable nascent Christianity in an often hostile Roman world. It is not surprising, therefore, that the *Catechism*'s reliance on theologies rooted in patristic thought would tend to encourage negative Hebrew/Jewish references.

This is seen in the frequent usage of views such as those of Hugh of St. Victor: "All Sacred Scripture is but one book, and that one book is Christ, because all divine Scripture speaks of Christ, and all divine Scripture is fulfilled in Christ."[14] Hence, "The Law is a pedagogy and prophecy of things to come" (St. Irenaeus);[15] the "Law of the Gospel 'fulfills,' refines, surpasses, and leads the Old Law to its perfection;"[16] and "[a]ll the old Covenant prefigurations find their fulfillment in Christ Jesus."[17]

The difficulty here is that instead of understanding the Bible as "a symphony of many voices,"[18] the *Catechism* presents basically only one way for Christians to comprehend the Hebrew tradition. More than half of the J/J references in the Hebrew Scriptures category alluded to the "Old Testament" according to a preparation/accomplishment pattern. While such a model has indeed prevailed in Christian history, so has the corollary anti-Jewish theology that the modern Church is seeking to reform. The words of the U.S. Bishops' Committee on the Liturgy are pertinent: "Communicate a reverence of the Hebrew Scriptures and avoid approaches that reduce them to a propaedeutic or background for the New Testament. It is God who speaks, communicating himself through divine revelation."[19]

The *Catechism* often uses typology to present the Hebrew Bible, which tends to devalue the Hebrew tradition or reduce it to one dimension:

> At the end of the flood, whose symbolism refers to Baptism, a dove released by Noah returns with a fresh olive-tree branch in its beak as a sign that the earth was again inhabitable (cf. Gen 8:8-12). When Christ comes up from the water of his baptism, the Holy Spirit, in the form of a dove, comes down upon him and remains with him (cf. Matt 3:16 and parallels).[20]

It must be stressed that the problem is not that such typology is ever used, but that the "typed" passages are inadequately presented on their own terms first. Such omissions implicitly teach that non-christological readings of the Hebrew Bible have little worth, and, presumably, that people who would prefer such non-christological readings are lacking in faith.

This is probably why other ecclesial documents had attempted to nuance and relativize the use of typology. For instance:

> Typology, however, makes many people uneasy and is perhaps the sign of a problem unresolved. . . . Typological reading only manifests the unfathomable riches of the Old Testament, its inexhaustible content and the mystery of which it is full, and should not lead us to forget that it retains its own value as revelation that the New Testament often does no more than resume (cf. Mark 12:29-31).[21]

It is unfortunate that the *Catechism* did not follow the Vatican "Notes" line of thought and use typology with more of a view to the ultimate fulfillment of God's designs when the Age to Come, Reign of God, or Return of Christ occurs. The *Catechism* is aware of section II of the "Notes," because it rewords it without citation in paragraph 840. The incorporation of a futuristic eschatology would do much to moderate the anti-Jewish potential of a less sophisticated sort of typology. This would be a worthy goal in a Church seeking to renounce its anti-Judaic past. For instance, the Noah reference quoted above could be reworked as follows:

> Water is often used as a symbol when the Bible teaches that God will be faithful to his promises to bring his People to new life. At the end of the flood, Noah learns this lesson when a dove released by him returns with a fresh olive-tree branch in its beak as a sign that the earth was again inhabitable (cf. Gen 8:8-12). When Christ comes up from the water of his baptism, he begins a ministry that will lead to his death and resurrection to new life. The Holy Spirit, in the form

of a dove, comes down upon him and remains with him (cf. Matt 3:16 and parallels), in token that God intends to keep his promises. Through our own baptisms we Christians have passed through water and will share in the fullness of the new life of God in Christ when all of God's purposes for his Creation have been accomplished (cf. Rom 8:18-25; 1 Cor 15:28; Eph 4:13).

This type of presentation utilizes the symbolic connections between Hebrew and Christian traditions that have characterized the Church's Tradition, but it leaves room for Jews to remain part of the ongoing and unfinished story of God's deeds in human history. It also better meets the mandate of the Vatican "Guidelines" (1974) that Catholics "acquire a better understanding of whatever in the Old Testament retains its own perpetual value."[22]

Turning now to the *Catechism*'s use of New Testament texts, there were again recurring practices that produced negative assessments in terms of Jews and Judaism. Although the *Catechism* teaches that the Gospels developed in three stages (see par. 126), it never reckons with the implications of this perception. Virtually all Gospel references to Jesus are offered as "Stage 1" materials.[23]

This encourages the *Catechism* to fail to distinguish between disputes in Jesus' ministry from those that arose between the early church and synagogue decades later. This distinction was urged by the Vatican "Notes" (1985): "The Gospels are the outcome of long and complicated editorial work. . . . Certain controversies [in them] reflect Christian-Jewish relations long after the time of Jesus. To establish this is of capital importance if we wish to bring out the meaning of certain Gospel texts for the Christians of today."[24]

The failure to distinguish among the three stages of Gospel development also promotes a portrayal of disputes in Jesus' ministry as proceeding along the lines of the later theological controversies. For example: "Jesus performed acts, such as pardoning sins, that manifested him to be the Savior God himself (cf. John 5:16-18). Certain Jews, who did not recognize God made man (cf. John 1:14), saw in him only a man who made himself God (John 10:33), and judged him as a blasphemer."[25]

It is notable that all of the Scripture references in this example are to the Gospel of John. It is all but an axiom of modern Scripture scholarship that this Gospel originated more than fifty years after Jesus' death in a church community whose Jewish members had recently been expelled from the local synagogue because of their claims about Jesus' divinity.[26]

If Jesus in Stage 1 was charged with blasphemy, it was not because he claimed to be the Son of God as understood in the later Church. Rather, it would have been because he was perceived as insolently invoking God in support of teachings often critical of the Temple leadership.[27]

Since the *Catechism* does not heed the difference between these Stage 1 and 3 contexts, its readers will anachronistically conclude that Jesus' divine identity was the primary reason for his death. This shifts responsibility for his execution away from the Roman political realities of his day and onto Jewish religious blindness. It is regrettable that such facts as the High Priest's appointment by Pilate are not included in the *Catechism,* for they would provide a more historically accurate background for the crucifixion.

It might be noted in passing that the *Catechism*'s collapsing of the three stages into one also has Christological consequences in that the Jesus of Nazareth described in such as places as paragraph 590 may be difficult to relate to as a human being. This may contribute to a stylization of the conflicts that led to his death as a Jewish failure to recognize his divinity.[28]

2. THE SELF-UNDERSTANDING OF JEWS IS NOT CONSIDERED

The *Catechism* rarely if ever observes the injunction of the 1974 Vatican "Guidelines" that "Christians must therefore strive to acquire a better knowledge of the basic components of the religious tradition of Judaism; they must strive to learn by what essential traits the Jews define themselves in the light of their own religious experience."[29] The *Catechism* consistently discusses Jews and Judaism in Christian categories, thereby creating an inaccurate portrait against which to contrast Jesus or the Church.

Three examples, two concerning the Law and the other the Temple cult, will demonstrate this point. For the first example, some of the accompanying scriptural citations will be quoted in footnotes.

> Jesus, Israel's Messiah and therefore the greatest in the kingdom of heaven, was to fulfill the Law by keeping it in its all-embracing detail—according to his own words, down to "the least of these commandments" (Matt 5:19). He is in fact the only one who could keep it perfectly (cf. John 8:46).[30] On their own admission the Jews were never able to observe the Law in its entirety without violating the least of its precepts (cf. John 7:19;[31] Acts 13:38-41;[32] 15:10).[33]

> This is why every year on the Day of Atonement the children of Israel ask God's forgiveness for their transgressions of the Law. The Law indeed makes up one inseparable whole, and St. James recalls, "Whoever keeps the whole law but fails in one point has become guilty of all of it" (Jas 2:10; cf. Gal 3:10; 5:3[34]).[35]

> The Law entrusted to Israel never sufficed to justify those subject to it; it even became the instrument of "lust" (cf. Rom 7:7). The gap between wanting and doing points to the conflict between God's Law which is the "law of my mind," and another law "making me cap-

tive to the law of sin which dwells in my members'' (Rom 7:23; cf. 7:10).[36]

Instituted to proclaim the Word of God and to restore communion with God by sacrifices and prayer (cf. Mal 2:7-9), this [Hebrew] priesthood nevertheless remains powerless to bring about salvation, needing to repeat its sacrifices ceaselessly and being unable to achieve a definitive sanctification, which only the sacrifice of Christ would accomplish (cf. Heb 5:3; 7:27; 10:1-4).[37]

In each of these three examples, the Hebrew tradition is evaluated according to Christian categories and concerns. In the first, the fact that a Jew is expected to treat the entire Torah as equally deserving of observance leads to the conclusion that no one could possibly keep the Torah. Highly polemical New Testament[!] passages are strung together as evidence that ''on their own admission'' Jews recognize this failure. (Paul's claim in Phil 3:6 that ''as to righteousness under the law [he is] blameless'' is not considered.) Failure to keep the whole law perfectly has never been an enormous problem in the Hebrew or Jewish traditions: it was expected the human beings would err. Forgiveness could be obtained through Temple or prayer, and motivation to try to follow the Torah was more important than actual performance in any case.[38]

In the second example, the failure of the Law to ''justify'' is stated. Justification is a Pauline theological term, of particular importance to his mission as apostle to the pagan Gentiles. The Law as a vehicle for justification is not a topic in the Hebrew/Jewish tradition. The Torah is to be followed out of gratitude to the God who has called Israel into being as the Chosen People beginning with the Exodus.[39] To fault the Law as having failed to justify makes little sense when the People observing that Law have never understood it that way.

Finally, example three faults Temple sacrifices for not providing ''salvation,'' using the Letter to the Hebrews as its primary foundation. Once more, salvation is a Christian term. It is not something pursued in the Hebrew or Jewish tradition. The Temple sought not to ''save,'' but to praise and sanctify, which are very different purposes.[40]

In all these cases, the Hebrew/Jewish heritage has been found wanting according to standards foreign to itself in order that the Church's superiority may be demonstrated. Such a practice will do little to achieve the aim of the 1985 Vatican ''Notes'' to remedy the ''painful ignorance of the history and traditions of Judaism, of which only negative aspects and often caricature seem to form part of the stock ideas of many Christians.''[41]

3. CARELESS DENIGRATING REMARKS

Scattered through the *Catechism* were unnecessary comments that served to belittle Judaism. For instance, "Abraham is the model of such obedience offered by Sacred Scripture. The Virgin Mary is its most perfect embodiment";[42] or "The Letter to the Hebrews proclaims its eulogy of the exemplary faith of the ancestors who 'received divine approval' (Heb 11:2, 39). Yet 'God had foreseen something better for us': the grace of believing in his Son Jesus, 'the pioneer and perfecter of our faith' (Heb 11:40; 12:2)";[43] or "Although to some extent the People of God in the Old Testament had tried to understand the pathos of the human condition in the light of the history of the fall narrated in Genesis, they could not grasp this story's ultimate meaning, which is revealed only in the light of the death and Resurrection of Jesus Christ."[44]

None of these statements required this sort of negative "spin" in order to present the Christian message. Mary could be presented as a true daughter of Abraham who marvelously embodied his obedience to God. The supersessionist tone of Hebrews could be avoided by drawing attention to how the model of the patriarchs inspired Christian authors over the centuries. Humanity's long and continuing grappling with the mystery of suffering could have been supplemented here by a reference to the Shoah.

On a slightly different note, although the *Catechism* strangely never cited any post-Vatican II ecclesial document concerning Jews and Judaism or biblical interpretation, it did occasionally paraphrase them, though sometimes with surprising twists. For example, paragraph 840 presents a version of the 1985 Vatican "Notes," but it goes its own way:

Vatican "Notes" (1985)
Furthermore, in underlining the eschatological dimension of Christianity, we shall reach a greater awareness that the people of God of the Old and New Testaments are tending towards a like end in the future: the coming or the return of the messiah—even if they start from two different points of view. It is more clearly understood that the person of the Messiah is not only a point of division for the people of God but also a point of convergence. Thus it can be said that Jews and Christians meet in a comparable hope, founded on the same promises made to Abraham (cf. Gen 12:1-3; Heb 6:13-18).[45] [The text goes on to speak about Jews and Christians working together to "prepare the world for the coming of the Messiah."[46]]

Catechism (1994)
And when one considers the future, God's People of the Old Covenant and the new People of God tend towards similar goals: expectation of the coming (or the return) of the Messiah. But one awaits the return of the Messiah who died and rose from the dead and is recognized as Lord and Son of God; the other awaits the coming of a Mes-

siah, whose features remain hidden till the end of time; and the latter waiting is accompanied by the drama of not knowing or of misunderstanding Christ Jesus.[47]

The inadequacy of the latter formulation for interfaith amity is shown by the fact that whereas the "Notes" were able to hope that young Christians would be taught "in a practical way to cooperate with Jews, going beyond simple dialogues,"[48] such a sentiment never appears anywhere in the *Catechism*. One wonders why a *Catechism* section on the Church's relationship to Judaism had to end on such a negative note.

Occasionally, the *Catechism* at least flirted with a violation of a principle contained in a post-*Nostra Aetate* document. Consider paragraph 1972:

> The New Law is a *law of love* because it makes us act out of love infused by the Holy Spirit, rather than from fear; a *law of grace,* because it confers the strength of grace to act [denied of the "Old Law" in par. 1963], by means of faith and sacraments; a *law of freedom*, because it sets us free from the ritual and juridical observances of the Old Law, inclines us to act spontaneously by the prompting of charity, and, finally, lets us pass from the condition of a servant who "does not know what his master is doing" to that of a friend of Christ—"For all that I have heard from my Father I have made known to you"—or even to the status of son and heir (John 15:15; cf. Jas 1:25; 2:12; Gal 4:1-7, 21-31; Rom 8:15).[49]

Without careful instruction it is hard to know how a reader of this paragraph would avoid embracing the stereotype condemned by the Vatican "Guidelines": "The Old Testament and the Jewish tradition founded upon it must not be set against the New Testament in such a way that the former seems to constitute a religion of only justice, fear, and legalism, with no appeal to the love of God and neighbor (cf. Deut 6:5; Lev 19:18; Matt 22:34-40)."[50]

Finally, paragraph 674 in the *Catechism* is very disturbing:

> The glorious Messiah's coming is suspended at every moment of history until his recognition by "all Israel," for "a hardening has come upon part of Israel" in their "unbelief" toward Jesus (Rom 11:20-26; cf. Matt 23:39). St. Peter says to the Jews of Jerusalem after Pentecost: "Repent therefore, and turn again, that your sins may be blotted out, that times of refreshing may come from the presence of the Lord, and that he may send the Christ appointed for you, Jesus, whom heaven must receive until the time for establishing all that God spoke by the mouth of his holy prophets from of old" (Acts 3:19-21). St. Paul echoes him: "For if their rejection means the reconciliation of the world, what will their acceptance mean but life from the dead?"

(Rom 11:15). The "full inclusion" of the Jews in the Messiah's salvation, in the wake of "the full number of the gentiles" (Rom 11:12, 25; cf. Luke 21:24), will enable the People of God to achieve "the measure of the stature of the fullness of Christ," in which "God may be all in all" (Eph 4:13; 1 Cor 15:28).[51]

Probably motivated by a praiseworthy effort to teach that Israel is destined for inclusion in God's Reign, the phrasing of this paragraph seems to be saying that Christ would have returned by now if only the Jews would believe! The exegetical mistake that produces this confusion is the use of Paul's ideas in Romans without recognizing that his eschatological expectations are different from our own. He anticipates the return of Jesus very soon and so can think of a brief, temporary exclusion of Israel from God's plans until all the Gentiles can be saved. We do not share Paul's expectation about Jesus' return, and so, two thousand years later, his temporary exclusion idea doesn't really work for us.[52]

The words of Pope John Paul II cited in the 1985 Vatican "Notes" come to mind here: " 'Work that is of poor quality or lacking in precision would be extremely detrimental' to Judaeo-Christian dialogue (John Paul II, speech of March 6, 1982). But it would be above all detrimental—since we are talking about teaching and education—to Christian identity" (ibid.).[53]

In sum, the *Catechism*'s relatively poor evaluation as compared with American religion textbooks stemmed from its often uncritical use of the Bible, its failure to describe Judaism on its own terms, and a certain carelessness of expression.

While not affecting the outcome of the statistical analysis, there were also notable gaps and lost opportunities in the *Catechism*. Among the topics that could have been treated but were not are: (1) the ongoing history and contributions of Judaism after the destruction of the Temple in 70 C.E.;[54] (2) the nature of the Jewish People's ongoing vocation in the world;[55] (3) the significance of the Shoah for both Christians and Jews;[56] (4) the importance of the Land and modern state of Israel for Jews;[57] and (5) the importance and benefits of Jewish and Catholic dialogue.[58]

C. Conclusion

At the end of chapter 3 earlier in this volume, it was noted that all recent Catholic ecclesial documents were not equally sensitive or aware of matters relating to the Jewish and Catholic relationship. This was seen as partly the result of the amazing reform in Church thought about Judaism inaugurated by *Nostra Aetate*. It was suggested that those documents which directly address topics relevant to the Church's understanding of

Judaism be given greater weight than instructions which impinge on them only indirectly in the process of discussing other topics.

This principle would also seem to be appropriate in the case of the *Catechism*, which "is intended to serve 'as a point of reference for the catechisms or compedia that are composed in the various countries.' ''[59] As a work primarily intended for bishops and "redactors of catechisms,"[60] it "is not intended to replace the local catechisms duly approved by the ecclesiastical authorities."[61] It is not envisioned to be used as a catechetical textbook, but as a reference work.

Therefore, local applications of the *Catechism* should always pursue the goal of meeting local needs and situations. Because the Church in the United States is a neighbor of the largest community of Jews in the world, it follows that there is a particular urgency here to employ the *Catechism* through the mediation of the developing post-*Nostra Aetate* documentary tradition, in both its universal (or Vatican) and local (or National [U.S.] Conference of Catholic Bishops) expressions.[62] This is all the more true when it is realized that the documents sparked by *Nostra Aetate* are seeking to implement a declaration of an ecumenical council, the highest ecclesial authority in the Roman Catholic tradition. In other words, the documentary legacy inspired by *Nostra Aetate*, which more fully articulates the growing theological rapprochement between Catholics and Jews than does the *Catechism,* should be used to supplement and refine catechesis on matters pertinent to the presentation of Jews and Judaism.

The directional criteria used to assess Catholic teaching materials in this regard, which are detailed in chapter 3 of this volume, are a distillation of this *Nostra Aetate* legacy. Together with the recommendations in chapter 7, they may prove useful to pastors, preachers, religious educators, and other ministers who are concerned about the Catholic and Jewish relationship and who wish to enhance their use of the *Catechism*. Textbook publishers and authors should find in them a helpful guide in maintaining and improving upon the relatively high ratings indicated by this book's textbook content analysis.

By increasing Catholic awareness of the effects of our teaching and theology on popular attitudes and behaviors toward the Jewish people and tradition, we will become more knowledgable about our own faith, be better witnesses to the Good News, and be more dedicated to education for *shalom*.

Notre Dame College
Manchester, N.H.
August 1994

Notes

[1] See *Origins* 23/29 (January 6, 1994) 497–524.

[2] Ibid., I,A.

[3] Ibid., III,C,1.

[4] Ibid., II,B,2.

[5] Ibid., I,C,1. The instruction expresses a similar idea about a related matter: "Jewish biblical scholarship in all its richness, from its origins in antiquity down to the present day, is an asset of highest value for the exegesis of both Testaments, provided. . . . [it is recognized that Jewish and Christian traditions have] two separate contexts, which for all their points of contact and similarity are in fact radically diverse" [I,C,2].

[6] Ibid., III,A,3. This conclusion recalls the statement in the Vatican "Notes" (1985) that the Hebrew Bible "retains its own value as revelation that the New Testament often does no more than resume" [II,7].

[7] Ibid., III,B,2.

[8] Idem, "The Bible and Christology," 1.2.1.

[9] Idem, "The Interpretation of the Bible in the Church" (1993) IV,A,3.

[10] Ibid., Conclusion.

[11] *Catechism of the Catholic Church* (Washington: United States Catholic Conference, 1994).

[12] See *Catechism,* pars. 207, 220, 839, 992, 2171 concerning the covenant; pars. 597–598 regarding the crucifixion.

[13] N.B., e.g., *Catechism,* pars. 78, 95, 128–130, 289, 1008.

[14] *Catechism*, par. 134, an "In Brief" summary statement.

[15] Ibid., par. 1967.

[16] Ibid., par. 1967.

[17] Ibid., par. 1223.

[18] Pontifical Biblical Commission, "Interpretation of the Bible in the Church" (1993) III,A,3.

[19] NCCB, *God's Mercy Endures Forever* (1988) 31c. See also 31a, b. In addition, consult Vatican "Guidelines" (1974) II; Vatican "Notes" (1985) II,3,7; and Pontifical Biblical Commission, "Interpretation of the Bible in the Church" (1993) III,B,2, quoted above.

[20] *Catechism,* par. 701.

[21] Vatican, "Notes" (1985) II,3,7; see also II,6,8-11; and NCCB, *God's Mercy Endures Forever* (1988) 11. In addition, refer to the Pontifical Biblical Commission, "Interpretation of the Bible in the Church" (1993) III,B,2, quoted above.

[22] Vatican, "Guidelines" (1974) II.

[23] Contrary to the warning in Pontifical Biblical Commission, "The Bible and Christology" (1984): "It can happen that the historical character of the texts is too easily admitted when . . . [these] might have had a theological purpose according to a literary convention of the time. Or the word-for-word authenticity of certain sayings attributed to Jesus is again too easily admitted" (1.2.1).

[24] Vatican, "Notes" (1985) IV,21,a.

[25] *Catechism*, #594, an "In Brief" summary statement.

[26] See, e.g., the remarks in two magisterial commentaries: Brown, *John*, LXX–LXXIII, 380; Schackenburg, *John,* I:165-167; II:250. N.B. *Catechism* par. 596, in which the notion that "[t]he Pharisees threatened to excommunicate his followers (John 11:48-50)" is set in a Stage 1 context!

[27] For an exhaustive treatment of the meaning of the blasphemy charge in the trial narratives, see the recently published Raymond E. Brown, *The Death of the Messiah* (New York: Doubleday, 1994) 480–483, 520–527, 530–547. Among other things, Brown states that "it is unlikely that this title [Son of God] was used of Jesus during his lifetime either by himself or by his followers" (p. 535), and that ". . . without doubt that [Sanhedrin] trial is phrased in the light of later Christian experience. In it we are hearing how Christians in the last third of the 1st cent. understood Jewish adversaries who considered Christian claims about Jesus to be blasphemous" (544). He concludes that blasphemy in Stage 1 centered on Jesus' behavior which ". . . could well have appeared religiously arrogant or presumptuous (and thus blasphemous) . . ." (545).

[28] N.B. *Catechism,* par. 443.

[29] Vatican "Guidelines" (1974) Preamble.

[30] "Which of you convicts me of sin? If I tell the truth why do you not believe me?"

[31] "Did not Moses give you the law? Yet none of you keeps the law. Why are you looking for an opportunity to kill me?"

[32] [Vs. 39:] ". . . by this Jesus everyone who believes is set free from all those sins from which you could not be freed by the law of Moses."

[33] "Now therefore why are you putting God to the test by placing on the neck of the disciples a yoke that neither we nor our ancestors have been able to bear?"

[34] "Once again I testify to every man who lets himself be circumcised that he is obliged to obey the entire law."

[35] *Catechism,* par. 578.

[36] Ibid., par. 2542.

[37] Ibid., par. 1540.

[38] See, e.g., Sanders, *Paul and Palestinian Judaism,* 93, 137.

[39] E.g., ibid., 422; Idem, *Judaism: Practice and Belief, 63 BCE–66 CE* (Philadelphia: Trinity Press, 1992) 241-278.

[40] E.g, see Sanders, *Judaism: Practice and Belief,* 251-257; Neusner, *Judaism in the Beginning of Christianity,* 35-44.

[41] Vatican, "Notes" (1985) Conclusion, 27.

[42] *Catechism,* par. 144.

[43] Ibid., par. 147.

[44] Ibid., par. 388.

[45] Vatican, "Notes" (1985) II,10.

[46] Ibid., II,11.

[47] *Catechism,* par. 840.

[48] Vatican, "Notes" (1985) II,11.

[49] *Catechism,* par. 1972. Italics in original. N.B. also par. 579 which has related difficulties.

[50] Vatican, "Guidelines" (1974) III.

[51] *Catechism,* par. 674.

[52] Those interested in this subject might consult my "Romans 9–11 and Modern Jewish-Catholic Relations: Reflections in Honor of the 30th Anniversary of *Nostra*

Aetate," to be printed in the September and October 1995 issues of *PACE (Professional Approaches in Christian Education).*

[53] Vatican, "Notes" (1985) I,6.

[54] N.B. Vatican, "Guidelines" (1974) III; Vatican, "Notes" (1985) VI,25.

[55] Considered by John Paul II, "To the Jews in Warsaw" (June 14, 1987).

[56] Vatican, "Notes" (1985) VI,25.

[57] Ibid.

[58] Vatican Council II, *Nostra Aetate,* 4; Vatican, "Guidelines" (1974).

[59] *Catechism,* par. 11, citing the *Final Report* of the 1985 Extraordinary Synod of Bishops, IIB a,4.

[60] Ibid., par. 12.

[61] John Paul II, *Fidei Depositum* (1992) 3.

[62] This is not meant to suggest that a concern for accuracy in Catholic teaching on Jews and Judaism should not be present elsewhere in the world. N.B. Vatican, "Guidelines" (1974) Conclusion: "[E]ven in areas where no Jewish communities exist, this remains an important problem." However, Catholics in the United States, because of our unique circumstances, have a special opportunity and responsibility in this regard, and can provide an invaluable service to the universal Church.

Appendix 1:

Definitions of Terms and Categories

[Based on Fisher, "Content Analysis," 38–39, 124–127.]

J/J References are statements clearly referring to Jews and Judaism or likely to be understood as such by the reader.

    For example, statements concerning "the Synagogue," "Israel," "the Israelites" (or "Israelis"), "Zionists," etc., all clearly refer to Jews and/or Judaism and were scored as such in this study. References to many specific theological and biblical concepts, such as "People of God," "Children of Abraham," etc., were judged according to context. A statement such as "The People of God were taken into exile in Babylonia in 586 B.C.E.," for example, would plainly indicate a treatment of Jews and Judaism, while a statement such as, "The Church is the People of God" would not. References to such well-known Jewish works and figures as the Talmud or Moses Maimonides would likewise be scored as treating of Jews and Judaism, but references to lesser-known Jewish figures, such as Victor Frankl, would need to be clearly identified as "Jewish" in the text or accompanying manual for the reference to be scored as a J/J reference.

Anti-Judaism is hostile speech or action against Jews or Judaism primarily for theological or religious motives. Thus, asserting that Jerusalem was destroyed in 70 C.E. because of a Jewish rejection of Jesus is an example of anti-Jewish thought.

Anti-Semitism is hostile speech or action against Jews or Judaism primarily on the basis of modern racial ideologies and/or economic stereotyping. Thus, asserting that the presence of Jews would corrupt society or that Jews control the banking industry would be instances

153

of anti-Semitic thought. This and the previous term are often used interchangably in textbooks.

Historical Period Categories

Hebrew Scriptures   While most textbooks typically use the term "Old Testament" to refer to the period of Hebrew/Israelite/Jewish history up to the birth of Jesus, the expression can carry negative connotations. Though the term as such has not been scored directionally in the study, the more neutral "Hebrew Scriptures" is used herein.

New Testament covers the period from the birth of Christ to the close of the Apostolic Age.

Rabbinic Judaism   covers the period of the writing of the Mishnah (200 C.E.) through the Bavli (c. 600 C.E.).

Middle Ages   includes the Crusades and here used as commonly understood in European History (sixth–fifteenth centuries).

Reformation   covers the sixteenth century to the twentieth century.

Twentieth Century   includes references to the *Shoah,* the modern State of Israel, and the Second Vatican Council.

General or Today   includes statements referring to Jews and Judaism in general, i.e., without a specific temporal relationship, as well as statements referring to contemporary Jews and Judaism. Non-period specific allusions to the Judaic origins of Christian beliefs or practices are also included.

Theme Categories

Jesus as a Jew includes references stating or implying the "Jewishness" of Jesus, his disciples, and the early Church.

Jesus and the Jews   the relationship between Jesus and Jewish contemporaries or between Jesus and the Jewish tradition. Comments about the relationship between Jewish apostles (e.g., Paul) and their Jewish contemporaries are also included. Also contained herein, on the negative pole, would be allegations of the supposed "Jewish rejection" of Jesus as Messiah, or of Jesus' "rejection" of Judaism.

Pharisees   specific references to the Pharisees as a religious movement or as individuals.

Crucifixion   includes the trial and death of Jesus, and surrounding events. The category would also subsume all statements regarding who should bear the historical "blame" for Jesus' death.

Divine Retribution   includes all statements referring to the historical plight of the Jews as "punishment" by God visited on the Chosen People for their alleged rejection of Jesus.

Shoah   the genocide against six million Jews in Nazi Germany, usually alluded to in the textbooks as the "Holocaust."

Modern Israel   includes references to Israeli history, songs, politics, etc., or to the modern State of Israel in general.

Relationship Between the Covenants   refers to the historical and theological relationship of Judaism and Christianity, the relative status of the Hebrew Scriptures and the New Testament, the place of Judaism in the Divine Plan of Salvation, or, especially, to the continued covenantal status of the Jewish people.

Crusades/ Inquisition   comments on any of the various Crusades or on the Roman or Spanish Inquisitions in which Jews are also mentioned. References to the Crusades, for instance, with no allusions to Jews would not be included.

Appendix 2

Bibliography

A. Ecclesial Documents

Abbott, Walter M., ed. *The Documents of Vatican II*. New York: Guild Press, 1966.

Bishops' Committee for Ecumenical and Interreligious Affairs, National Conference of Catholic Bishops. *Criteria for the Evaluation of Dramatizations of the Passion*. Washington: United States Catholic Conference, 1988.

Bishops' Committee on the Liturgy, National Conference of Catholic Bishops. *God's Mercy Endures Forever: Guidelines on the Presentation of Jews and Judaism in Catholic Preaching*. Washington: United States Catholic Conference, 1988.

Bishops' Conferences of the German Federal Republic, of Austria, and of Berlin. "Accepting the Burden of History." *SIDIC* 22/1-2 (1989) 36-42.

Catholic-Jewish Respect Life Committee, Los Angeles Archdiocese and the American Jewish Committee. "The Holocaust: At the Edge of Comprehension." *Origins* 19/37 (February 15, 1990) 601-604.

Croner, Helga, ed. *More Stepping Stones to Jewish-Christian Relations: An Unabridged Collection of Christian Documents, 1975-1983*. New York/Mahwah: Paulist Press/Stimulus Books, 1985.

_____. *Stepping Stones to Further Jewish-Christian Relations: An Unabridged Collection of Christian Documents*. New York/London: Stimulus Books, 1977.

Fisher, Eugene J., and Leon Klenicki, eds. *Pope John Paul II on Jews and Judaism: 1979-1986*. Washington: United States Catholic Conference, 1987.

Fitzmyer, Joseph A. *Scripture and Christology: A Statement of the Biblical Commission with a Commentary*. New York/Mahwah: Paulist Press, 1986.

Flannery, Austin, ed. *Vatican Council II: The Conciliar and Post-Conciliar Documents*. Northport, N.Y.: Costello Publishing, 1975.

_____. *Vatican Council II: More Post-Conciliar Documents*. Vol. 2. Northport, N.Y.: Costello Publishing, 1982.

International Catholic-Jewish Liaison Committee, sponsored by the Vatican Commission for Religious Relations with the Jews and the International Jewish Committee on Interreligious Consultations. "Uprooting Anti-Semitism." *Origins* 20/15 (September 20, 1990) 233-236.

John Paul II, Pope. "Address to American Jewish Leaders." *Origins* 17/15 (September 24, 1987) 241-243.

_____. "Apostolic Letter on the 50th Anniversary of the Beginning of World War II." *Origins* 19/15 (September 14, 1989) 253-256.

_____. "Letter to Archbishop John May." *Origins* 17/12 (September 3, 1987) 181-183.

_____. *John Paul II on Jews and Judaism, 1979-1986.* Edited by Eugene J. Fisher and Leon Klenicki. Washington: United States Catholic Conference, 1987.

_____. "To a Delegation of the American Jewish Committee." *Origins* 19/43 (March 29, 1990) 714-716.

_____. "To European Bishops Preparing for the 1991 European Synod of Bishops." *Origins* 20/6 (June 21, 1990) 90-93.

_____. "To the Jews in Warsaw." *Origins* 17/13 (September 10, 1987) 200.

_____. "To the Jewish Community in Warsaw." *Origins* 21/6 (June 20, 1991) 100-101.

National Conference of Catholic Bishops. "Guidelines on Doctrine for Catechetical Materials." *Origins* 20/27 (December 13, 1990) 429-436.

_____. "Toward Peace in the Middle East: Perspectives, Principles, and Hopes." *Origins* 19/25 (November 23, 1989) 401-413.

Polish Bishops. "Pastoral Letter on Jewish-Catholic Relations." *Origins* 20/36 (February 14, 1991) 593-595.

Pontifical Biblical Commission. "Instruction on the Historical Truth of the Gospels." In *A Christological Catechism: New Testament Answers* by Joseph A. Fitzmyer, 131-142. New York/Ramsey: Paulist Press, 1982.

Pontifical Council on Interreligious Dialogue. "Dialogue and Proclamation." *Origins* 21/8 (July 4, 1991) 121-135.

Pontifical Justice and Peace Commission. "The Church and Racism: Toward a More Fraternal Society." *Origins* 18/37 (February 23, 1989) 613-626.

Secretariat for Catholic-Jewish Relations, Bishops' Committee on Ecumenical and Interreligious Affairs, National Conference of Catholic Bishops. *Guidelines for Catholic-Jewish Relations.* 1985 Revision. Washington: United States Catholic Conference, 1985.

_____. Adult Education Section, the Education Department, United States Catholic Conference; and Interfaith Affairs Department, Anti-Defamation League of B'nai B'rith. *Within Context: Guidelines for the Catechetical Presentation of Jews and Judaism in the New Testament.* Morristown, N.J.: Silver Burdett & Ginn, 1987.

Ratzinger, Joseph Cardinal. "Report to the 1990 Synod of Bishops on the Universal Catechism." *Origins* 20/22 (November 8, 1990) 356-359.

Vatican Commission for Religious Relations with the Jews, "Notes on the Correct Way to Present Jews and Judaism in Preaching and Catechesis in the Roman Catholic Church." *Origins* 15/7 (July 4, 1985) 102-107.

Vatican Congregation for Catholic Education. "Instruction on the Study of the Fathers of the Church in the Formation of Priests." *Origins* 19/34 (January 25, 1990) 549–561.

World Council of Churches and Member Churches. *The Theology of the Churches and the Jewish People: Statements by the World Council of Churches and Its Member Churches.* Geneva: WCC Publications, 1988.

B. Bible and Theology

Achtemeier, Paul J. *Mark.* Proclamation Commentaries. Philadelphia: Fortress Press, 1975.

_____. *The Quest for Unity in the New Testament Church.* Philadelphia: Fortress Press, 1987.

Attridge, Harold W. *Hebrews.* Hermeneia Commentary. Philadelphia: Fortress Press, 1989.

Augustine. *De Catechizandis Rudibus.* Translated by Joseph Patrick Christopher. Washington: The Catholic University of America, 1926.

Best, Ernest. *Disciples and Discipleship: Studies in the Gospel According to Mark.* Edinburgh: T & T Clark, 1986.

Boomershine, Thomas E. "Intentionality and the Ethics of Interpretation: The Pilate Trial in Mark and Christian Anti-Semitism." Paper read at the annual meeting of the Society of Biblical Literature, Boston, December 7, 1987.

Borowitz, Eugene B. *Contemporary Christologies: A Jewish Response.* New York/Ramsey: Paulist Press, 1980.

Boys, Mary C. *Biblical Interpretation in Religious Education.* Birmingham, Ala.: Religious Education Press, 1980.

Brawley, Robert L. *Luke-Acts and the Jews: Conflict, Apology, and Conciliation.* Atlanta: Scholars Press, 1987.

Brooks, Roger. *The Spirit of the Ten Commandments: Shattering the Myth of Rabbinic Legalism.* San Francisco: Harper & Row, 1990.

Brown, Raymond E. *Biblical Exegesis and Church Doctrine.* New York/Mahwah: Paulist Press, 1985.

_____. *The Gospel According to John I-XII.* Anchor Bible, 29. Garden City, N.Y.: Doubleday, 1966.

_____. *The Gospel According to John XIII-XXI.* Anchor Bible, 29a. Garden City, N.Y.: Doubleday, 1970.

_____. *The Birth of the Messiah: A Commentary on the Infancy Narratives in Matthew and Luke.* Garden City, N.Y.: Image Books, 1977.

_____. *The Churches the Apostles Left Behind.* New York/ Mahwah: Paulist Press, 1984.

_____. *The Community of the Beloved Disciple: The Life, Loves, and Hates of an Individual Church in New Testament Times.* New York/Ramsey: Paulist Press, 1979.

_____ and John P. Meier. *Antioch and Rome: New Testament Cradles of Catholic Christianity.* New York/ Ramsey: Paulist Press, 1983.

_____, Joseph A. Fitzmyer, and Roland E. Murphy. *The New Jerome Biblical Commentary.* Englewood Cliffs, N.J.: Prentice Hall, 1990.

Brueggemann, Walter. *Genesis.* Interpretation Commentary. Atlanta: John Knox Press, 1982.

Buchanan, George Wesley. *To the Hebrews.* Anchor Bible, 36. Garden City, N.Y.: Doubleday, 1972.

Burghardt, Walter J. "On Early Christian Exegesis." *Theological Studies* 9/1: (1950) 78–116.

Callan, Terrence. *Forgetting the Root: The Emergence of Christianity from Judaism.* New York/Mahwah: Paulist Press, 1986.

Charlesworth, James A. *Jesus Within Judaism: New Light From Exciting Archaeological Discoveries.* New York: Doubleday, 1988.

Cohen, Arthur A. *The Tremendum: A Theological Interpretation of the Holocaust.* New York: Crossroad, 1988.

Collins, John J. *Between Athens and Jerusalem: Jewish Identity in the Hellenistic Diaspora.* New York: Crossroad, 1986.

Conzelmann, Hans. *Acts of the Apostles.* Hermeneia Commentaries. Philadelphia: Fortress Press, 1987.

Coote, Robert B. and David Robert Ord. *The Bible's First History: From Eden to the Court of David with the Yahwist.* Philadelphia: Fortress Press, 1989.

Cope, O. Lamar. *Matthew: A Scribe Trained for the Kingdom of Heaven.* Washington: Catholic Biblical Association of America, 1976.

Cunningham, Philip A. *Jesus and the Evangelists: The Ministry of Jesus in the Synoptic Gospels.* Lanham, Md.: University Press of America, 1993.

_____. *Jewish Apostle to the Gentiles: Paul as He Saw Himself.* Mystic, Conn.: Twenty-Third Publications, 1986.

Davies, W. D. *Jewish and Pauline Studies.* Philadelphia: Fortress Press, 1984.

_____. *Paul and Rabbinic Judaism.* 3rd ed. Philadelphia: Fortress Press, 1970.

Deferrari, Roy J., trans. *Saint Cyprian: Treatises.* New York: Fathers of the Church, Inc., 1958.

Donfried, Karl P., ed. *The Romans Debate.* Minneapolis: Augsburg Press, 1977.

Efroymson, David P., Eugene J. Fisher, Leon Klenicki, eds., *Within Context: Essays on Jews and Judaism in the New Testament.* Collegeville: The Liturgical Press, 1993.

Fackenheim, Emil L. *To Mend the World: Foundations of Future Jewish Thought.* New York: Schocken Books, 1982.

Falk, Harvey. *Jesus the Pharisee: A New Look at the Jewishness of Jesus.* New York/Mahwah: Paulist Press, 1985.

Feldman, Louis H. "Proselytes and 'Sympathizers' in the Light of the New Inscriptions from Aphrodisias." *Revue des Etudes Juives* 148 (March–April, 1989) 265–305.

Fitzmyer, Joseph A. *The Gospel According to Luke I-IX.* Anchor Bible, 28. Garden City, N.Y.: Doubleday, 1981.

_____. *The Gospel According to Luke X-XXIV.* Anchor Bible, 28a. Garden City, N.Y.: Doubleday, 1983.

_____. *Luke the Theologian: Aspects of His Teaching.* New York/Mahwah: Paulist Press, 1989.

_____. *Paul and His Theology: A Brief Sketch.* Englewood Cliffs, N.J.: Prentice Hall, 1989.

————. *A Christological Catechism: New Testament Answers.* New York/Ramsey: Paulist Press, 1981.

Fredriksen, Paula. *From Jesus to Christ: The Origins of the New Testament Images of Jesus.* New Haven: Yale University Press, 1988.

Friedman, Richard Elliott. *The Exile and Biblical Narrative: The Formation of the Deuteronomistic and Priestly Works.* Chico, Calif.: Scholars Press, 1981.

Gaston, Lloyd. *Paul and the Torah.* Vancouver: University of British Columbia Press, 1987.

Good, R.S. "Jesus, Protagonist of the Old, in Lk. 5:33-39." *Novum Testamentum.* 25/1 (1983) 19-36.

Green, Arthur, ed. *Jewish Spirituality from the Bible Through the Middle Ages.* New York: Crossroad, 1987.

————. *Jewish Spirituality from the Sixteenth Century Revival to the Present.* New York: Crossroad, 1987.

Haenchen, Ernst. *The Acts of the Apostles: A Commentary.* Philadelphia: Westminster, 1971.

Hare, Douglas R. A. *The Theme of Jewish Persecution of Christians in the Gospel According to St. Matthew.* Cambridge, England: Cambridge University Press, 1967.

Harrington, Daniel J. *God's People in Christ: New Testament Perspectives on the Church and Judaism.* Philadelphia: Fortress Press, 1980.

Hengel, Martin. *Acts and the History of Earliest Christianity.* Philadelphia: Fortress Press, 1979.

————. *Between Jesus and Paul.* Philadelphia: Fortress, 1983.

————. *Judaism and Hellenism.* Philadelphia: Fortress Press, 1974.

————. *Studies in Mark.* Philadelphia: Fortress, 1985.

————. *The "Hellenization" of Judea in the First Century After Christ.* Philadelphia: Trinity Press, 1989.

Horsley, Richard A. *Jesus and the Spiral of Violence: Popular Jewish Resistance in Roman Palestine.* San Francisco: Harper & Row, 1987.

————. *Sociology and the Jesus Movement.* New York: Crossroad, 1989.

————. *The Liberation of Christmas: The Infancy Narratives in Social Context.* New York: Crossroad, 1989.

———— with John S. Hanson. *Bandits, Prophets, and Messiahs: Popular Movements at the Time of Jesus.* San Francisco: Harper & Row, 1985.

Hurtado, Larry W. *One God, One Lord: Early Christian Devotion and Ancient Jewish Monotheism.* Philadelphia: Fortress Press, 1988.

Jervell, Jacob. *Luke and the People of God: A New Look At Luke-Acts.* Minneapolis: Augsburg Press, 1972.

————. *The Unknown Paul: Essays on Luke-Acts and Early Christian History.* Minneapolis: Augsburg Press, 1984.

Johnson, Luke T. "The New Testament's Anti-Jewish Slander and the Conventions of Ancient Polemic." *Journal of Biblical Literature* 108/3 (Fall 1989) 419-441.

Juel, Donald. *Messianic Exegesis: Christological Interpretation of the Old Testament in Early Christianity.* Philadelphia: Fortress Press, 1988.

Kaylor, R. David. *Paul's Covenant Community: Jew and Gentile in Romans.* Atlanta: John Knox Press, 1988.

Keck, Leander E. and J. Louis Martyn, eds. *Studies in Luke/Acts*. Philadelphia: Fortress Press, 1980.

Kingsbury, Jack Dean. *The Christology of Mark's Gospel*. Philadelphia: Fortress Press, 1983.

Koester, Craig. "The Origins and Significance of the Flight to Pella Tradition." *Catholic Biblical Quarterly* 51/1 (January 1989) 90–106.

Kraft, Robert A. and George W. E. Nickelsburg, eds. *Early Judaism and Its Modern Interpreters*. Atlanta: Scholars Press, 1986.

Kysar, Robert. *John: The Maverick Gospel*. Atlanta: John Knox Press, 1976.

Lachs, Samuel Tobias. *A Rabbinic Commentary on the New Testament: The Gospels of Matthew, Mark, and Luke*. New York: Crossroad, 1987.

Lapide, Pinchas and Peter Stuhlmacher. *Paul: Rabbi and Apostle*. Minneapolis: Augsburg, 1984.

Lee, Bernard J. *The Galilean Jewishness of Jesus: Retrieving the Jewish Origins of Christianity*. New York/Mahwah: Paulist Press, 1988.

Liddell, Henry George and Robert Scott. *A Greek-English Lexicon*. 9th ed. Oxford: Clarendon Press, 1940.

Lindars, Barnabas. *The Gospel of John*. New Century Bible Commentary. Grand Rapids: Eerdmans, 1972.

Linder, Amnon. *The Jews in Roman Imperial Legislation*. Detroit: Wayne State University Press, 1987.

Mann, C. S. *Mark*. Anchor Bible, 27. Garden City, N.Y.: Doubleday, 1986.

Marrow, Stanley B. *Paul: His Letters and His Theology*. New York/Mahwah: Paulist Press, 1986.

Marshall, I. Howard. *The Acts of the Apostles: An Introduction and Commentary*. Grand Rapids: Eerdmans, 1980.

Martyn, J. Louis. *History and Theology of the Fourth Gospel*. Rev. ed. Nashville: Abingdon Press, 1979.

Matera, Frank J. *Passion Narratives and Gospel Theologies*. New York/Mahwah: Paulist, 1986.

_____. *What Are They Saying About Mark?* New York/ Mahwah: Paulist Press, 1987.

McBrien, Richard P. *Catholicism*. Minneapolis: Winston Press, 1980.

McKenzie, John L. *Second Isaiah*. Anchor Bible, 20. Garden City, N.Y.: Doubleday, 1968.

McKnight, Scot. *A Light Among the Gentiles: Jewish Missionary Activity in the Second Temple Period*. Minneapolis: Fortress Press, 1991.

Meeks, Wayne A. *The First Urban Christians*. New Haven: Yale University Press, 1983.

_____ and Robert L. Wilken. *Jews and Christians in Antioch in the First Four Centuries of the Common Era*. Missoula, Mont.: Scholars Press, 1978.

Meyer, Ben F. *The Aims of Jesus*. London: SCM Press, 1979.

_____. *The Early Christians: World Mission and Self-Discovery*. Wilmington, Del.: Michael Glazier, 1986.

Munck, Johannes. *The Acts of the Apostles*. Anchor Bible, 31. Garden City, N.Y.: Doubleday, 1967.

Murphy-O'Connor, Jerome. *Becoming Human Together: The Pastoral Anthropology of St. Paul*. Wilmington, Del.: Michael Glazier, 1982.

Neusner, Jacob. *Invitation to the Talmud: A Teaching Book.* 1984 revision. San Francisco: Harper & Row, 1973.

_____. " 'Israel': Judaism and Its Social Metaphors." *Journal of the American Academcy of Religion* 55/2 (Summer 1987) 331–361.

_____. *Judaism in the Beginning of Christianity.* Philadelphia: Fortress Press, 1984.

_____. *Method and Meaning in Ancient Judaism.* Chico, Calif.: Scholars Press, 1979.

_____. "Money Changers in the Temple: The Mishnah's Explanation." *New Testament Studies* 35 (1989) 287–290.

_____. *Scriptures of the Oral Torah.* San Francisco: Harper & Row, 1987.

_____. *Self-Fulfilling Prophecy: Exile and Return in the History of Judaism.* Boston: Beacon Press, 1987.

_____. *The Incarnation of God: The Character of Divinity in Formative Judaism.* Philadelphia: Fortress Press, 1988.

_____. *The Oral Torah: The Sacred Books of Judaism.* San Francisco: Harper & Row, 1986.

_____. *The Pharisees—Rabbinic Perspectives.* Hoboken, N.J.: KTAV, 1973.

_____. "Two Pictures of the Pharisees: Philosophical Circle or Eating Club." *Anglican Theological Review* 64/4 (October 1982) 525–538.

_____, William S. Green, and Ernest Frerichs. *Judaisms and Their Messiahs: At the Turn of the Christian Era.* New York: Cambridge University Press, 1987.

Neyrey, Jerome H. *An Ideology of Revolt: John's Christology in Social Science Perspective.* Philadelphia: Fortress Press, 1988.

Nickelsburg, George W. E. *Jewish Literature Between the Bible and the Mishnah.* Philadelphia: Fortress Press, 1981.

_____ and Michael E. Stone. *Faith and Piety in Early Judaism: Texts and Documents.* Philadelphia: Fortress Press, 1983.

Overman, J. Andrew. *Matthew's Gospel and Formative Judaism: The Social World of the Matthean Community.* Minneapolis: Fortress Press, 1991.

Patte, Daniel. *Paul's Faith and the Power of the Gospel.* Philadelphia: Fortress Press, 1983.

Perkins, Pheme. *Resurrection: New Testament Witness and Contemporary Reflection.* Garden City, N.Y.: Doubleday, 1984.

Raisanen, Heikki. *Paul and the Law.* Philadelphia: Fortress Press, 1986.

Reynolds, Joyce and Robert Tannenbaum. *Jews and Godfearers at Aphrodisias: Greek Inscriptions with Commentary.* Cambridge, England: Cambridge Philological Society, 1987.

Reese, W. L. *Dictionary of Philosophy and Religion.* New Jersey: Humanities Press, 1980.

Saldarini, Anthony J. "Delegitimation of Leaders in Matthew 23." *The Catholic Biblical Quarterly* 54/4 (October 1992) 659–680.

_____. "The Gospel of Matthew and Jewish-Christian Conflict in Galilee." Paper to appear in the English and Hebrew Proceedings of the First International Conference on Galilean Studies in Late Antiquity, 1991.

_____. *Jesus and Passover.* New York/Ramsey: Paulist Press, 1984.

_____. *Pharisees, Scribes, and Sadducees in Palestinian Society*. Wilmington, Del.: Michael Glazier, 1988.

Sanders, E. P. *Jesus and Judaism*. Philadelphia: Fortress Press, 1985.

_____. *Jewish Law From Jesus to the Mishnah*. Philadelphia: Trinity Press, 1990.

_____. *Paul and Palestinian Judaism: A Comparison of Patterns of Religion*. Philadelphia: Fortress Press, 1977.

_____. *Paul, the Law, and the Jewish People*. Philadelphia: Fortress Press, 1983.

Sanders, Jack T. *The Jews in Luke-Acts*. Philadelphia: Fortress Press, 1987.

Sandmel, Samuel. *Judaism and Christian Beginnings*. New York: Oxford University Press, 1978.

Sarna, Nahum M. *Exploring Exodus*. New York: Schocken Books, 1986.

_____. *Genesis*. The JPS Torah Commentary. Philadelphia: Jewish Publication Society, 1989.

_____. *Understanding Genesis*. New York: Schocken Books, 1966.

Schiffman, Lawrence H. *Who Was a Jew? Rabbinic and Halakhic Perspectives on the Jewish-Christian Schism*. Hoboken, N.J.: KTAV, 1985.

Schillebeeckx, Edward. *Christ: The Experience of Jesus as Lord*. New York: Crossroad, 1981.

_____. *Jesus: An Experiment in Christology*. New York: Crossroad, 1981.

Schineller, J. Peter. "Christ and Church: A Spectrum of Views." *Theological Studies* 37 (January 1976) 545–566.

Schmithals, Walter. *Paul and James*. Naperville, Ill.: Alec R. Allenson, Inc., January 1965.

Schnackenburg, Rudolph. *The Gospel According to St. John*. 3 vols. New York: Crossroad, 1982.

Segal, Alan F. *Paul the Convert: The Apostolate and Apostasy of Saul the Pharisee*. New Haven: Yale University Press, 1990.

_____. *Rebecca's Children: Judaism and Christianity in the Roman World*. Cambridge: Harvard University Press, 1986.

Skinner, John. *Genesis*. International Critical Commentary 2nd ed. Edinburgh: T & T Clark, 1930.

Speiser, E.A. *Genesis*. Anchor Bible, 1. Garden City, N.Y.: Doubleday, 1964.

Stanton, Graham, ed. *The Interpretation of Matthew*. Philadelphia: Fortress Press, 1983.

Steinsaltz, Adin. *The Essential Talmud*. New York: Basic Books, 1986.

Stendahl, Krister. *Paul Among Jews and Gentiles*. Philadelphia: Fortress Press, 1980.

Terrien, Samuel. *The Elusive Presence: Toward a New Biblical Theology*. San Francisco: Harper & Row, 1978.

Theissen, Gerd. *Sociology of Early Palestinian Christianity*. Philadelphia: Fortress Press, 1978.

_____. *The Miracle Stories of the Early Christian Tradition*. Philadelphia: Fortress Press, 1983.

Tyson, Joseph B., ed. *Luke-Acts and the Jewish People: Eight Critical Perspectives*. Minneapolis: Augsburg Press, 1988.

Vermes, Geza. *Jesus the Jew: A Historian's Reading of the Gospels.* Philadelphia: Fortress Press, 1983.

————. *The Dead Sea Scrolls in English.* 3rd ed. New York: Penguin Books, 1987.

————. *The Dead Sea Scrolls: Qumran in Perspective.* Philadelphia: Fortress Press, 1977.

Watson, Francis. *Paul, Judaism, and the Gentiles: A Sociological Approach.* New York: Cambridge University Press, 1986.

Weeden, Theodore J., Sr. *Mark: Traditions in Conflict.* Philadelphia: Fortress Press, 1971.

Westerholm, Stephen. *Israel's Law and the Church's Faith: Paul and His Recent Interpreters.* Grand Rapids: Eerdmans, 1988.

Wilken, Robert L. *The Christians as the Romans Saw Them.* New Haven: Yale University Press, 1984.

Williamson, Clark. "Jesus of Nazareth." Paper read at the meeting of the Christian Study Group on Jews and Judaism, Baltimore, March 25, 1990.

Wyschogrod, Michael. *The Body of Faith: Judaism as Corporeal Election.* Minneapolis: Seabury Press, 1983.

Zeitlin, Irving M. *Jesus and the Judaism of His Time.* New York: Polity Press, 1988.

C. Jewish-Christian Relations

Allport, Gordon W. *The Nature of Prejudice.* Reading, Mass.: Addison-Wesley, 1954.

Bandura, Albert. *Aggression: A Social Learning Analysis.* Englewood Cliffs: Prentice Hall, 1973.

Banki, Judith H. "The Image of Jews in Christian Teaching." *Journal of Ecumenical Studies* 21:3 (1984) 437–451.

Beck, Norman A. *Mature Christianity: The Recognition and Repudiation of the Anti-Jewish Polemic of the New Testament.* Selinsgrove: Susquehana University Press, 1985.

Berger, David, ed. *History and Hate: The Dimensions of Anti-Semitism.* Philadelphia: Jewish Publication Society, 1986.

————. "Jewish-Christian Relations: A Jewish Perspective." *Journal of Ecumenical Studies* 20/1 (1983) 5–32.

Bishop, Claire Hutchet. *How Catholics Look at Jews: Inquiries into Italian, Spanish, and French Teaching Materials.* New York/Ramsey: Paulist Press, 1974.

Boadt, Lawrence, Helga Croner, and Leon Klenicki. *Biblical Studies: Meeting Ground of Jews and Christians.* New York/Ramsey: Paulist Press/Stimulus Books, 1980.

Boys, Mary C. "Questions 'Which Touch on the Heart of Our Faith.' " *Religious Education* 76/6 (November-December 1981) 636–656.

Braybrooke, Marcus. *Time to Meet: Towards a Deeper Relationship Between Jews and Christians.* Philadelphia: Trinity Press, 1990.

Charlesworth, James H., ed. *Jews and Christians: Exploring the Past, Present, and Future.* New York: Crossroad, 1990.

Cohen, Martin A. and Helga Croner, eds. *Christian Mission-Jewish Mission.* New York/Ramsey: Paulist Press/Stimulus Books, 1982.

Croner, Helga and Leon Klenicki, eds. *Issues in the Jewish-Christian Dialogue.* New York/Ramsey: Paulist Press/Stimulus Books, 1979.

Culbertson, Philip. "Changing Christian Images of the Pharisees." *Anglican Theological Review* 64/4 (October 1982) 539–561.

_____. "Doing Our Own Homework: Fifteen Steps Toward Christian-Jewish Dialogue in Local Congregations." *Journal of Ecumenical Studies* 20/1 (1983) 118–123.

_____. "Eretz Israel: Sacred Space, Icon, Sign, or Sacrament?" *Shofar* 6/3 (Spring 1988) 9–17.

_____. "Toward a Christian Theology of Loyal Opposition to Israel." Paper read at the meeting of the Christian Study Group on Jews and Judaism, Baltimore, April 8, 1989.

Cunningham, Philip A. "A Content Analysis of the Presentation of Jews and Judaism in Current Roman Catholic Religion Textbooks." Ph.D. dissertation, Boston College, 1992. [U.M.I. Order # 9217440]

Davies, Alan T., ed. *Antisemitism and the Foundations of Christianity.* New York/Ramsey: Paulist Press, 1979.

_____. "Love and Law in Judaism and Christianity." *Anglican Theological Review* 64/4 (October 1982) 454–466.

Eckardt, A. Roy. *Jews and Christians: The Contemporary Meeting.* Bloomington: Indiana University Press, 1986.

Ellis, Marc H. *Beyond Innocence and Redemption: Confronting the Holocaust and Israeli Power.* San Francisco: Harper & Row, 1990.

_____. *Toward a Jewish Theology of Liberation: The Uprising and the Future.* 2nd ed. Maryknoll, N.Y.: Orbis Books, 1989.

Ericksen, Robert P. *Theologians Under Hitler.* New Haven: Yale University Press, 1985.

Fackre, Gabriel. *The Christian Story: A Pastoral Systematics.* Vol. 2. *Authority: Scripture in the Church for the World.* Grand Rapids: Eerdmans, 1987.

Fiedler, Peter. "Categories for a Correct Presentation of Jews and Judaism in Catholic Religious Teaching." *Journal of Ecumenical Studies* 21:3 (1984) 470–488.

Fisher, Eugene J. "A Content Analysis of Treatment of Jews and Judaism in Current Roman Catholic Religion Textbooks and Manuals on the Primary and Secondary Levels." Ph.D. dissertation, New York University, 1976.

_____. "Covenant Theology and Jewish-Christian Dialogue." *American Journal of Theology and Philosophy* 9/1-2 (January–May, 1988) 5–39.

_____. *Faith Without Prejudice: Rebuilding Christian Attitudes Toward Judaism.* New York/Ramsey: Paulist Press, 1977.

_____. "The Holy See and the State of Israel: The Evolution of Attitudes and Policies." *Journal of Ecumenical Studies* 24/2 (1987) 191–211.

_____. "Implementing the Vatican Document: 'Notes on Jews and Judaism in Preaching and Catechesis.' " *Living Light* 22/2 (January 1986) 103–111.

_____. "Research on Christian Teaching Concerning Jews and Judaism: Past Research and Present Needs." *Journal of Ecumenical Studies* 21/3 (1984) 421–436.

_____. *Seminary Education and Christian-Jewish Relations: A Curriculum and Resource Handbook*. Washington: National Catholic Education Association, 1983.

_____ and Leon Klenicki. *In Our Time: The Flowering of Jewish-Catholic Dialogue*. New York/Mahwah: Paulist Press/Stimulus Books, 1990.

_____, A. James Rudin, and Marc H. Tanenbaum, eds. *Twenty Years of Jewish-Catholic Relations*. New York/Mahwah: Paulist Press, 1986.

Flannery, Edward H. *The Anguish of the Jews: Twenty-Three Centuries of Anti-semitism*. Revised and updated. New York/Mahwah: Paulist Press/Stimulus Books, 1985.

Gager, John G. *The Origins of Anti-Semitism: Attitudes Toward Judaism in Pagan and Christianity*. New York: Oxford University Press, 1985.

Greeley, Andrew M. and Jacob Neusner. *The Bible and Us: A Priest and a Rabbi Read Scripture Together*. New York: Warner Books, 1990.

Hauerwas, Stanley. "Jews and Christians Among the Nations: The Social Significance of the Holocaust." *Cross Currents* (Spring 1981): 15–34.

Jenson, Joseph. "Prediction-Fulfillment in Bible and Liturgy." *Catholic Biblical Quarterly* 50/4 (October 1988) 646–662.

Kastning-Olmesdahl, Ruth. "Theological and Pyschological Barriers to Changing the Image of Jews and Judaism in Education." *Journal of Ecumenical Studies* 21/3 (452–469) 1984.

Klenicki, Leon and Eugene J. Fisher. *Root and Branches: Biblical Judaism, Rabbinic Judaism and Early Christianity*. Winona, Minn.: St. Mary's Press, 1987.

Klenicki, Leon and Geoffrey Wigoder, eds. *A Dictionary of the Jewish-Christian Dialogue*. New York/Ramsey: Paulist Press/Stimulus Books, 1984.

Koenig, John. "The Jewishness of the Gospel: A Lutheran's Thoughts." *Journal of Ecumenical Studies* 19/1 (January 1982) 57–68.

Lapide, Pinchas. *The Resurrection of Jesus: A Jewish Perspective*. Minneapolis: Augsburg Press, 1983.

_____ and Ulrich Luz. *Jesus in Two Perspectives: A Jewish-Christian Dialog*. Minneapolis: Augsburg Press, 1979.

Levenson, Jon D. "Is There a Counterpart in the Hebrew Bible to New Testament Antisemitism?" *Journal of Ecumenical Studies* 22/2 (1985) 242–260.

Levine, Samuel. *You Take Jesus, I'll Take God: How to Refute Christian Missionaries*. Los Angeles: Hamoroh Press, 1980.

Littell, Franklin H. "Editorial: Teaching the Holocaust and Its Lessons." *Journal of Ecumenical Studies*. 21/3 (1984) 531–535.

Lux, Richard C. "Covenant Interpretations: A New Model for the Christian-Jewish Relationship." *Schola* 5 (1982) 25–62.

Maher, Trafford P. "The Catholic School Curriculum and Intergroup Relations." *Religious Education* 55/2 (March–April, 1960) 117–122.

Marcus, Jacob R. *The Jew in the Medieval World—A Source Book: 315–1791*. New York: Atheneum Press, 1938.

McGarry, Michael B. *Christology After Auschwitz*. New York/ Ramsey: Paulist Press, 1977.

_____. "A Question of Motive: A Conversation on Mission and Contemporary Jewish-Christian Relations." Paper read at the meeting of the Christian Study Group on Jews and Judaism, Baltimore, November 1989.

McInnes, Val Ambrose, ed. *Renewing the Judeo-Christian Wellsprings*. New York: Crossroad, 1987.

Mussner, Franz. *Tractate on the Jews*. Leonard Swidler, trans. Philadelphia: Fortress Press, 1984.

Neusner, Jacob. *Jews and Christians: The Myth of a Common Tradition*. Philadelphia: Trinity Press, 1991.

Novak, David. *Jewish-Christian Dialogue: A Jewish Justification*. New York: Oxford University Press, 1989.

Oesterreicher, John M. *The New Encounter Between Christians and Jews*. New York: Philosophical Library, 1986.

Olson, Bernhard E. *Faith and Prejudice: Intergroup Problems in Protestant Curricula*. New Haven: Yale University Press, 1963.

_____. "Intergroup Relations in Protestant Teaching Materials." *Religious Education* 55/2 (March–April, 1960) 123–138.

Osten-Sacken, Peter von der. *Christian-Jewish Dialogue*. Translated by Margaret Kohl. Philadelphia: Fortress Press, 1986.

Parkes, James. *The Conflict of the Church and the Synagogue*. New York: Atheneum Press, 1969.

Pawlikowski, John T. *Catechetics and Prejudice: How Catholic Teaching Materials View Jews, Protestants, and Racial Minorities*. New York/Ramsey: Paulist Press, 1973.

_____. *Christ in the Light of the Jewish-Christian Dialogue*. New York/Ramsey: Paulist Press/Stimulus Books, 1982.

_____. "Christian Ethics and the Holocaust: A Dialogue with Post-Auschwitz Judaism." *Theological Studies* 49 (1988) 649–669.

_____. "Ethical Issues in the Israeli-Palestinian Conflict: One Christian's Viewpoint." Paper read at lecture sponsored by the American Jewish Committee, Cambridge, November 1988.

_____. *Jesus and the Theology of Israel*. Wilmington, Del.: Michael Glazier, 1989.

_____. *What Are They Saying About Christian-Jewish Relations?* New York/Ramsey: Paulist Press, 1980.

_____. "Worship After the Holocaust: An Ethician's Reflections." *Worship* 58/4 (July 1984) 315–329.

_____ and James A. Wilde. *When Catholics Speak About Jews*. Chicago: Liturgy Training Publications, 1987.

Peck, Abraham, J., ed. *Jews and Christians After the Holocaust*. Philadelphia: Fortress Press, 1982.

Perelmuter, Hayim Goren. *Siblings: Rabbinic Judaism and Early Christianity at Their Beginnings*. New York/ Mahwah: Paulist Press, 1989.

Petuchowski, Jakob B. *When Jews and Christians Meet*. Albany: State University of New York Press, 1988.

_____, ed. *Defining a Discipline: The Aims and Objectives of Judaeo-Christian*

Studies. Cincinnati: Hebrew Union College, 1984.

Pratt, Douglas and Dov Bing, eds. *Judaism and Christianity: Toward Dialogue.* Auckland, New Zealand: College Communications, 1987.

Rabinowitz, A. H. *Israel: The Christian Dilemma.* Jerusalem: Gefen Publishing, 1985.

Rahner, Karl and Pinchas Lapide. *Encountering Jesus—Encountering Judaism: A Dialogue.* New York: Crossroad, 1987.

Reese, Thomas J., ed. *The Universal Catechism Reader: Reflections and Responses.* San Francisco: Harper and Row, 1990.

Richardson, Peter, ed. *Anti-Judaism in Early Christianity.* Vol. 1: *Paul and the Gospels.* Waterloo, Ont.: Wilfrid Laurier University Press, 1986.

Rothschild, Fritz A., ed. *Jewish Perspectives on Christianity.* New York: Crossroad, 1990.

Rubenstein, Richard L. and John K. Roth. *Approaches to Auschwitz: The Holocaust and Its Legacy.* Atlanta: John Knox Press, 1987.

Ruether, Rosemary. *Faith and Fratricide: The Theological Roots of Anti-Semitism.* Minneapolis: Seabury Press, 1974.

Saperstein, Marc. *Moments of Crisis in Jewish-Christian Relations.* Philadelphia: Trinity Press, 1989.

Schussler Fiorenza, Elisabeth & David Tracy. *The Holocaust as Interruption.* Concilium. Edinburgh: T & T Clark, 1984.

Shermis, Michael. *Jewish-Christian Relations: An Annotated Bibliography and Resource Guide.* Bloomington: Indiana University Press, 1988.

Siegman, Henry. "A Decade of Catholic-Jewish Relations—A Reassessment." *Journal of Ecumenical Studies* 15 (1978) 243–260.

Staub, Ervin. *The Roots of Evil: The Origins of Genocide and Other Group Violence.* New York: Cambridge University Press, 1990.

Strober, Gerald S. *Portrait of the Elder Brother: Jews and Judaism in Protestant Teaching Materials.* New York: American Jewish Committee, 1972.

Swidler, Leonard. "The Dialogue Decalogue: Ground Rules for Interreligious Dialogue." *Journal of Ecumenical Studies* 20/1 (1983) 1–4.

_____. *Yeshua: A Model for Moderns.* Kansas City: Sheed & Ward, 1988.

Talmage, F. E., ed. *Disputation and Dialogue: Readings in the Jewish-Christian Encounter.* New York: KTAV/Anti-Defamatation League of B'nai B'rith, 1975.

Tannebaum, Marc H., Marvin R. Wilson, and A. James Rudin, eds. *Evangelicals and Jews in an Age of Pluralism.* Grand Rapids: Baker Book House, 1984.

Thering, Rose. "Potential in Religious Textbooks for Developing a Realistic Self-Concept." Ph.D. dissertation, St. Louis University, 1961.

Thoma, Clemens. *A Christian Theology of Judaism.* New York/Ramsey: Paulist Press/Stimulus Books, 1980.

_____ and Michael Wyschogrod, eds. *Understanding Scripture: Explorations of Jewish and Christian Traditions of Interpretation.* New York/Mahwah: Paulist Press/Stimulus Books, 1987.

_____, eds. *Parable and Story in Judaism and Christianity.* New York/Mahwah: Paulist Press/Stimulus Books, 1989.

Trachtenberg, Joshua. *The Devil and the Jews: The Medieval Conception of the Jews and Its Relation to Modern Anti-Semitism.* Philadelphia: Jewish Publication Society, 1943.

van Beeck, Franz Jozef. *Loving the Torah More Than God?—Toward a Catholic Appreciation of Judaism.* Chicago: Loyola University Press, 1989.

van Buren, Paul M. *A Theology of the Jewish-Christian Reality.* Vol. 1. *Discerning the Way.* San Francisco: Harper and Row, 1980.

_____. *A Theology of the Jewish-Christian Reality.* Vol. 2. *A Christian Theology of the People Israel.* San Francisco: Harper and Row, 1983.

_____. *A Theology of the Jewish-Christian Reality.* Vol. 3. *Christ in Context.* San Francisco: Harper and Row, 1988.

_____. "Theological Education for the Church's Relationship to the Jewish People." *Journal of Ecumenical Studies* 21/3 (1984) 489–505.

Weinryb, Bernard D. "Intergroup Content in Jewish Textbooks." *Religious Education* 55/2 (March–April, 1960) 109–116.

Wilken, Robert L. *John Chrysostom and the Jews: Rhetoric and Reality in the Late Fourth Century.* Berkeley: University of California Press, 1983.

_____. *Judaism and the Early Christian Mind: A Study of Cyril of Alexandria's Exegesis and Theology.* New Haven: Yale University Press, 1971.

Williamson, Clark M. and Ronald J. Allen. *Interpreting Difficult Texts: Anti-Judaism and Christian Preaching.* Philadelphia: Trinity Press, 1989.

Wilson, Marvin R. *Our Father Abraham: Jewish Roots of the Christian Faith.* Grand Rapids: Eerdmans, 1989.

Wilson, Stephen G., ed. *Anti-Judaism in Early Christianity.* Vol. 2. *Separation and Polemic.* Waterloo, Ont.: Wilfrid Laurier University Press, 1986.

Zerin, Edward. *What Catholics Should Know About Jews.* Dubuque: William C. Brown: 1980.